Ministry through Word and Sacrament

THOMAS C. ODEN

Classical Pastoral Care

VOLUME TWO
MINISTRY THROUGH
WORD & SACRAMENT

Baker Books

A Division of Baker Book House Co
Grand Rapids, Michigan 49516

For John F. Ollom and James M. O'Kane

© 1987 by Thomas C. Oden
Originally published 1987 by The Crossroad Publishing Company

Published by Baker Books
a division of Baker Book House Company
P.O. Box 6287, Grand Rapids, MI 49516-6287

Printed in the United States of America

ISBN 0-8010-6764-2

Library of Congress Cataloging-in-Publication data on file in Washington, D.C.

Contents

Preface to the Baker Edition

EVANGELICALS STAND POISED to rediscover the classical pastoral tradition. This series seeks the revitalization of a discipline once familiar to evangelical Protestant scholarship, but now regrettably crippled and enervated.

It has been commonly observed that there is a deep hunger and profound readiness among evangelicals for neglected classical Christian roots as a resource for counsel, teaching, exegesis, and the work of ministry (see the writings of Robert Webber, Mark Noll, Ward Gasque, Donald Bloesch, James I. Packer, Michael Horton, Clark Pinnock, and Os Guinness).

It is well known that classic Protestant and evangelical teachers made frequent and informed references to the ancient Christian pastoral writers. Calvin was exceptionally well grounded in Augustine, but was also thoroughly familiar with the texts of Cyprian, Tertullian, John Chrysostom, Ambrose, Jerome, Leo, and Gregory the Great, and ecumenical council definitions such as those of Nicea, Constantinople I, and Chalcedon. Philipp Melancthon and Martin Chemnitz were especially gifted scholars of classical pastoral care. This tradition was carried forth and deepened by Reformed pastoral theologians (Gerhard, Quenstedt, Bucanus, Ursinus, Wollebius, and Cocceius), and survived healthily well into the eighteenth-century evangelical revival among leading teachers like J.A. Bengel, Philip Doddridge, Jonathan Edwards, John Wesley, and Johann Neander, all of whom read classic Christian writers handily in their original languages. Not until the late nineteenth century did the study of the ancient pastoral writers atrophy among Protestant pastors.

What is notably missing in today's picture is the classic pastoral texts themselves in accessible form, and a vital community of pastors and care-givers in living dialogue with these foundational prototypes.

A major long-range objective of this edition is the mentoring of young evangelical pastors and counselors toward greater competence in the classical pastoral tradition. Deliberately included in this collection are the voices of women from the classic Eastern and Western traditions of spiritual formation, exegesis, martyrology, catechesis, and piety. While the documentation of their poignant utterances is regrettably infrequent, they still are exceedingly powerful commentators on care-giving—I am thinking of such voices as Amma Theodora, Julian of Norwich, Hildegaard of Bingen, and Teresa of Avila.

Will benefits accrue to persons in teaching and helping professions who have no evangelical commitments or interests? The study of classical pastoral care is fitting not only for pastors and professionals, but for lay readers interested in their own inward spiritual formation. The arguments contained in this series tend to elicit ripple effects on diverse readers in such widely varied fields as psychology, Western cultural history, liturgies, homiletics, and education. Classical pastoral care is long overdue in contributing something distinctive of its own to the larger dialogue on care-giving, empathy, behavioral change, and therapeutic effectiveness.

By the early eighties it began to be evident that someone needed to pull together a substantial collection of essential sources of classic Christian writers on major themes of pastoral care. The series was first published by Crossroad/Continuum Publishing Company, a general academic publisher of religious books with strong ties to the erudite Herder tradition of Catholic scholarship. In the intervening years, no serious rival or alternative to this collection has appeared. There exists no other anthology of texts of classical pastoral care that presents the variety of textual material offered in this series. I am now deeply pleased to see it come out in an edition more accessible to Protestants. This is the first time the series has been made available in paperback.

The four books can be read either as a single, unified sequence or separately as stand-alone volumes. To this day some readers know of only one or two volumes, but are not aware that each volume is part of a cohesive series. Baker has made this unity clearer by offering the four volumes as a series.

I am deeply grateful for the interest that many working pastors, counselors, and lay persons have shown in this Classical Pastoral Care series. Even though these volumes were chosen as a Religious Book Club selection over several years, the circulation has been disseminated largely through academic audiences. I am pleased that it is now being offered by Baker for the first time to evangelical pastors and evangelically oriented pastoral and lay counselors and lay readers.

These texts are sometimes hard to locate if one is approaching them topically in crumbling, antiquated editions with poor indexes. This edition provides for the first time a well-devised index for the whole series that makes the anthology much more accessible to readers who wish to dip into it thematically.

These four volumes are designed to display the broad range of classical Christian reflections on all major questions of pastoral care. Many practical subjects are included, such as care of the dying, care of the poor, marriage and family counseling, pastoral visitation and care of the sick, counsel on addictive behaviors, vocational counsel, the timing of good counsel, the necessary and sufficient conditions of a helping relationship, body language in pastoral counsel, pastoral care through preaching, pastoral care through prayer, the pastor as educator of the soul, preparing for the Lord's table, clergy homosexuality and sexual ethics, equality of souls beyond sexual difference, the path to ordination, charismatic, healing ministries, and preparation for the care of souls.

The four volumes are:

I. *On Becoming a Minister* (first published 1987)
II. *Ministry through Word and Sacrament* (1989)
III. *Pastoral Counsel* (1989)
IV. *Crisis Ministries* (1986)

This edition for the first time identifies the order of volumes more clearly. Since in the first edition the fourth volume (*Crisis Ministries*, with its bio-bibliographical addendum) appeared first, the sequential order of the series has been confusing to some readers. Many have never seen the four volumes in a collection together, and do not yet realize that the whole sequence is constructed in a well-designed order to cover all major topics of pastoral theology.

There is reason to believe that this series is already being regarded as a standard necessary accession of theological seminary libraries, as well as of the libraries of most colleges and universities in which religious studies are taught, and in many general public libraries.

Meanwhile, out of rootless hunger the prefix "pastoral" has come to mean almost anything. There is no constraint on ascribing any subject matter to the category of pastoral care. In this game pastoral can mean my ultimate concern, transcendental meditation, or worse, my immediate feeling process or group hugging or my racial identity or crystal-gazing—you name it, anything. Then what is called pastoral is no longer related to the work of Christian ministry at all.

The preaching and counseling pastor needs to know that current pastoral care stands in a tradition of two millennia of reflection on the tasks of soul care. If deprived of these sources, the practice of pastoral care may become artificially constricted to modern psychotherapeutic procedures or pragmatic agendas. During the sixties and seventies, these reductionistic models prevailed among many old-line Protestant pastors, and to some degree as the eighties proceeded they also took root among evangelicals. This anthology shows the classic historic roots of contemporary approaches to psychological change, and provides to some degree a critique of those contemporary models.

Pastors today are rediscovering the distinctiveness of pastoral method as distinguished from other methods of inquiry (historical, philosophical, literary, psychological, etc.). Pastoral care is a unique enterprise that has its own distinctive subject-matter (care of souls); its own methodological premise (revelation); its own way of inquiring into its subject-matter (attentiveness to the revealed Word through Scripture and its consensual tradition of exegesis); its own criteria of scholarly authenticity (accountability to canonical text and tradition); its own way of knowing (listening to sacred Scripture with the historic church); its own mode of cultural analysis (with worldly powers bracketed and divine providence appreciated); and its own logic (internal consistency premised upon revealed truth).

The richness of the classic Christian pastoral tradition remains pertinent to ministry today. The laity have a right to competent, historically grounded pastoral care. The pastor has a right to the texts that teach how pastors have understood their work over the centuries. Modern chauvinism has falsely taught us a theory of moral inferiority: that new ideas are intrinsically superior, and old patterns inferior. This attitude has robbed the laity of the pastoral care they deserve, and the ministry of the texts that can best inform the recovery of pastoral identity.

Thomas C. Oden
June, 1994

Introduction

"SOUL" (*psyche, anima*) IS THAT WHICH ENLIVENS, energizes, animates human existence, as distinguished but not separated from the body which is animated. Body minus soul equals corpse. A warm body is one with soul—alive.

The term *soul care* translates the ancient Latin idea of *cura animarum:* the nourishment, guidance, and care of that which animates human existence. Curacy, or soul care, is a vocation set aside to guide souls in their journey through life toward fulfillment of their genuine freedom and possibility.

The previous Volume I, *Becoming a Minister,* set forth classic pastoral writings on the calling and work of the minister. This present Volume II, *Ministry through Word and Sacrament,* asks how that care-giver acts to provide nourishment and guidance for souls in eight crucial arenas of ministry: care of oneself; ministry of the Word; soul care through prayer; ministry of the sacrament of beginnings—baptism; ministry of holy communion; the education of the soul; the nurture of community; and the engendering of support for ministry. The following Volume III, *Pastoral Counsel,* will focus upon individual one-on-one conversations as a major concern of pastoral care. Our present purpose is to show that soul care occurs not only in individual conversations, but also in a community of care, in public settings like preaching and worship, and in sacramental life, in baptizing and celebrating the Eucharist, in the teaching of children and adults, and in the nurturing of community in the parish and the civil order.

The eight questions of this volume are:

- Why do *care-givers themselves need soul care?* And what special nourishment is required to transcend despair over the burdens of care for others?

5

- How does soul care occur through community by means of public witness and the *preaching of good news*?
- In what sense does *the worshipping community and the life of prayer* provide the broader social and necessary spiritual matrix for individual soul care?
- How do sacramental ministries constitute central acts of soul care, beginning with the ministry of *baptism*?
- Why is *confession* intrinsically connected with holy *communion* so as to constitute the quintessential service of soul care?
- How does the pastor *teach* the soul to increase in faith and behavioral excellence?
- How does the pastor nurture *community* in the parish, and *civil justice* beyond the parish?
- How may the care-giver best find and order resources *properly to support ministry* without eliciting abuses?

The Christian pastor struggles for the health of the person and the life of the soul simultaneously in these diverse developmental phases and arenas.

1 On the Pastoral Obligation to Care for Oneself

PASTORAL BURN-OUT is thought to be a distinctively modern dilemma, but the classic pastoral writers repeatedly faced it thoughtfully and resourcefully. They thought that burnout could best be averted by wise preparation and by following the ancient injunction to take care of oneself. This injunction was closely linked with pastoral care in Acts 20:28: "Keep watch over yourselves and over all the flock of which the Holy Spirit has given you charge."

This volume, therefore, begins its search into the diverse arenas of pastoral care by inquiring at closest quarters into the nearest of these: oneself as pastor, one's own needs and dreams. Caring for the flock cannot occur unless one first cares for oneself, watches over one's own welfare, feeds and nurtures one's own body and soul.

The first step toward doing unto others as one would have them do unto oneself is to learn what one's ownself truly needs, proportionally loves, freely fantasizes, and uniquely requires. For if one does not know how one would wish to be treated, one cannot treat others as one would wish to be treated. In pursuit of soul care for the pastor, the pastoral tradition has candidly faced the distinctive challenges of pastoral service, difficulties intrinsic to soul care, reasons for pastoral burnout, and how to avert it.

I ❧ CARE OF THE CARE-GIVER

The principle was firmly established by the classic writers that the care-giver needs regular and special care. Since so much attention in ministry focusses on offering pastoral care to others, the point is easily missed that the pastor often seriously needs to be cared for. Luther stated the principle succinctly:

> Those who take care of souls are worthy of all care. (Luther, *Table Talk*, W-T 5, #6287; WLS 2, p. 939)

Gregory the Great reflected deliberately on ways in which pastors are called to care for themselves. Gregory thought it a specific hazard of ministry that one becomes so focussed upon others' needs that one's own health and well-being may be jeopardized. The sudden death of highly competent ministers may be an oblique witness to their own myopia about their omnicompetencies:

In restoring others to health by healing their wounds, he must not disregard his own health. . . . Let him not, while helping his neighbours, neglect himself, let him not, while lifting up others, fall himself. In many instances, indeed, the greatness of certain men's virtues has been an occasion of their perdition, in that they have felt inordinately secure in the assurance of their strength, and they died suddenly because of their negligence. (Gregory the Great, *Pastoral Care*, Part IV, ACW 11, p. 234)

John Chrysostom argued that pastors need more help and care than the average person due to the heavy demands and extraordinary expectations associated with the pastoral office:

The priest's wounds require greater help, indeed as much as those of all the people together. They would not have required greater help if they had not been more serious, and their seriousness is not increased by their own nature but by the extra weight of dignity belonging to the priest who dares to commit them. (Chrysostom, *On the Priesthood*, Ch. VI.10, sec. 16, p. 151)

Keeping guard over oneself is likened to the need of each ship in a crowded harbor to steer carefully to avoid collisions. This is especially so where there is silent anger within, of which one has remained unaware:

Let us keep guard over ourselves with all care. For when a harbour is full of ships, it is easy for them to get crushed by each other, especially if they are secretly riddled with bad temper as by some worm. (John Climacus, *The Ladder of Divine Ascent*, Step 4, sec. 77, p. 43)

With characteristic balance and good judgment, Gregory the Great grasped the point that effective care of souls is conjointly composed of two aspects—care of others and care of oneself—neither of which should inordinately dominate the other:

Pastors are called to fulfil their charge over others in such a way as not to fail to accomplish the charge over themselves, and to be ardently solicitous on their own account in such as way as not to grow slack in watching over those entrusted to them. (Gregory the Great, *Pastoral Care*, Part III, Ch. 4, ACW 11, p. 97)*

An appropriate concern for oneself, or proportional self-interest (or-dinate self-love), is frequently cited as a pastoral duty. It is not unseemly or selfish for pastors to pray for their own needs. The depth of these needs is seen in this prayer of Aelred:

You know well, O Searcher of my heart, that there is nothing in my soul that I would hide from you, even had I the power to escape your eyes. . . . Further, against the vices and the evil pas-sions which still assault my soul, (whether they come from past bad habit, or from my immeasurable daily negligence, whether their source is in the weakness of my corrupt and vitiated nature, or in the secret tempting of malignant spirits) against these vices, Lord, may your sweet grace afford me strength and courage; that I may not consent thereto, nor let them reign in this my mortal body. (Aelred of Rievaulx, *The Pastoral Prayer*, sec. 5, CFS 2, pp. 110-111)

The notion of ministers sharing in support groups is very old indeed. Anglican Bishop Burnet underscored the need for pastors to care for one another:

The clergy ought to contrive ways to meet often together, to enter into a brotherly correspondence, and into the concerns one of another, both in order to their progress in knowledge, and for consulting together in all their affairs. This would be a means to cement them into one body: hereby they might understand what were amiss in the conduct of any in their division, and try to cor-rect it either by private advices and endeavours, or by laying it before the bishop, by whose private Labours, if his clergy would be assisting to him, and give him free and full informations of things, many disorders might be cured, without rising to a public scandal, or forcing him to extreme censures. It is a false pity in any of the clergy, who see their brethren running into ill courses, to look on and say nothing: it is a cruelty to the church, and may prove a cruelty to the person of whom they are so unseasonably tender: for things may be more easily corrected at first, before they have grown to be public, or are hardened by habit and cus-tom. Upon all these accounts it is of great advantage, and may be matter of great edification to the clergy, to enter into a strict union together, to meet often, and to be helpful to one another. (Gilbert Burnet, *Of the Pastoral Care*, Ch. VIII, pp. 175-176)

If clergy remain passively silent while a fellow pastor is stumbling and falling, it amounts to cruel indifference and "unseasonable tenderness."

II ⚘ DIFFICULTIES INTRINSIC TO CARE-GIVING

Suppose one came upon a description of a vocational profile in which hours were long, pay minimal, risks high, accomplishments largely unnoticed, and the level of conflict at times intense. Would it not seem reasonable to avoid it at all costs? Yet if ministry is viewed primarily in terms of hedonic costs/benefits, much of it could be described in this way. Nonetheless the pastoral literature frequently attests to a deep sense of joy in genuine ministry. Amid these struggles there emerges a unique form of happiness and fulfillment from the distinctive pastoral tasks of liturgy, intercession, meditative study, teaching, proclamation, pastoral care, and intimate interpersonal communication.

The classical pastoral writers have tried to make it clear that the office of the pastor is not an easy street, and that there are certain persistent problems and dilemmas that often accompany the task—difficulties intrinsically connected with care-giving.

The household sweat is great; the political sweat is greater; the church sweat is the greatest. (Luther, "Lectures on Genesis Chapters One to Five, 1535–36," WA 42, 159, WLS 2, p. 951; cf. in LW, 1, p. 213)

It is impossible to list in advance all the difficulties one might expect to encounter in ministry:

Making a list of all the difficulties involved is like trying to measure the ocean. (Chrysostom, *On the Priesthood*, Ch. VI, sec. 8, p. 149)

The perplexity is that the deepest joys of ministry are intrinsically related precisely to what makes ministry at times very difficult:

We can engage in no sublimer and greater work on earth than educating people by preaching and teaching. . . . But no work is more difficult than making other people good. Yet this is the best service we can render God. (Luther, WA 36, 216; WLS 2, p. 951)

In the astonishing medieval poetry of Ramon Lull, Christ is the Lover and he the beloved. Lull portrays the joys and trials of ministry as intricately connected. Modern readers may mistake for masochism the subtlety of this intrinsic connection:

The Beloved asked the Lover, "Have you remembered any way in which I have rewarded you for you to love me thus?" "Yes," replied the Lover, "for I make no distinction between the trials which you send and the joys."

The Beloved asked, "Tell me, Lover, if I double your sorrows, will you still be patient?" "Yes," replied the Lover, "so that you will also double my love." (Ramon Lull, *The Book of the Lover and the Beloved*, sec. 8-9, pp. 14-15)

Benedict of Nursia in the sixth century showed the complexity of reasons why care of souls is a demanding task. For it requires at the same time honesty, compassion, accountability, and prudence. It is not meant for one lacking in courage, candor, or imagination:

Let him reflect how difficult and perplexing a business he undertakes, at once to govern many souls and to be subject to as many humours: to suit himself to everyone with regard to their capacity and condition; to win some by fair means, others by reprimands, others by dint of reason: that he may not suffer damage to his flock, but rather rejoice at the increase and improvement of it.

Above all, he is not to dissemble or undervalue the care of souls committed to his charge, for the sake of temporal concerns, which are earthly, transitory, and fleeting; but ever to reflect that the government of souls is his business, and that he is accountable for them. (Benedict of Nursia, Rule, LCC IX, p. 296)

To engage in ministry without succumbing to numerous temptations is like walking a tightrope or balancing on a razor's edge. Without denying the difficulties of the task, Luther commented on how the pastor is to find inner certitude and physical energy to persist in this exacting work:

Thus there are many temptations and hindrances for this ministry on both the right and the left side, the temptation of keeping quiet either to escape harm and persecution or to gain popularity, property, or pleasure. Besides, we are weak, lazy, and listless. Therefore we let ourselves be distracted, and we get tired when we see that things do not progress as we would like, when it all seems useless and the people despise our rebukes and even become the worse on account of them. . . . Our consolation is in the fact that He makes us His salt and will sustain us in our salting. He commands us to do that salting with good cheer, regardless of whether the world refuses to tolerate it and persecutes us. (Luther, "Commentary on the Sermon on the Mount, 1532," LW 21, pp. 57-58)

Among temptations to the church's ministry, Luther described three in particular: persecution, heresy, and antinomianism. First there is the tyrannical persecution of faith's witness by coercive state powers, then false teachings parading as faith, and most subtly, the antinomian spirit of license against the law that imagines the gospel no longer needs the law.

The first trial of the church (from the beginning of the world) always comes from the tyrants, who shed our blood. When the tyrants are almost at an end, the far more harmful trial brought on by heretics follows, reinforcing the violence of the tyrants. After the heretics have been somewhat suppressed, there follows the most harmful trial of all in the time of peace, namely, license and worldly-mindedness in living, life without the Law, without the Word, since we are satiated and surfeited with the Word, which is no longer necessary "because the enemies are defeated." So the worst enemies of a man are those of his own household. These three trials tempt to sin against the Father, the Son, and the Holy Ghost. (Luther, W-Br. 9, pp. 510f.; WLS 1, p. 281)

The tempter is formidable, deceitful, and determined. The temptation of ministers is often treated, but never with more subtlety than by Baxter. That our own highest ideals and principles may cause our downfall anticipates much post-Niebuhrian social criticism:

As wise and learned as you are, take heed to yourselves, lest he outwit you. The devil is a greater scholar than you, and a nimbler disputant: he can transform himself into an angel of light to deceive: he will get within you, and trip up your heels before you are aware: he will play the juggler with you undiscerned, and cheat you of your faith or innocency, and you shall not know that you have lost it; nay he will make you believe it is multiplied or increased, when it is lost. . . . He will be sure to find advantages within you, and make your own principles and inclinations betray you; and whenever he ruineth you, he will make you the instruments of ruin to others. (Baxter, *RP*, pp. 74-75)

Those called to ministry, if faithful to the apostolic tradition, will be given grace to persevere:

We show forth our diligence in preaching the same doctrines that they taught, beside which, according to the admonition of the Apostle, we are forbidden to add anything. For the office of keeping what is committed to our trust is no less dignified than that of handing it down. . . . Shouldn't you expect that God would give you grace to preserve in that which he has given you to preach? So being filled with the Holy Spirit, as it is written, you may set forth that one truth which the Spirit himself has taught you, although with diverse voices. (Ephesus, A.D. 431, The Letter of Pope Celestine to the Synod of Ephesus, The Seven Ecumenical Councils, NPNF 2, XIV, pp. 220-221)*

III ❧ PASTORAL BURNOUT

Given the difficulties that necessarily accompany the care of souls, it is not surprising that some should experience periods of intense demoralization. This phenomena, which has more recently been called "pastoral burnout," has been recognized, wisely analyzed and creatively faced in previous periods of pastoral care.

Catherine of Siena provides a poignant example. At one point she experienced an overwhelming sense of failure and defeat as a care-giver, as expressed in these dramatic terms in the solitude of prayer:

Oh, unhappy one that I am! Thou hast placed me in charge of souls, assigning to me so many beloved sons, that I should love them with singular love and direct them to Thee by the way of Life, but I have been to them nothing but a mirror of human weakness. I have had no care of them. I have not helped them with continuous and humble prayer in Thy presence, nor have I given them sufficient examples of the good life or the warnings of salutary doctrine. (Catherine of Siena, *Transit of the Saint*, p. 341)*

Similarly Luther wrote of certain periods in which his feelings of frustration, anger, despair, disgust, and weariness caused him to wish to decline the struggle altogether. When despair over the burdens of soul care approached, Luther took comfort in Jesus' specific promise to those who are reviled:

I often become so angry and impatient with our peasants, townsfolk, and nobility that I think I never want to deliver another sermon; for they carry on so shamefully that a person is inclined to be disgusted with life. Besides this, the devil does not stop plaguing me without and within. Therefore I would almost like to say: Let someone else be preacher in my place. I will let matters take their course, for I am getting nothing but the hatred and envy of the world and all sorts of trouble from the devil. Thus flesh and blood rise in revolt, and human nature becomes dejected and disheartened. In such conditions I must find counsel in the Word of God. . . . "How blest are you, when you suffer insults and persecution and every kind of calumny for my sake.

Accept it with gladness and exultation, for you have a rich reward in heaven; in the same way they persecuted the prophets before you" (Matt. 5:11). To these words I cling. (Luther, WA 34 II, pp. 527f.; WLS 3, p. 1120, NEB)*

Some mystical writers have imagined that Christ was the beckoner as one moves into a period of depression. Luther stubbornly asserted the opposite. It is the influence of the adversary that elicits depression. This provided him with a partial clarification of the otherwise complete absurdity of recurrent *Anfechtung* (affliction) accompanying his soul care. During periods of depression about ministry, which he experienced often, he thought that it was not Christ but the demonic that confronted him. The adversary's motive: to drive him out of ministry. Luther's remedy: confront and renounce the demonic, and confess Christ:

We must know this and be guided by it when we must step forth to preach and confess the Word. Then indeed we shall find out, both on the outside among our enemies and on the inside among ourselves, when the devil himself will attack you and show you how hostile he is to you, in order that he may bring you into sorrow, impatience, and heaviness of heart, and inflict every plague on you. Who does all this? Surely not Christ or any good spirit; it is the accursed, desperate enemy. He shoots such darts into your heart, not because you are a sinner as others are, adulterers, thieves, and the like. No, he does so because he is hostile to you for being a Christian. . . . Therefore be prepared, so that when you experience and feel these temptations either in your official capacity or especially in your heart, you can confront the devil and say: "Now I see why the devil assails me this way. He wants to scare and drive me from my office, from my preaching, and confession, and my faith, and to make me despondent. He does not want me to expect anything good from my Lord Christ or to praise, honor, or call upon Him. For the devil is Christ's sworn and declared enemy. But I despise you and your power, you accursed devil. I am determined to defy you and to preach and praise this Man all the more, to comfort my heart with His blood and death, and to put my trust in Him, even if you and all hell should burst asunder." (Luther, "Sermons on the Gospel of St. John Chapter Fifteen, 1537," LW 24, p. 289)

Luther provided the classic description of the crisis of burnout, by speaking in a sermon of his own temptation to depression. He assumed that it could only be the adversary who was saying to him: Cease ministry.

For I know [says Christ] that the devil will harass you severely for My sake, to sadden and weary you, to make you impatient, to induce you to defect, and to make you say: "I wish I had never had anything to do with this!" That is the sentiment of many right now. I myself have been assailed by such aversion and weariness, and the thought has come to me: "If I had not begun to do so, I would never again preach another word; I would let everything take whatever course it may." ... But Christ declares: "That is not the right attitude. Do not let the devil, the world, or your own flesh overcome you; but think of how I have loved you and still love you." (Luther, "Sermons on the Gospel of St. John Chapter Fifteen, 1537," LW 24, p. 247)

The beleaguered pastor may not always find support among clergy colleagues. Menno Simons is a case in point. In discussing the problem of integrity in ministry, Menno applied the trenchant metaphor of a prostitute talking incessantly about virtue. Having found many hypocrisies among clergy, this persecuted clergyman wrote:

O preachers, preachers, how aptly has the Holy Spirit likened you to wells without water, clouds without rain from which no helpful water can be received, trees without fruit from which nothing edible can be picked. I know not to what you may be better compared than to a woman who lives in all manner of shame and wantonness, but likes to talk about modesty and virtue. (Menno Simons, *Foundations of Christian Doctrine*, 1539, *CWMS*, p. 168)*

In a Sermon of 1531 on Titus 2:13, Luther stated his conviction that the power and goodness of God at times become hidden from view, even while one is actively engaged in Christ's ministry. God allows his power to be perceived as weakness and dying, in order that subsequently it might become known as love and resurrection:

He allows His prophets and apostles to be expelled and murdered: Paul to be beheaded, Peter to be crucified, His holy martyrs to be flung into bonds and prison, to be scourged, stoned, hacked, and stabbed to pieces and miserably done away with. He allows His Christians to suffer want, trouble, and misfortune in the world. He acts as He did in the days of His flesh, when John the Baptist had to lose his head for the sake of a desperate harlot, while He, the Savior and Helper, said nothing about it, departed thence in a ship and withdrew to the solitude of a wilderness (Matt. 14:10ff, Mark 6:27, 32). Is He not a petty, childish God, who does not save Himself and allows His children to suffer as if

He did not see how badly they were faring?

Then, as the writings of the prophets and the psalms state, the godless boast; they mock the Christians and their God, saying: "Where is now their God?" (Ps. 115:2; cf. John 16:20). If He is God, let Him contend for His rights and the rights of His people so that His name may not be rooted out and His people may not suffer. If he does not see what is going on, then He has no eyes to see and no reason to understand. On the other hand, if He does see and know but allows these things to happen, then He is no good, faithful God and has no heart for His people. Likewise, if He sees and knows but cannot help, then He has no hands that are able to do anything, nor does He have power to enable Him to save.

Hence the prophet Isaiah correctly says of God: "Verily Thou art a God that hidest Thyself, O God of Israel, the Savior" (45:15). For He hides His omnipotence, wisdom, power, and might and acts so childishly as though He could do nothing, knew nothing, understood nothing or did not want to do anything. Now He lets our adversaries treat His Word, Sacraments, and Christians as they please. He lets us call and cry and says nothing, as though He were deep in thought or were busy or were out in the field or asleep and heard nothing, as Elijah says of Baal (1 Kings 18:27). (Luther, WA 34 II, pp. 128f.; WLS 1, p. 282)

John Chrysostom thought that the strength of a ministry could only be known through testing. The life of monk and priest are contrasted just at this point—the priestly life is subjected to more severe testing:

In harbour the man at the helm cannot yet give sure proof of his skill. . . . I should have no claim to admiration if I did not commit sin only because I was sleeping, or did not get a fall only because I was not wrestling, or was not wounded only because I was not fighting! . . . What am I to do? Nothing is as useless for church government as this inactivity and detachment, which other people regard as a form of self-discipline, but which I have more as a veil for my own worthlessness, using it to cloak most my failings and keep them from becoming obvious. . . . [In pastoral work] all his faults are exposed, and as fire tests metals, so the touchstone of the ministry distinguishes men's souls. (Chrysostom, *On the Priesthood*, Ch. VI, sec. 5, pp. 144-147)

The pastor does well to expect good outcomes under the guidance of divine grace. The distortable theme of positive thinking, rediscovered in the last century by William James and Norman Vincent Peale, was anticipated by Richard Baxter:

If you would prosper in your work, be sure to keep up earnest desires and expectations of success. . . . I have observed that God seldom blesses any one's work so much as one whose heart is set upon the success of it. (Baxter, *RP*, p. 121)*

IV ❧ On Leaving the Ministry

The laying on of hands in ordination has been considered, like baptism, an act that occurs only once, that is not repeated, and not reversible once enacted. A distinction recurs in classical pastoral care between between those liturgical acts that are are repeated, and those that are administered only once. The Lord's Supper, preaching, teaching, and prayer are among actions done repeatedly. But baptism, confirmation, and marriage are among the actions ordinarily taken only once, and the commitment is understood or assumed in principle to be once for all. Ordination has usually been placed in this latter category. Thus a debate has ensued as to whether orders are "indelible," i.e., undeletable. The heart of the issue: Once one has been duly called and ordained to the care of souls, how it is possible justly and legitimately to abandon or take leave of it?

The Athanasian Canons stated the rigorist view, that one having taken up ministry shall not leave it:

None shall take upon him this call, that is the priesthood, and despise it. Rather he shall perform his service faithfully, even as did the Levites.

Let none say,"I desire to have nothing to do with the altar, nor do I have time for the ministry." For this cannot be. For the Saviour will say to him, "Either do my law or go forth from my city". . . . If you say, "I take nothing from the altar, and neither do I serve," then think of the parable of the talents, of what God did to the one who had ten pounds and to the other who had one pound and hid it in the earth, and no profit came from it. God took it from him and gave it unto him that had the ten pounds. (*Athanasian Canons*, pp. 36-37)*

Luther and Lutheran scholastics such as Chemnitz took a moderating view that the church does not have the right to remove one called by God to ministry, but it does have the right to remove one not so called:

As long as God lets in the ministry His minister who teaches rightly and lives blamelessly, the church does not have the power, without divine command to remove an unwanted man, namely [if he is] a servant of God. But when he does not build up the church by either doctrine or life, but rather destroys [it], God Himself removes him, 1 Sam 2:30; Hos 4:6. And then the church not only properly can but by all means should remove such a one from the ministry. For just as God calls ministers of the church, so He also removes them through legitimate means. (Chemnitz, *MWS*, Part I, Sec. 31, p. 37)

In the background of the complex debate on indelible orders is the problem of whether it is possible to receive divine gifts from unworthy priests. Augustine had influentially established the point in the controversy with the Donatists that even bad ministers may continue to receive the dignity of the pastoral office when their ordination has been duly authorized. Catherine of Siena made the same point later and with even greater force, that unworthy ministers are due to be revered, since they are not revered for their personal worthwhileness, but for their office. Catherine's striking metaphor is of a tramp bearing kingly gifts:

This reverence should never diminish in the case of priests whose virtue grows weak.... This dignity belongs to good and bad alike—all have the Sun to administer, as has been said, and perfect priests are themselves in a condition of light, that is to say, they illuminate and warm their neighbours through their love. And with this heat they cause virtues to spring up and bear fruit in the souls of their subjects. I have appointed them to be in very truth your guardian angels to protect you; to inspire your hearts with good thoughts by their holy prayers, and to teach you My doctrine reflected in the mirror of their life, and to serve you by administering to you the holy Sacraments, thus serving you, watching over you, and inspiring you with good and holy thoughts as does an angel.... You know well that if a filthy and badly dressed person brought you a great treasure from which you obtained life, you would not hate the bearer, however ragged and filthy he might be, through love of the treasure and of the lord who sent it to you. His state would indeed displease you, and you would be anxious through love of his master that he should be cleansed from his foulness and properly clothed. This, then, is your duty according to the demands of charity, and thus I wish you to act with regard to such badly ordered priests, who themselves filthy and clothed in garments ragged with vice through their separation from My love, bring you great Treasures. (Catherine of Siena, *A Treatise of Prayer*, pp. 255-257)

The crow is an ancient metaphor of abandonment. In his Table Talk of 1531, Luther compared the abrupt pastoral abandonment of those in one's care to crow deserting their young:

Crows are said to be very heartless in that they desert their young after they have hatched them and fly away. Thereafter God miraculously feeds them (Ps. 147:9). By these crows the false and faithless teachers, and pastors of the church are pictured. For the sake of the belly (*ventris gratia*) or danger, they desert their young ones (*pullos*), that is, the Christians entrusted to their care. (Luther, *Table Talk*, W-T 2, #2154; WLS 1, p. 283)

Ignatius Loyola viewed the authentic choice of priesthood as immutable, binding further choice, for that is the nature of immutable choice. But if the divine call has been misunderstood, one had best not compound one bad choice with another:

There are some things that are the objects of an immutable choice, such as the priesthood, matrimony, etc. There are others in which the choice is not immutable, as for example, accepting or relinquishing a benefice, accepting or renouncing temporal goods.

Once an immutable choice has been made there is no further choice, for it cannot be dissolved, as is true with marriage, the priesthood, etc. It should be noted only that if one has not made this choice properly, with due consideration, and without inordinate attachments, he should repent and try to lead a good life in the choice that he has made. Since this choice was ill considered and improperly made, it does not seem to be a vocation from God, as many err in believing, wishing to interpret an ill-considered or bad choice as a divine call. For every divine call is always pure and clean without any admixture of flesh or other inordinate attachments. (Ignatius Loyola, *Spiritual Exercises*, pp. 83-84)

Luther argued against the strict interpretation of indelibility:

A priest is no longer a priest when he is deposed. But now they have invented *characteres indelebiles* (indelible marks) and prate that a deposed priest is nevertheless something different from a mere layman. They even dream that a priest can nevermore become a layman or be anything else than a priest. All this is mere talk and man-made law. (Luther, "To the Christian Nobility of the German Nation, 1520," WA 6, p. 407; WLS 2, p. 944; cf. LW, 44, p. 129)

Again, Luther:

In this view of the ministry, the so-called "indelible character" vanishes and the perpetuity of the office is shown to be fictitious. A minister may be deposed if he proves unfaithful. (Luther, "Concerning the Ministry, 1523," LW 40, p. 35)

What about pastors who leave parishes and invest their entire time seeking to influence bureaucracies and secondary church organizations? Although it may seem to be only a modern phenomenon, this problem was being debated already at the Council of Chalcedon (451 A.D.). Priests were leaving their parishes to try to influence the bureaucracy at Constantinople, lobbying, scheming, and making trouble:

It has come to the hearing of the holy Synod that certain clergymen and monks, having no authority from their own bishop, and sometimes, indeed, while under sentence of excommunication by him, betake themselves to the imperial Constantinople, and remain there for a long time, raising disturbances and troubling the ecclesiastical state, and turning men's houses upside down. Therefore the holy Synod has determined that such persons be first notified by the Advocate of the most holy Church of Constantinople to depart from the imperial city; and if they shall shamelessly continue in the same practices, that they shall be expelled by the same Advocate even against their will, and return to their own places. (Chalcedon, A.D. 451, Canon XXIII, The Seven Ecumenical Councils, NPNF 2, XIV, pp. 283-284)

Shortly after the Diocletian persecution, the Council of Ancyra rigorously assessed those conditions under which it should not be considered blameworthy to flee from persecution:

Those who have fled and been apprehended, or have been betrayed by their servants; or those who have been otherwise despoiled of their goods, or have endured tortures, or have been imprisoned and abused, declaring themselves to be Christians; or who have been forced to receive something which their persecutors violently thrust into their hands, or meat (offered to idols), continually professing that they were Christians; and who, by their whole apparel, and demeanour, and humility of life, always give evidence of grief at what has happened; these persons, inasmuch as they are free from sin, are not to be repelled from the communion; and if, through an extreme strictness or ignorance of some things, they have been repelled, let them forthwith be re-admitted. (Council of Ancyra, A.D. 314, Canon III, The Seven Ecumenical Councils, NPNF 2, XIV, p. 64)

V ❧ On Healing the Corruptions of Sacred Ministry

Lapse comes from *lapsare*, to slip, stumble, slide or fall. The stumbling of pastors may occasion the stumbling of many others. Thus the lapsing of clergy (an extension of the analogy of the fall of humanity) has been a recurrent point of debate and analysis for classical pastoral writers.

In this Part we have discussed the pastoral duty to care for oneself, especially as it takes the form of vocational demoralization, burnout, and the temptation of abandonment of ministry. In examining these subjects, the pastoral writers have been intensely aware of *the special corruptions to which ministry is prone*, and have sought alertly to identify, circumvent, and where they occur, reform and heal them.

The pastor, like all others, is liable to stumble along the way, but pastoral stumbling may too quickly elicit a crisis in self-esteem, partly due to the inordinate quality of idealism that sometimes attaches itself to the vocation to ministry. So it is pertinent to ask of the classical writers how they understood the proneness of ministry to fall. This is considered under the category of the pastoral duty to care for oneself because the struggle takes place primarily in the self-consciousness, conscience, and inner life of the pastor.

Some vices or undesirable behavior patterns have been thought to be more directly opposed to the nature and spirit of care of souls than others. Luther thought that two in particular, pride and avarice, were most commonly destructive of the foundation of pastoral service:

> The sum and substance of this epistle is that in a preacher or teacher no vice is more hurtful or harmful than vainglory, although avarice is also an evil trait in them, and both commonly appear together. For the sake of profit—that they may gain more—preachers and teachers want to be something outstanding, special and superior. . . . All other vices are more endurable in a preacher, although, of course, none of them are good; and a preacher should, in fairness, be blameless and perfect, as St. Paul teaches (Titus 1:7). Nor is this surprising, for both vices are naturally and directly opposed to the nature of the ministry. (Luther, WA 17 II, p. 144; WLS 2, pp. 952-953)

On the occasion of his being burned at the stake in Oxford, October 16, 1555, Anglican Bishop Nicolas Ridley of London recounted how repeatedly the ministry has failed the people, and how quickly a corrupted ministry was able to do injury to church and society:

> You that are my kinsfold and countrymen, know that however much the blind, ignorant, and wicked world hereafter shall rail upon my death, they cannot do worse than their fathers did of the death of Christ. . . . Now you also know, my true lovers in

God, my kinsfolk and countrymen, that the cause for which I am put to death is the same sort and condition. . . . For you all know that when the poor true man is robbed by the thief of his own truly-gotten goods, by which he and his household should live, he is greatly wronged. For the thief in stealing and robbing with violence the poor man's goods, offends God, transgresses his laws, and is injurious both to the poor man and to the commonwealth. So I say it is with the Church of England in the cause of my death, as you all know. . . . This Church of England had of late, of the infinite goodness and abundant Almighty God, great substance, great riches of heavenly treasure, great plenty of God's true and sincere word, the true and wholesome administration of Christ's holy sacraments, the whole profession of Christ's religion, truly and plainly set forth in baptism, the plain declaration and understanding of the faith taught in the holy catechism to be learned of all true Christians. . . . But, alas! of late, into this spiritual possession of the heavenly treasure of these godly riches, thieves have entered in who have robbed and spoiled all this heavenly treasure away. I may well complain of these thieves, and cry out upon them with the prophet, saying: "O God, the heathen have set foot in thy domain, defiled thy holy temple, and laid Jerusalem in ruins" (Ps. 79:1)—that is, they have broken and beat down to the ground your holy city. This heathen generation, these thieves of Samaria, these Sabaeans and Chaldeans, these robbers, have rushed out of their dens and robbed the Church of England of all the holy treasure of God. They have carried it away, and overthrown it, and in the place of God's holy Word, the true and right administration of Christ's holy sacraments, as of baptism and others, they mixed their ministry with foolish fantasies, and many wicked and ungodly traditions. (Bishop Ridley, 1555, Confessorsand Martyrs, OCC I, p. 64-67)*

There is no absolute guarantee that once approved and ordained for care of souls, the pastor's integrity will remain inviolable. Tertullian looked to biblical precedent (Saul, David, and Solomon) to show that one could at one time be called and approved of God in performing a special office, and then at a later time fall into abuses:

This again is, I suppose, an extraordinary thing, that one who has been approved should afterwards fall back? Saul, who was good beyond all others, is afterwards subverted by envy. David, a good man "after the Lord's own heart," is guilty afterwards of murder and adultery. Solomon, endowed by the Lord with all grace and wisdom, is led into idolatry by women. (Tertullian, *On Prescription Against Heretics*, Ch. III, ANF III, p. 244)

Accountability in caring for souls depends upon something more than formal ecclesiastical approval. Menno Simons, the sixteenth century Anabaptist leader who had suffered so much at the hands of ordained ministers, had good reason to doubt that ordination, once given, would necessarily guarantee its continued authenticity, charity, and fairness. False ministries will be called into account, if not by human, then by divine judgment:

A portion of them are useless, haughty, immoral men; some are avaricious, usurers, liars, deceivers; some are drunkards, gamblers, licentious, open seducers, idolaters, etc., concerning whom it is written that they shall not inherit the kingdom of God if they do not repent (1 Cor. 6:9, 10). Some also are idle profligates, young and haughty, wholly unlearned in the Scriptures, anointed and shaven by Antichrist, just so they have a smattering of Latin, as if the office of God and cure of souls depended not on piety and the gift of grace, but on linguistic attainment. No, my reader, no, we shall have to look deeper than that. . . . It is much worse than I can write. The blind call the blind; the one idolater calls the other; one ungodly man calls the other. The saying of the prophet comes true: deceivers, liars, drunkards, and gluttons are good prophets for this people (Micah 2:11). . . . No doubt it suits perverted fleshly ease to live in luxury here on earth with bodies fat and sleek and with gloved hands putting on airs; to be greeted as doctor, lord, and master by men. But when the messenger of death shall knock at the door of your souls and say: "Give account," you may no longer be stewards. When you must appear before the throne of the eternal majesty and before the poor miserable souls which you have led off the true highway of Christ with your deceiving, false doctrine, idolatrous witchcraft, and wickedly liberal life; when you must be wrenched from your lying mouths, your blind and infidel hearts, and your sleek and lazy bodies, oh, where will you conceal yourselves then from the wrath of God? Then men will cry, ye mountains, fall on us; and ye hills, cover us (Rev. 6:16). Ah, then you will know what kind of calling you had, what office and life you led, that you served no one but your impotent god, the belly, the devil, and your self-seeking evil flesh, that you came without being called, that you have sought nothing but the milk, wool, and flesh of the sheep. (Menno Simons, *Foundations of Christian Doctrine*, 1539, *CWMS*, pp. 162-163)

Ministry is entrusted with power that can greatly harm, as well as help, the community of faith. It is because the people have come to depend so profoundly upon the genuine caring of ministers, that the abuses of ministry become so wrenching. The office of ministry bears special responsibilities, just as physicians or magistrates, which others need not bear. If one had chosen to live a private life without taking a pastoral charge, there would be less grounds for complaint; but ministers have voluntarily accepted and taken on these unique responsibilities:

When reproofs themselves prove so ineffectual, that they are more offended at the reproof than at the sin, and had rather that we should cease reproving than that themselves should cease sinning, I think it is time to sharpen the remedy. . . . To bear with the vices of the ministry is to promote the ruin of the Church, for what speedier way is there for the depraving and undoing of the people, than the depravity of their guides? And how can we more effectually further a reformation, than by endeavouring to reform the leaders of the Church? . . . If thousands of you were in a leaking ship, and those that should pump out of the water, and stop the leaks, should be sporting or asleep, or even but favouring themselves in their labours, to the hazarding of you all, would you not awaken them to their work and call of them labour as for your lives? . . . Neither God nor good men will let you alone in such sins. Yet if you had betaken yourselves to another calling, and would sin to yourselves only, and would perish alone, we should not have so much necessity of molesting you, as now we have; but if you will enter into the office of the ministry, which is for the necessary preservation of us all, so that by letting you alone in your sin, we must give up the Church to loss and hazard, blame us not if we talk to you more freely than you would have us do. If your own body were sick, and you will despise the remedy, or if your own house were on fire, and you will be singing or quarrelling in the streets, I could possibly bear it, and let you alone (which yet, in charity, I should not easily do), but, if you will undertake to be the physician of an hospital, or to a whole town that is infected with the plague, or will undertake to quench all the fires that shall be kindled in the town, there is no bearing with your remissness, how much soever it may displease you. Take it how you will, you must be told of it. (Baxter, *RP*, pp. 39-41)

When the trust offered to the pastoral counselor is abused, as when the counselor has sexual intercourse with a parishioner, the integrity of the whole of the clergy may be thrown in question. That such abuses are ancient is evident in this fourth century account by Socrates Scholasticus. The remedy for such abuses, however, must not itself create greater problems:

A woman of noble family coming to the rite of penitence, made a general confession of those sins she had committed since her baptism. The presbyter urged fasting and prayer continually, that together with the acknowledgment of error, she might have to show works also meet for repentance. Some time after this, the same lady again presented herself, and confessed that she had been guilty of another crime, a deacon of the church having slept with her. When this was proved the deacon was removed from the church; but the people were very indignant, being not only offended at what had taken place, but also because the deed had brought scandal and degradation upon the Church. When in consequence of this, ecclesiastics were subjected to taunting and reproach, Eudaemon a presbyter of the church, by birth an Alexandrian, persuaded Nectarius the bishop to abolish the office of penitential presbyter, and to leave every one to his own conscience with regard to the participation of the sacred mysteries; for in his judgment, only in this way could the Church be preserved from bad repute. . . . My observation to Eudaemon, when he first related the circumstance, was this: "Whether, O presbyter, your counsel has been profitable for the Church or otherwise, God knows; but I see that it takes away from all the means of admonishing one another's faults, and prevents our acting upon that precept of the apostle." (Socrates Scholasticus, *Ecclesiastical History*, Bk. V, Ch. XIX, NPNF 2, II, p. 128)*

Several conclusions may be derived from this vignette: Due to the unique closeness of confessional conversation that brings men and women together on a confidential and personal basis, clergy are brought near the possibilities of sexual irresponsibilities (or more often simply suspicion of sexual misdeeds). However abusable, the answer to potential sexual abuses of confession is not to do away with confession altogether.

Fourth century canon law strictly forbade clergy to do any form of violence to persons. For lay persons become vulnerable in the care of clergy, and put themselves trustfully into the hands of clergy. This rule remains in broad intent still applicable to pastoral counseling relationships—do no harm:

We command that clergy, whether bishop, presbyter or deacon, who resort to violent acts to correct believers, be deprived of their office. They imagine that they are going to terrify people into faith. Yet our Lord has nowhere taught us such things. On the contrary, "when he was abused he did not retort with abuse, when he suffered he uttered no threats" (1 Pet. 2:23). (*Constitutions of the Holy Apostles*, Ecclesiastical Canons, Book VIII, Sec. v, Canon 28, ANF VII, p. 501, NEB)*

There is a strong antinomian temptation almost unique to sacred ministry, which believing that God has especially chosen ministers, consequently tends to view ministers as above or beyond the law. With this false premise, it is difficult to prevent the pastoral office from becoming a cloak for abuses, insensitivities, and deceptions, according to John Chrysostom:

A man who has received an honour beyond his deserving should not use its greatness as a cloak for his faults. He ought rather to use God's abundant favour towards him as a stronger incentive to improvement. But because he has been so highly honoured, he thinks he is allowed to make mistakes, and is determined to prove that the cause of his own sins is the kindness of God. This is always the argument of irreverent men who manage their lives carelessly. We must not be like that. (John Chrysostom, *On the Priesthood*, Ch. IV, sec. 1, p. 106)

This contorted temptation centers on the presumed premise of the lenience of God, as if to say, since God forgives all, why not sin that grace may abound? Such a misguided ministry is candidly likened by Luther to pandering:

In no place have people blasphemed God more and put Him to shame more than in those churches and houses of God, as they were called. Therefore I may well say: It would be better for all churches to be dance halls than churches in which the tomfoolery is preached and practiced with which men rob God of His honor and ruin countless souls. In fact, I would even say more: that such churches are worse than all public houses of ill fame (*alle gemeine Frauenhaeuser*); for there thousands of souls are poisoned and prostituted at once, and the preacher is a thousand times worse than a panderer. He prostitutes so many tender souls by his sermons. (Luther, WA 17 II, p. 342f; WLS 1, #873, p. 298)

According to Tertullian, God the Spirit knew in advance the special vulnerabilities of clergy, that they would be tempted more strongly than others to licence and antinomianism:

The Holy Spirit saw that in the future some would say: "All things are permitted to bishops!" And, in fact, your bishop of Uthina is a case in point: he did not scruple to violate even the edict of Scantinius! And how many bigamists are there who rule in your churches, obviously insulting the Apostle, or at least unembarrassed, even as his words on this subject are read out while they are presiding! (Tertullian, *On Monogamy*, ACW 13, p. 99)

Clergy are capable of elaborate rationalizations. Much more than normal damage can be done under the guise of righteousness. Luther preferred open theivery to deceptive ministry:

There is no more terrible plague, calamity, and misfortune on earth than a preacher who does not preach God's Word. Unfortunately, the world is now full of such preachers. Yet they imagine that they are doing well and are pious. However, they are doing nothing but murdering souls, blaspheming God, and establishing idolatry. It would be far better for them to be robbers, murderers, and the worst rogues; then they would at least know that they are doing wrong. (Luther, WA 10 I, p. 85; WLS 3, p. 1124)

John Donne prayed in his parting days that he be spared those who would abuse the pastoral office:

Keep me back, O Lord, from them who misprofess arts of healing the soul . . . by means not imprinted by thee in the church for the soul. (John Donne, *Devotions*, p. 28)

Every care-giver needs care. The selections of Part One have focussed upon soul care for the care-giver, and the pastoral obligation to care for oneself, to receive due care for one's own soul. Special nourishment is required to transcend despair over the burdens of care for others. Caring for the flock cannot occur unless one first insures that one's own soul is fed. This requires facing the distinctive challenges of pastoral service and the difficulties intrinsic to soul care, so that ministry will not have to be abandoned under fire, and the temptations and corruptions closest to soul care will be resisted.

2 Pastoral Care Through Preaching

PASTORAL CARE HAS BEEN DISJOINED from preaching in modern curricula. In previous periods, pastoral care was thought to include preaching, and preaching was viewed as a task intrinsic to pastoral care. In this Part we will review key texts that make clear the nature of preaching and its integral relation with the care of souls.

I ፠ THE MINISTRY OF THE WORD

In Romans 10:12-15, Paul set forth the primary reason for preaching: "Scripture says: . . . 'Everyone who invokes the name of the Lord will be saved.' How could they invoke one in whom they had no faith? And how could they have faith in one they had never heard of? And how hear without someone to spread the news? And how could anyone spread the news without a commission to do so? And that is what Scripture affirms: 'How welcome are the feet of the messengers of good news!' " Following Paul, the pastoral writers have spoken frequently of the human need for being counseled through the word of preaching. Major classic definitions of soul care, whether of patristic, medieval, or Reformation periods, include proclamation of the gospel. It is not a task that Christianity expects God unilaterally to do for us or without our human voices, as Luther noted:

It would not be surprising if I threw the keys at the Lord's feet and said: Lord, do Your own preaching. No doubt You are able to do better; for we have preached to them, but they will not listen to us. But God wants us to stand fast in our calling and office, to administer them, and to give rebukes. For He wants to rule His church through preachers, through the external word and Sacrament, just as He rules the world through burgomasters, kings, princes, and lords, and punishes the wicked with the sword. (Luther, WA 47, p. 95; WLS 3, p. 1115)

28

As the external, political life of the world needs the ordering provided by government, so does the inner life of the soul need the guidance of preaching. Alan of Lille defined preaching as a highly public activity which nonetheless seeks to reach deeply into the hidden recesses of the soul:

Preaching is an open and public instruction in faith and behavior, whose purpose is the forming of men; it derives from the path of reason and from the fountainhead of the "authorities." Preaching should be public, because it must be delivered openly. That is why Christ says: "What you hear whispered you must shout from the housetops" (Matt. 10:27). For if preaching were hidden, it would be suspect. (Alan of Lille, *The Art of Preaching*, Ch. I, CFS, 23, pp. 16-17, NEB)*

The best pastoral preaching does not focus autobiographically upon the preacher's inward feelings or sentiments, but upon God's own Word addressed through scripture. Martin Chemnitz asked: What is the preacher called to preach about?

Neither his dreams, nor the visions of his heart, nor whatever seemed good or right to him (Jer. 23:16, 25); also not human traditions or ordinances (Is. 29:13; Mt. 15:9). But let him who teaches in the church teach the Word of God (1 Pt. 4:11), so that the heart of the ministry is and remains this, Is. 59:21: "I have put My words in your mouth," and as Augustine aptly says: "Let us not hear in the church: I say this, you say this, he says that; but: Thus says the Lord." (Chemnitz, *MWS*, Part 2, sec. 34, p. 39)

The essential subject matter of preaching is the good news of God's coming to humanity that we might come to share in God's life, as set forth by Anglican theologian Ralph Cudworth:

Though the gospel be not God, as He is in His own brightness, but God veiled and masked to us, God in a state of humiliation and condescendent as the sun in a rainbow, yet it is nothing else but a clear and unspotted mirror of Divine holiness, goodness, purity, in which attributes lies the very life and essence of God Himself. The gospel is nothing else but God, descending into the world in our form and conversing with us in our likeness, that He might allure and draw us up to God and make us partakers of His Divine form. *Theos gegonen anthropos* (as Athanasius speaks) *hina hemas en eauto theopoiese*; "God was therefore incarnated and made man, that He might deify us," that is (as St. Peter expresses

it), "make us partakers of the Divine Nature" (cf. 2 Pet. 1:4). . . .
God Who is absolute goodness cannot love any of His creatures
and take pleasure in them without bestowing a communication of
His goodness and likeness upon them. (Ralph Cudworth, Sermon
Preached Before the House of Commons, 1647, pp. 16-21, *Angl.*,
p. 782)*

The freedom of the pulpit will be maintained only with vigilance. Yet
the free pulpit does not give the preacher the general license to express
any and every private opinion about whatever happens to be of personal
interest. Luther, who did as much as anyone to free the pulpit from
intrusions from state power, argued the case rigorously:

If any man would preach, let him suppress his own words. Let
him make them count in family matters and secular affairs. But
here in the church he should speak nothing except the Word of
this rich Head of the household; otherwise it is not the true
church. Therefore this must be the rule: God is speaking. . . .
That is why a preacher, by virtue of his commission and office, is
administering the household of God and dare say nothing but
what God says and commands. And although much talking is
done which is outside the Word of God, yet the church is not
established by such talk, though men were to turn mad in their
insistence on it. (Luther, WA 47, p. 773f; WLS 1, p. 287)

If Luther is correct, the best pastoral preaching is clear, forceful, rel-
evant exposition of the texts of scripture. That is what distinguishes the
ministry of the Word from editorial opinion on economics, politics and
domestic affairs. Jeremy Taylor, the Anglican defender of religious toleration, warned against the pulpit being used crassly as an arena for
divisive debates, or a platform for the propagation of teachings inconsis-
tent with Christian faith. The guiding rule for what is to be preached is
canonical scripture and ancient ecumenical tradition:

Every minister ought to be careful, that he never expound
Scriptures in public contrary to the known sense of the catholic
Church, and particularly of the churches of England and Ireland,
nor introduce any doctrine against any of the four first general
councils; for these, as they are measures of truth, so also of necessity; that is, as they are safe, so they are sufficient; and besides
what is taught by these, no matter of belief is necessary to salvation.
Let no preacher bring before the people, in his sermons or discourses, the arguments of great and dangerous heresies, though

with a purpose to confute them; for they will much easier retain the objection than understand the answer.

Let not the preacher make an article of faith to be a matter of dispute; but teach it with plainness and simplicity, and confirm it with easy arguments and plain words of Scripture, but without objection; let them be taught to believe, but not to argue. (Jeremy Taylor, *RAC*, sec. 56, *CS*, pp. 18-19)

With wry humor, Luther mused about hyper-creative preachers who imagine that they are called to preach new ideas so as to improve upon the gospel of Christ:

There are some ministers who imagine that they cannot be preachers unless they teach more than Christ and above the level of our preaching. These are the ambitious eccentrics, who forsake our simplicity and rush on with their peculiar wisdom, so that people cast admiring glances at them and exclaim: What a preacher! They should be sent to Athens, where people desired to hear something new every day (Acts 17:21). They seek their own honor, not Christ's, therefore they will also end in shame. Beware of them and stay with Paul, who desired to know nothing save Christ and Him crucified. (Luther, WA 10 II, p. 167f; WLS 3, p. 1116)

II ⚘ THE AUTHORITY OF THE WORD

Classic pastoral writers have generally viewed Paul as the key biblical prototype of the ministry of the Word. In his work, *On the Priesthood*, John Chrysostom sought to analyze why this man, who ostensibly had only the fragile power of speech, had such remarkable influence through preaching:

He had a greater power than speech, a power which was able to effect greater results. By his mere presence, and without a word, he terrified the devils. . . . Let a man's diction be beggarly and his verbal composition simple and artless, but do not let him be inexpert in the knowledge and careful statement of doctrine. . . . How did he confute the Grecians? Why was he sent to Tarsus? Was it not because he powerfully prevailed by his words and so far routed them that they were provoked to murder him, not being able to bear their defeat? Then he had not yet begun to work wonders and no one could say that the crowds thought him wonderful because of the fame of his miracles or that the people who opposed him were overthrown by his reputation. For at that time his only power was the power of speech. How did he contend and dispute with those who tried to live like Jews at Antioch? Did not the Areopagite, who belonged to that very superstitious city, follow him with his wife because of his speech alone? How did Eutychus come to fall from the window? Was it not because he was engrossed until midnight in the word of his teaching? What happened at Thessalonica and Corinth? What at Ephesus and Rome itself? Did he not spend whole days and nights continuously in expounding the Scriptures? ... Why did the Lycaonians believe him to be Hermes? The idea that he and Barnabas were gods was due to their miracles; but the idea that he was Hermes was due not to his miracles but to his eloquence. . . . Listen also to what he says to his disciple in a letter: "Devote your attention to the public reading of the scriptures, to exhortation, and to teaching" (1 Tim. 4:13). And he adds the fruit which develops from this: "For in doing so," he says, "you will further the salvation of yourself and your hearers," and again, "The servant of the Lord must not be quarrelsome, but kindly towards all. He should be a good teacher, tolerant" (2 Tim. 2:24). . . . "Let your conversation be always gracious, and never insipid; study how best to talk with each person you meet" (Col. 4:6). And the command to be ready to give an answer was given to all alike. Writing to the Thessalonians, Paul says, "Fortify one another—as indeed you do." But when he speaks of priests, he says, "Elders who do well as leaders should be reckoned worthy of a double stipend, in particular those who labour at preaching and teaching." (John Chrysostom, *On the Priesthood*, Ch. IV.6-8, pp. 120-125)

Luther was realistically aware that parishioners were not naturally drawn to hear rigorous preaching:

It happened to Ambrosius. He was once told by his parishioners, after they had been admonished to hear the Word and the sermon: The truth is, dear pastor, that if you were to tap a keg of beer in church and call us to enjoy it, we would be glad to come. (Luther, W-T 3, #3663, WLS 1, #890, p. 303)

Nonetheless, since preaching is God's own purpose and intention, God will in due time find listeners for the faithful preacher:

Since God creates people whom He bids to preach, He will no doubt also create and send listeners who will take their teaching to heart. (Luther, WA 46, p. 540; WLS 1, #889, p. 303)

Although the cultural settings in which the Word is proclaimed may be always changing, the Word does not change. Irenaeus contrasted the diversity of false teaching with the fundamental unity of ecumenical teaching amid highly diverse cultures:

The Church, having received this preaching and this faith, although scattered throughout the whole world, yet, as if occupying but one house, carefully preserves it. She also believes these points [of doctrine] just as if she had but one soul, and one and the same heart, and she proclaims them, and teaches them, and hands them down with perfect harmony, as if she possessed only one mouth. For, although the languages of the world are dissimilar, yet the import of the tradition is one and the same. For the Churches which have been planted in Germany do not believe or hand down anything different, nor do those in Spain, nor those in Gaul, nor those in the East, nor those in Egypt, nor those in Libya. . . . Nor will any one of the rulers in the churches, however highly gifted he may be in point of eloquence, teach doctrines different from these. . . . It does not follow because men are endowed with greater and less degrees of intelligence, that they should therefore change the subject-matter [of the faith] itself, and should conceive of some other God besides Him who is the framer, Maker, and Preserver of this universe (as if He were not sufficient for them), or of another Christ, or another Only-begotten. But the fact referred to simply implies this, that one may [more accurately than another] bring out the meaning of those things which have been spoken in parables, and accommodate them to the general scheme of the faith. (Irenaeus, *Against Heresies*, Bk. I, Ch. x, sec. 2-3, ANF I, p. 331)

The authenticity of preaching is to be insured from generation to generation primarily by its accountability to and continuity with the apostolic teaching:

It is within the power of all, therefore, in every Church, who may wish to see the truth, to contemplate clearly the tradition of the apostles manifested throughout the whole world; and we are in a position to reckon up those who were by the apostles instituted bishops in the Churches, and [to demonstrate] the succession of these men to our own times; those who neither taught nor knew of anything like what these [heretics] rave about. For if the apostles had known hidden mysteries, which they were in the habit of imparting to "the perfect" apart and privily from the rest, they would have delivered them especially to those to whom they were also committing the Churches themselves. . . . The faith preached to men. . . . comes down to our time by means of the successions of the bishops. For it is a matter of necessity that every Church should agree with this Church, on account of its pre-eminent authority, that is, the faithful everywhere, inasmuch as the apostolical tradition has been preserved continuously by those [faithful men] who exist everywhere.

The blessed apostles, then, having founded and built up the Church, committed into the hands of Linus the office of the episcopate. Of this Linus, Paul makes mention in the Epistles to Timothy. To him succeeded Anacletus; and after him, in the third place from the apostles, Clement was allotted the bishopric. . . . Polycarp also was not only instructed by apostles, and conversed with many who had seen Christ, but was also, by apostles in Asia, appointed bishop of the Church in Smyrna, whom I also saw in my early youth, for he tarried [on earth] a very long time, and, when a very old man, gloriously and most nobly suffering martyrdom, departed this life, having always taught the things which he had learned from the apostles, and which the Church has handed down and which alone are true. . . . Suppose there arise a dispute relative to some important question among us, should we not have recourse to the most ancient Churches with which the apostles held constant intercourse, and learn from them what is certain and clear in regard to the present question? For how should it be if the apostles themselves had not left us writings? (Irenaeus, *Against Heresies*, Bk. III, Ch. iii-iv, ANF I, pp. 415-417)

The best pastoral preaching lives out of Holy Writ. The Westminster Confession set forth the complex inward process by which scripture works to transform life, self-evidencing its authority, working in our hearts:

We may be moved and induced by the testimony of the Church to an high and reverent esteem of the holy Scripture; and the heavenliness of the matter, the efficacy of the doctrine, the majesty of the style, the consent of all the parts, the scope of the whole (which is to give all glory to God), the full discovery it makes of the only way of man's salvation, the many other incomparable excellencies, and the entire perfection thereof, are arguments whereby it doth abundantly evidence itself to be the Word of God; yet, notwithstanding our full persuasion and assurance of the infallible truth and divine authority thereof, is from the inward work of the Holy Spirit, bearing witness by and with the

Word in our hearts. . . . All things in Scripture are not alike plain in themselves, nor alike clear unto all; yet those things which are necessary to be known, believed, and observed, for salvation, are so clearly propounded and opened in some place of Scripture or other, that not only the learned, but the unlearned, in a due use of the ordinary means, may attain unto a sufficient understanding of them. (Westminster Confession, Ch. I, sec. v-vii, *CC*, pp. 195-196)

This statement concisely defines six common arguments for the inspiration of scripture: (1) its subject matter transcends natural reasoning; (2) its teachings have good effect; (3) its style is authoritative, as if God himself were speaking; (4) its various parts, properly understood, agree; (5) its scope is necessary and sufficient to salvation; and (6) above all the Holy Spirit bears witness through it that we are children of God.

Using a metaphor of fire igniting fire, Guerric of Igny taught that inspired preaching comes directly from inspired scripture:

Tongues indeed of fire they were that that fire distributed from itself and they so set not only the minds but also the tongues of the Apostles on fire that even now the devout listener is set on fire by their word. A tongue indeed of fire was Peter's! A tongue of fire was Paul's! In their utterances there lives even now a perpetual fire which casts its sparks upon our hearts too if we draw near, if we do not turn our ears or our mind away from their words. (Guerric of Igny, *Liturgical Sermons*, Vol. 2, Sermon 39, sec. 1, CFS 32, p. 117)

Alan of Lille used the metaphor of Jacob's ladder to speak of the steps leading toward effective pastoral preaching. It portrays the intrinsic interconnection of prayer, biblical study and preaching:

Jacob beheld a ladder reaching from earth to heaven, on which angels were ascending and descending. The ladder represents the progress of the catholic man in his ascent from the beginning of faith to the full development of the perfect man. The first rung of this ladder is confession; the second, prayer; the third, thanksgiving; the fourth, the careful study of the Scriptures; the fifth, to inquire of someone more experienced if one comes upon any point in Scripture which is not clear; the sixth, the expounding of Scripture; the seventh, preaching.

The man who repents his sin then should first set his foot on the first rung of this ladder by confessing his sin. He should mount to the second rung by praying to God that grace may be bestowed on him. The third rung is reached through thanksgiving for the grace which is given. The ascent to the fourth rung is made by studying Scripture so as to preserve the gift of grace—for Holy Scripture teaches how grace, once given, may be held fast. In this way the fifth rung is seen in sight, when a doubtful point arises, and the reader asks someone senior to help him understand it. The sixth rung is reached when the reader himself expounds Holy Scripture to others. He climbs the seventh rung when he preaches in public what he has learned from Scripture. (Alan of Lille, *The Art of Preaching*, CSS 23, pp. 15-16)

III ❧ Pastoral Preaching

Directness is an elementary rule of preaching:

It is commonly said that these are the three qualifications which mark a good preacher: First, that he step up; secondly, that he speak up and say something (worthwhile); thirdly, that he know when to stop. (Luther, WA 32, p. 302; WLS 3, #3544, p. 1109)

Eloquence, to the pastoral writers, meant expressing oneself with force and fluency. While preaching requires eloquence in this sense, it also requires a strong self-identity that does not depend hungrily upon positive feedback. John Chrysostom, the greatest preacher of the patristic age, noted two principal requirements of effective preaching:

It is impossible to acquire this power [preaching] except by these two qualities: contempt of praise and the force of eloquence. If either is lacking, the one left is made useless through divorce from the other. If a preacher despises praise, yet does not produce the kind of teaching which is "with grace, seasoned with salt" (Col. 4:6), he is despised by the people and gets no advantage from his sublimity. And if he manages this side of things perfectly well, but is a slave to the sound of applause, again an equal damage threatens both him and the people, because through his passion for praise he aims to speak more for the pleasure than the profit of his hearers. . . . So, like a good charioteer, the preacher should have reached perfection in both these qualities, in order to be able to handle both of them as need requires. (John Chrysostom, *On the Priesthood*, Ch. V.2-3, pp. 128-129)

The preacher must first enter deeply into his own feeling process and experience if he is to drive home a point profoundly in the hearts of others. Luther spoke candidly of getting in touch with his anger as an emotive exercise that stimulated and improved his preaching:

If I want to write, pray, preach well, then I must be angry. Then my entire blood supply refreshes itself, my mind is made keen, and all temptations depart. (Luther, W-T 2, #241a; WLS 1, #80, p. 29)

Although preaching may appear easy, it requires great labor and enormous concentration of energies, as Luther wittily observed:

It is true, to ride in armor would be hard work for me. But, on the other hand, I should like to see the horseman who could sit still for an entire day and merely look into a book, even if he had nothing to worry about, to compose, to think, or to read. Ask a writer, preacher, or speaker what labor writing and speaking are; ask a schoolmaster what labor teaching and training boys is. The pen is light, that is true; nor is any tool of any of the trades easier to get than the tool of the writer, for all you need is goose feathers, and plenty of these may be had anywhere for nothing. At the same time, however, the best part of the body (which is the head) and the noblest of its members (which is the tongue) and the highest of its faculties (which is speech) must here bear the burden and do most of the work. In other occupations only the fist or the foot or the back or some other such member has to work. Meanwhile people can cheerfully sing and freely jest, which a writer certainly must forego. Three fingers do the work, people say of writers; but a man's entire body and soul are at work. (Luther, WA 30 II, p. 573; WLS 1, #333, p. 110)

Richard Baxter understood why preaching is such a difficult and subtle task—for it must appeal to both mind and heart, elicit decision, and meet objections, in making the truth plain:

To preach a sermon, I think, is not the hardest part; and yet what skill is necessary to make the truth plain; to convince the hearers, to let irresistible light in to their consciences, and to keep it there, and drive all home; to screw the truth into their minds, and work Christ into their affections; to meet every objection and clearly to resolve it; to drive sinners to a stand. (Baxter, *RP*, p. 70)

The purpose of preaching is misconceived when the congregation becomes the spectator of an aesthetic performance. Sermons are not occasions for literary criticism, but rather a unique moment of expected divine address:

Most of those who are under authority refuse to treat preachers as their instructor. They rise above the status of disciples and assume that of spectators sitting in judgement on secular speech-making. . . . For most people usually listen to a preacher for pleasure, not profit, like critics of a play or concert. (John Chrysostom, *On the Priesthood*, Ch. V.1, p. 127)*

Popular preachers have regrettably found ways of exploiting preaching to their own benefit. Preaching may become the servant of avarice, celebrity status, and bland civil religion. Socrates of Constantinople (c. 380-450) offered this early account of two cases of the abuse of preaching:

Severian presided over the church at Gabala, a city of Syria, and Antiochus over that of Ptolemais in Phoenicia. They were both renowned for their eloquence; but although Severian was a very learned man, he did not succeed in using the Greek language perfectly; and so while speaking Greek he betrayed his Syrian origin. Antiochus came first to Constantinople, and having preached in the churches for some time with great zeal and ability, and having thus amassed a large sum of money, he returned to his own church. Severian hearing that Antiochus had collected a fortune by his visit to Constantinople, determined to follow his example. He therefore exercised himself for the occasion, and having composed a number of sermons, set out for Constantinople. Being most kindly received by John, to a certain point, he soothed and flattered the man, and was himself no less beloved and honored by him: meanwhile his discourses gained him great celebrity, so that he attracted the notice of many persons of rank, and even of the emperor himself. (Socrates Scholasticus, *Ecclesiastical History*, Bk. VI, Ch. XI, NPNF 2, II, p. 146)

Effectiveness in a church is not measured by size of congregation, but by depth of genuine hearing of the Word of God. Luther urged against trying to collect great numbers of people to preach to:

Great numbers do not make the church . . . We must look to the Word alone and judge on the basis of that. . . . The church is a daughter, born of the Word; she is not the mother of the Word. Therefore, whoever loses the Word and instead eagerly looks to influential persons ceases to be the church and lapses into blindness; neither numbers nor power will do him any good. (Luther, WA 42, p. 334; WLS 1, #844, p. 287)

Hearers cannot be expected to follow a pastor who does not follow his own teachings:

They will think that he does not mean as he speaks, if he does not live as he speaks. They will hardly believe a man that seems not to believe himself. . . .they are more apt to believe their sight than their hearing, as being the more perfect sense of the two. All that a minister does is a kind of preaching. (Baxter, *RP*, pp. 84-85)*

IV ℣ THE GIFT AND CRAFT OF HOMILY

Christian homily (from *homilia*, discourse in an assembly) consists of practical discourse with a view to spiritual edification. The homily originated as a highly personal reappropriation of scriptural wisdom.

There were strong injunctions by some early writers against using materials taken from another in a homily. The prevailing assumption was that a given text or series of texts of scripture was addressing a particular congregation of the faithful at a particular time through a particular preacher who knew the pastoral needs of that congregation at that time. For this reason:

It is as unseemly for teachers to give instruction from notes taken from other men's writings, as it is for painters to take inspiration from other men's compositions. (John Climacus, To the Shepherd, sec. 5, *Ladder of Divine Ascent*, p. 231)

John Chrysostom, whose sermons have been plundered more often than any in the pastoral tradition, deplored the widespread practice of sermonic borrowing:

If it happens that a preacher weaves among his own words a proportion of other men's flowers, he falls into worse disgrace than a common thief. (John Chrysostom, *On the Priesthood*, Ch. V.1, p. 127)

Sermon preparation consists first of all in prayerfully searching the scriptures with utmost inwardness, not pirating nicely turned phrases from popular authors:

Some pastors [rely on commentaries] and other good books to get a sermon out of them. They do not pray; they do not study; they do not read; they do not search the Scripture. It is just as if there were no need to read the Bible for this purpose. They use such books as offer them homiletical helps in order to earn their yearly living; they are nothing but parrots and jackdaws, which learn to repeat without understanding, though our purpose and the purpose of these theologians is to direct preachers to Scripture. (Luther, WA 53, p. 218; WLS 3, #3547, p. 1110)*

Luther, however, did not rule out the use of classical Christian preaching in sermon preparation:

Whoever has no cement must build his wall with mud. . . . If Dr. Martin cannot write such good epistles as St. Paul did to the Romans, or cannot preach as well as St. Augustine did, then it is honorable for him to open the book, to beg a morsel, from St. Paul or from St. Augustine, and to follow the pattern of their preaching. (Luther, WA 51, p. 213; WLS 3, #3511, pp. 1130-1131)

The pastor need not choose between didactic strength and rhetorical appeal, for it is better that both be present in fit proportion:

Dialectic teaches, rhetoric moves; the latter pertains to the will, the former to the intellect. Paul embraces both in Rom. 12:7f: "He that teaches [let him wait] on teaching, or he that exhorteth, on exhortation." And these two constitute the method of preaching. (Luther, W-T 2, #2199a; WLS 3, #3604, p. 1129)

Alan of Lille employed striking metaphor and humor to caution preachers against both excessive fanciness and dullness:

Preaching should not glitter with verbal trappings, with purple patches, nor should it be too much enervated by the hue of colorless words: the blessed keep to a middle way. If it were too heavily-embroidered (the sermon) would seem to have been contrived with excessive care, and elaborated to win the admiration of man, rather than for the benefit of our neighbors, and so it would move less the hearts of those who heard it. Those who preach in this way are to be compared with the pharisees, who made the tassels of their garments long, and wore large phylacteries. . . . He must make it clear that the sermon is not designed to arouse the foolish acclaim of the mob, nor tempered to win popular favor, nor shaped to evoke applause, as in a theatre. It is composed to instruct the souls of the listeners, so that they may concentrate, not on who is speaking to them, but on what he is saying. . . . But let the sermon be brief, in case prolixity should cause boredom. When the preacher sees that his hearers' minds are moved, and that they weep freely, and that their expressions are downcast, he should hold back a little, but not too much, for, as Lucretius says: "Nothing dries up faster than a tear (Cicero, Orat. xvii:57)." (Alan of Lille, *The Art of Preaching*, Ch. 1, CFS 23, pp. 18-19, 21-22)

Jeremy Taylor also warned against the tendency of the novice preacher to use technical or ornate language in sermons:

In your sermons and discourses of religion, use primitive, known, and accustomed words, and effect not new, fantastical, or schismatical terms. Let the Sunday-festival be called the Lord's day; and pretend no fears from the common use of words amongst Christians. For they that make a business of the words of common use, and reform religion by introducing a new word, intend to make a change but no amendment; they spend themselves in trifles, like the barren turf that sends forth no medicinable herbs, but a store of mushrooms. (Jeremy Taylor, *RAC*, sec. 54, *CS*, pp. 17-18)

We sometimes imagine we can change long-established patterns and customs by instantly changing our language about them. The fantasy is that by linguistic revisions we may make actual historical reversals, while in truth we are not looking for signficant amendment but only change (as Kierkegaard's "Rotation Method" in Either/Or, Vol. I, out of boredom hungered constantly for change). Pastoral communication is best when it uses ordinary words known to all.

George Herbert artfully described the diverse means by which the preacher seeks to gain a hearing:

When he preaches, he procures attention by all possible art, both by earnestness of speech, for it is natural that men think that where there is much earnestness there is something worth hearing, and by a diligent and busy cast of his eye on his auditors, without letting them know that he observes who marks and who not. . . . Sometimes he tells them stories and sayings of others, according as his text invites him; for them also men heed, and remember better than exhortations; which, though earnest, yet often die with the sermon, especially with country people; who are thick and heavy and hard to raise to a point of zeal and fervency, and need a mountain of fire to kindle them; but stories and sayings they will well remember. He often tells them, that sermons are dangerous things; that none goes out of church as he came in, but either better or worse; . . . He is not witty or learned or eloquent, but Holy. A character that *Hermogenes* never dreamed of, and therefore he could offer no precepts for it. But it is gained, first, by choosing texts of devotions, not controversy; moving and ravishing texts, of which the scriptures are full. Secondly, by dipping and seasoning all our words and sentences in our hearts before they come into our mouths; truly affecting, and cordially expressing all that we say, so that the auditors may plainly perceive that every word is heart-deep. (George Herbert, *CP*, Ch. vii, CWS, p. 63)*

Although preaching is done by means of human language, under the address of scripture it becomes God's own address:

Let every minister be diligent in preaching the word of God, according to the ability that God gives him: ever remembering, that to minister God's word unto the people is the one half of his great office and employment.

Let every minister be careful that what he delivers be indeed the word of God; that his sermon be answerable to the text; for this is God's word, the other ought to be according to it; that although in itself it be but the word of man, yet by the purpose, truth, and signification of it, it may, in a secondary sense, be the word of God. (Jeremy Taylor, *RAC*, sec. 40-41, CS, p. 14)

Assuming that every word of scripture is understood in relation to the whole witness of scripture, Luther with characteristic hyperbole proposed that a better sermon could be preached on a single biblical word than all human words:

He who has only one word of the Word of God and cannot preach a whole sermon on the basis of this one word is not worthy ever to preach. (Luther, W-T 2, #2287; WLS 3, #3546, p. 1110)

Like a crude barbarian glancing with boredom at an artistic master-piece—so are our hard-won sermons sometimes received, according to John Chrysostom. Likewise when bad sermons are praised, it is like bad art being superficially admired:

If a painter of first rank who excelled all others in skill, saw the picture he had painted with great care scoffed at by men ignorant of art, he ought not to be dejected or to regard his painting as poor, because of the judgement of the ignorant; just as little should he regard a really poor work as wonderful and charming because the unlearned admired it. . . . So too the man who has accepted the task of teaching should pay no attention to the commendation of outsiders, any more than he should let them cause him dejection. When he has composed his sermons to please God (and let this alone be his rule and standard of good oratory in sermons, not applause or commendation), then if he should be approved by men too, let him not spurn their praise. But if his hearers do not accord it, let him neither seek it or sorrow for it. It will be sufficient encouragement for his efforts, and one much better than anything else, if his conscience tells him that he is organizing and regulating his teaching to please God. For in fact, if he has already been overtaken by the desire for unmerited praise, neither his great efforts nor his powers of speech will be any use. . . . Do you not know what a passion for oratory has recently infatuated Christians? Do you not know that its exponents are respected above everyone else, not just by outsiders, but by those of the household of faith? How, then, can anyone endure the deep disgrace of having his sermon received with blank silence and feelings of boredom, and his listeners waiting for the end of the sermon as if it were a relief after fatigue; whereas they listen to someone else's sermon, however long, with eagerness, and are annoyed when he is about to finish and quite exasperated when he decides to say no more?

Perhaps this seems to you a trifling, negligible matter, because you have no experience of it. Yet it is enough to kill enthusiasm and paralyse spiritual energy, unless a man dispossesses himself of all human passions and studies to live like the disembodied spirits who are not hounded by envy or vain glory or any other disease of that sort. (John Chrysostom, *On the Priesthood*, Ch. V.6-8, pp. 132-135)

John Chrysostom recognized that the preacher will feel extraordinary pressure to perform, to make the public happy, to play for popularity, to please everyone. Just at this point the inner dictates of the true preacher, like those of the true artist, will deliberately resist applause and follow a narrower way.

Preaching well requires living well:

All the week long is little enough, to study how to speak two hours; and yet one hour seems too much to study how to live all the week. [Some preachers] are loath to misplace a word in their sermons, or to be guilty of any notable infirmity (and I blame them not, for the matter is holy and weighty), but they make nothing of misplacing their affections, words, and actions, in the course of their lives. Oh how curiously have I heard some preach; and how carelessly have I seen them live! . . . Those who seemed most impatient of barbarisms, solecisms, and paralogisms in a sermon, seemed to easily tolerate them in their life and conversation. . . . A practical doctrine must be practically preached. We must study as hard how to live well, as how to preach well. We must think and think again how we may so compose our lives as may most tend to men's salvation, as well as to our sermons. (Baxter, *RP*, p. 64)*

The reason why humor in homily has been resisted is that it tends to be used manipulatively to gain approval, or reduce worship to theatre:

Of all preaching in the world (that speaks not stark lies) I hate that preaching which tends to make the hearers laugh, or to move their minds with tickling levity, and affect them as stageplays do, instead of affecting them with a holy reverence of the name of God. Jerome says, "Teach in thy church, not to get the applause of the people, but to set in motion the groan." (Baxter, *RP*, pp. 119-120)

George Herbert warned against constructing a sermon by dissecting a sentence so that each word becomes the basis of an extended discourse:

The way of crumbling a text into small parts (such as, the person speaking or spoken to, the subject, the object, and the like), has in it neither sweetness nor gravity nor variety. For the words apart are not Scripture, but a dictionary. (George Herbert, *CP*, Ch. VII, CWS, p. 64)*

Those who preach too long make their hearers despise what they are saying:

The Parson exceeds not an hour in preaching, because all ages have thought that a competency, and he that profits not in that time, will less afterwards; the same affection which made him not profit before, making him then weary, and so he grows from not relishing, to loathing. (George Herbert, *CP*, Ch. VII, CWS, p. 64)

V ❧ Word and Counsel

It is a modern misjudgment to bifurcate preaching and pastoral care, splitting them into two entirely different fields, as they appear in modern theological school curricula. Classical pastoral writers regarded proclamation as a task intrinsic to the nature of pastoral care, and the ministry of the Word through preaching as inextricably interwoven with the ministry of the Word through conversation. Anglican bishop Jeremy Taylor viewed preaching and pastoral care as so closely allied that neither could stand alone without the other:

Let every minister exhort his people to a frequent confession of their sins, and a declaration of the state of their souls; to a conversation with their minister in spiritual things, to an inquiry concerning all the parts of their duty: for by preaching, and catechising, and private intercourse, all the needs of souls can best be served; but by preaching alone they cannot. (Jeremy Taylor, *RAC*, V.68, *CS*, p. 21)

The inward integrity that characterizes good pastoral conversation also characterizes good preaching. Only ministers who have dealt with their own feelings and passions can be trusted to responsibly preach the Word of God, according to Clement:

He who is incapable of speaking what is true respecting himself, is he not much less reliable in what concerns God? (Clement of Alexandria, *The Stromata, or Miscellanies*, Bk. VI, Ch. XVIII, ANF II, p. 519)

Counsel (*nouthesia*, admonition, warning, sometimes translated reproof) has been consistently thought to be a crucial function of the pastor. But this counsel is not to occur only in one-on-one situations, but also in the context of public worship through preaching. However, as Taylor warned, when admonition occurs in a public setting, the pastor must be careful to avoid directing the admonition only to one party instead of to the whole body of hearers. Thus admonitory preaching differs from, yet is closely correlated with, the highly personal level of admonitory conversation. Yet public admonition is not addressed abstractly to "the times," but to the body of actual hearers.

Every minister, in reproofs of sin and sinners, ought to concern himself in the faults of them that are present, but not of the absent; not in reproof of the times: for this can serve no end but of faction and sedition, public murmur and private discontent. Besides this, it does nothing but amuse the people in the faults of others, teaching them to revile their betters, and neglect the dangers of their own souls. . . . Every minister ought to preach to his parish, and urge their duty: St. John the Baptist told the soldiers what the soldiers should do, but did not trouble their heads with what was the duty of the scribes and pharisees. (Jeremy Taylor, *RAC*, IV.44-45, *CS*, p. 15)*

Since preaching constitutes a general act of congregational pastoral care, or a general admonition, it is confusing to direct it toward a particular, small group of scholarly hearers:

When we are in the pulpit, we should nurse people and give them milk to drink; for a new church is growing up daily which needs to know the first principles. Therefore one should not hesitate to teach the Catechism diligently and to distribute its milk. The lofty speculations and matters should be reserved for the wiseacres. I will not consider Drs. Pomeranus, Jonas, and Philipp while I am preaching; for they know what I am presenting better than I do. Nor do I preach to them, but to my little Hans and Elizabeth; these I consider. He must be a harebrained gardener who wants to consider only one flower in a large garden and neglects all the others. Therefore see to it that you preach purely and simply and have regard for the unlearned people. (Luther, W-T 3, #3421; WLS 3, #3610, p. 1130)

It is not sufficient merely to decry sin. Preaching is aimed at spiritual conversion and behavioral transformation:

Publicans and harlots enter heaven sooner than Pharisees because they are sooner convinced of their sin and misery. . . . Although many may seem excellent preachers, and may shout down sin as loudly as others, yet it often amounts to little more than emotive fervency, and too commonly but a mere useless bawling. . . . The perverse preacher may more strongly will the reformation of others than of his own behavior, and hence may show a kind of earnestness in dissuading others from their evil ways. He can preach against sin at an easier rate than he can forsake it. . . . He is like a traitorous commander who shoots nothing against the enemy but powder. His guns may make as great a sound or report as those loaded with bullets. (Baxter, *RP*, pp. 83-84)*

Preaching that perennially elicits doubt is misconceived, since the purpose of preaching is to elicit faith:

If you want to preach to a person in a comforting way, then do it so that he who hears you is certain that he is in God's favor, or be silent altogether. . . . For all preachers who make their hearers doubt are good for nothing. For in the kingdom of God we must be sure that we have a gracious God, forgiveness of sins, and eternal life. (Luther, WA 47, p. 307f; WLS 3, #3566, p. 1116)

Prosper of Aquitaine concisely defined the complex interaction that occurs in preaching between the divine Word, the human word, and the human hearer, so as to awaken behavioral transformation and the regeneration of the fallen will:

Whenever, then, the word of God enters into the ears of the body through the ministry of the preachers, the action of the divine power fuses with the sound of a human voice, and He who is the inspirer of the preacher's office is also the strength of the hearer's heart. Then the food of the word becomes sweet to the soul; the darkness of old is expelled by the new light; the interior eye is freed from the cataracts of the ancient error; the soul passes from one will to another, and although the will that is driven out lingers on for a while, yet the new-born one claims for itself all that is better in man, so that the law of sin and the law of God do not dwell in the same way and together in the same man. (Prosper of Aquitaine, *The Call of All Nations*, Bk. 1, Ch. 8, ACW 14, pp. 38-39)

Alan of Lille viewed the preached word as a precious gift that should not be thrown away miscellaneously to those who might trample on it and abuse it:

Preaching should be withheld from the unworthy and obstinate, for those who reject the word of God make themselves unworthy. . . . (Acts 13:46). He who divulges secrets to the unworthy lessens the greatness of the secrets; and the vessels of the Lord are not to be set before the Babylonians. (Alan of Lille, *The Art of Preaching*, Ch. xxxix, CS 23, p. 146)

VI ❧ THE HERMENEUTICAL TASK

Since counsel is central to pastoral care, the pastor studies scripture carefully seeking to communicate its message accurately, gauging it properly to speak within concrete situations. The classical pastors wrote so extensively on the interpretation of scripture that the resulting literature has in time become a distinct area of study itself: hermeneutics, the study of interpretation.

The work of interpreting ancient scripture for modern hearers requires careful, responsible study. One aspect of that study hinges on the awareness that oral traditioning has often preceded the written word. Twentieth century scholars of the oral tradition that predates written New Testament documents may think of their studies as completely unprecedented. Yet there is evidence that early pastoral writers were well aware that an oral traditon of preaching existed, for example, prior to the record of the four evangelists:

Perhaps many of the things which were said to them were said to all who virtually believed; for not to the Apostles alone did the saying apply, "Before governors and kings also shall ye be brought for My sake for a testimony to them and to the Gentiles" (Matt. 10:13). . . . "Whosoever shall confess Me," etc. (Matt. 10:31), is said not specially to the Apostles, but also to all believers. According to this, then, through that which was said to the

Apostles an outline was given beforehand of the teaching which would afterwards come to be of service both to them and to every teacher. (Origen, *Commentary on Matthew*, Bk. XII, sec. 16, ANF X, p. 460)

Origen had already grasped in the early third century that an oral tradition preceded the written scriptures. The testimony of this oral tradition was addressed to general audiences of believers in varied cultural settings. The apostles remembered it in an outline form and later wrote it down in order to be of service to those who were not eyewitnesses. Origen nonetheless strongly argued for the historical accuracy of biblical reports of events. Although a few passages are provided for mystical or anagogic interpretation, most are accurate historical accounts. Origen thought the scriptures should be searched for their spiritual meaning wherever a literal truth is not evident:

But that no one may suppose that we assert respecting the whole that no history is real because a certain one is not; and that no law is to be literally observed, because a certain one, (understood) according to the letter, is absurd or impossible; or that the statements regarding the Saviour are not true in a manner perceptible to the senses; or that no commandment and precept of His ought to be obeyed;—we have to answer that, with regard to certain things, it is perfectly clear to us that the historical account is true; as that Abraham was buried in the double cave at Hebron, as also Isaac and Jacob, and the wives of each of them; and that Shechem was given as a portion to Joseph; and that Jerusalem is the metropolis of Judea, in which the temple of God was built by Solomon; and innumerable other statements. For the passages that are true in their historical meaning are much more numerous than those which are interspersed with a purely spiritual signification. . . . The careful (reader), however, will be in doubt as to certain points, being unable to show without long investigation whether this history so deemed literally occurred or not, and whether the literal meaning of this law is to be observed or not. And therefore the exact reader must, in obedience to the Saviour's injunction to "search the Scriptures," (John 5:39), carefully ascertain in how far the literal meaning is true, and in how far impossible; and so far as he can, trace out, by means of similar statements, the meaning everywhere scattered through Scripture of that which cannot be understood in a literal signification.

Since, therefore, as will be clear to those who read, the connection taken literally is impossible, while the sense preferred is not impossible, but even the true one, it must be our object to grasp the whole meaning, which connects the account of what is literally impossible in an intelligible manner with what is not only not impossible, but also historically true, and which is allegorically understood, in respect of its not having literally occurred. (Origen, *De Principiis*, Bk. IV, Ch. I, sec. 19-20, ANF IV, pp. 368-369)

Historical research does not elicit faith. Origen thought explicitly about the extent to which faith may be dependent upon historical research:

Suppose we knew the place in the wilderness, for example, said to be where the children of Israel camped as they were passing through. What use would that be to me, or what progress could it afford to those who read and meditate on the Law of God day and night? (cf. Ps. 1:2). (Origen, Homily XXVII On Numbers, sec. 6, CWS, p. 253)

Origen was aware that scripture is not always self-evident. He recommended that the preacher struggle candidly and non-defensively with difficulties of exegesis. Like many pastoral writers, Origen thought that the scripture was open to debate among serious readers who encountered difficulties in interpreting it, and that it is better to leave some exegetical issues open for continuing theological discussion:

It is fitting to inquire why He now at all commands the disciples that they should not say that He was the Christ? . . . Matthew then, according to some of the manuscripts, has written, "Then He commanded His disciples that they should tell no man that He was the Christ," (Matt. 16:20) but Mark says, "He charged them that they should tell no man of Him;" (Mark 8:30) and Luke, "He charged them and commanded them to tell this to no man" (Luke 9:21). But what is the "this"? . . . The difficulty thus stated seems to me a very real difficulty; but let a solution which cannot be impugned be sought out, and let the finder of it bring it forward before all, if it be more credible than that which shall be advanced by us as a fairly temperate view. (Origen, *Commentary on Matthew*, Bk. XII, sec. 15, ANF X, p. 459)

VII ❧ COMFORTING OTHERS AS GOD HAS COMFORTED US

The assurance of divine care is a prevailing theme of pastoral care. The aim of pastoral preaching is the awakening of awareness that one is loved by God in Christ, freed from sin and death, and given new life. The pastor's task is to help that awareness come into full bloom both in consciousness and in daily behavior. From this derives the principle connection between pastoral care and preaching: The pastoral preacher hopes to make plausible the assuring word of divine comfort. The caregiver seeks to make clear God's own caring.

The pastor seeks daily to enable parishioners to receive the Spirit of forgiveness, enjoy Christian freedom, pray with boldness, understand that their being corrected is for their good, as by a loving Father, and stand assured of their continuing in the divine favor. Main features of the preaching of assurance were summarized in the Westminster Confession:

All those that are justified God has vouchsafed, in and for his only Son Jesus Christ, to make partakers of the grace of adoption. They are taken into the number, and enjoy the liberties and privileges of the children of God; have his name put upon them; receive the Spirit of adoption; have access to the throne of grace with boldness; are enabled to cry, Abba, Father; are pitied, protected, provided for, and chastened by him as by a father; yet never cast off, but sealed to the day of redemption, and inherit the promises, as heirs of everlasting salvation. (Westminister Confession, Ch. XII, *CC*, p. 208)*

While ministers seek deeply to address the feeling processes, they know that faith is not reducible to an emotion, or to the level of a passing feeling, or to a malleable human experience. Luther argued that faith is prior to experience, in the sense that faith shapes the life of feelings, and is not merely shaped by them:

We must not judge by what we feel or by what we see before us. The Word must be followed, and we must firmly hold that these truths are to be believed, not experienced; for to believe is not to experience. Not indeed that what we believe is never to be experienced but that faith is to precede experience. And the Word must be believed even when we feel and experience what differs entirely from the Word. (Luther, WA 40 III, p. 370f; WLS 1, #1539, p. 513)

Having believed the good news, it is quite possible that doubts of its truthfulness may again invade. This is why the preacher of the good news will be prepared to continue to nurture the believer in the Christian life subsequent to the first dawning of faith, in order that the awareness of God's mercy may be sustained through various crises:

Such as truly believe in the Lord Jesus, and love him in sincerity, endeavoring to walk in all good conscience before him, may in this life be certainly assured that they are in a state of grace, and may rejoice in the hope of the glory of God, which hope shall never make them ashamed.

This certainty is not a bare conjectural and probable persuasion, grounded upon a fallible hope; but an infallible assurance of faith, founded upon the divine truth of the promises of salvation, the inward evidence of those graces unto which these promises are made, the testimony of the Spirit of adoption witnessing with our spirits that we are the children of God: which Spirit is the earnest of our inheritance, whereby we are sealed to the day of redemption.

This infallible assurance does not so belong to the essence of faith, but that a true believer may wait long, and conflict with many difficulties before he be partaker of it: yet, being enabled by the Spirit to know the things which are freely given him of God, he may, without extraordinary revelation, in the right use of ordinary means, attain thereunto. . . . True believers may have the assurance of their salvation [in] divers ways shaken, diminished, and intermitted; as, by negligence in preserving of it; by falling into some special sin, which wounds the conscience, and grieves the Spirit; by some sudden or vehement temptation; by God's withdrawing the light of his countenance, and suffering even such as fear him to walk in darkness and to have no light: yet are they never utterly destitute of the seed of God, and the life of faith, that love of Christ and the brethren, that sincerity of heart and conscience of duty, out of which, by the operation of the Spirit, this assurance may in due time be revived, and by the which, in the mean time, they are supported from utter despair. (Westminister Confession, Ch. XVIII, *CC*, pp. 212-213)

Quality pastoral preaching seeks to make credible to the individual hearer the good news of divine forgiveness in Christ. But what if such attempts meet with the objection: "If good works gain no merit, why do them?"

These good works, done in obedience to God's commandments, are the fruits and evidences of a true and lively faith; and by them believers manifest their thankfulness, strengthen their assurance, edify their brethren, adorn the profession of the gospel, stop the mouths of the adversaries, and glorify God, whose workmanship they are, created in Christ Jesus thereunto, that, having their fruit unto holiness, they may have the end, eternal life. . . . We can not, by our best works, merit pardon of sin, or eternal life at the hand of God, by reason of the great disproportion that is between them and the glory to come, and the infinite distance that is between us and God, whom by them we can neither profit nor satisfy for the debt of our former sins; but when we have done all we can, we have done but our duty, and are unprofitable servants; and because, as they are good, they proceed from his Spirit; and as they are wrought by us, they are defiled and mixed with so much weakness and imperfection that they can not endure the severity of God's judgment.

Yet notwithstanding, the persons of believers being accepted through Christ, their good works also are accepted in him, not as though they were in this life wholly unblamable and unreprovable in God's sight; but that he, looking upon them in his Son, is pleased to accept and reward that which is sincere, although accompanied with many weaknesses and imperfections. (Westminister Confession, Ch. XIV, *CC*, pp. 210-211)

VIII ❦ Enabling Christian Freedom

Pastoral preaching intends to enable freedom. It seeks to set the inner self free from guilt, sin and death; free for the neighbor; free for responsible love. Through the ministry of the Word, the pastor seeks to breathe Christian freedom into life, nurture and sustain it. Yet several dilemmas persist concerning what sort of freedom it is to which the Christian is set free.

The liberty which Christ hath purchased for believers under the gospel consists in their freedom from the guilt of sin, the condemning wrath of God, the curse of the moral law; and in their being delivered from this present evil world, bondage to Satan, and dominion of sin, from the evil of afflictions, the sting of death, the victory of the grave, and everlasting damnation; as also in their free access to God, and their yielding obedience unto him, not out of slavish fear, but a child-like love and willing mind. (Westminister Confession, Ch. XX, *CC*, p. 215)

Suppose the good news of freely-given divine grace is met with an attitude of licentious, law-disavowing, anarchism or antinomianism. Then it might seem better not to take the risk of preaching freedom, but soften the promise that faith makes one free. Luther struggled with this dilemma: Which is worse—to preach faith that turns to license, or to fail altogether to preach faith?

If you preach faith, people become lax, want to do no good, serve and help no one. But if you do not preach faith, hearts become frightened and dejected and establish one idolatrous practice after another. Do as you please; nothing seems to help. Yet faith in Christ should and must be preached, no matter what happens. I would much rather hear people say of me that I preach too sweetly and that my sermon hinders people in doing good works (although it does not do so) than not preach faith in Christ at all; for then there would be no help for timid, frightened consciences.

I see and experience this: here is a man who is lax and lazy, who falsely boasts of faith and says that he relies on the grace and mercy of God and that these will no doubt help him even though he clings to sins. But as soon as death comes to him, it appears that he has never really grasped and believed the grace and mercy of God. Therefore one will have enough to do to cheer and comfort him, even though he has not practiced any particular idolatry. But when the message of faith has been extinguished and the heart is completely swamped by sadness, there is neither counsel nor help. Say something about grace to such a heart, and it will answer: You preach much to me about grace and mercy; but if you felt what I feel, you would speak differently. So a frightened, inconsolable heart goes on. I have heard people speak like this when I tried to comfort them. Therefore I should like to have the message of faith in Christ not forgotten but generally known. It is so sweet a message, full of sheer joy, comfort, mercy, and grace. I must confess that I myself have as yet not fully grasped it. We shall have to let it happen that some of our people turn the message into an occasion for security and presumption; but others, the work-righteous, slander us on this account and say that we make people lazy and thus keep them from reaching perfection. Christ Himself had to hear that He was a friend of publicans and sinners (Luke 15:2), that He broke the Sabbath, etc. We shall not fare any better. (Luther, WA 37, p. 394f; WLS 3, #3603, pp. 1128-1129)

Nothing is more deadly for pastoral preaching than unqualified legalisms and endless hortatory harangue. Luther argued that one cannot experience genuine freedom with a good conscience by following many intricate rules and legal maxims, but only by trusting God's reclaiming, freeing Word. He used the metaphor of two persons in love:

When a man and a woman love and are pleased with each other, and thoroughly believe in their love, who teaches them how they are to behave, what they are to do, leave undone, say, not say, think? Confidence alone teaches them all this, and more. They make no difference in works: they do the great, the long, the much, as gladly as the small, the short, the little, and vice versa; and that too with joyful, peaceful, confident hearts, and each is a free companion of the other. But where there is a doubt, search is made for what is best; then a distinction of works is imagined whereby a man may win favor; and yet he goes about it with a heavy heart, and great disrelish; he is, as it were, taken captive, more than half in despair, and often makes a fool of himself.

So a Christian who lives in this confidence toward God, knows all things, can do all things, undertakes all things that are to be done, and does everything cheerfully and freely; not that he may gather many merits and good works, but because it is a pleasure for him to please God thereby, and he serves God purely for nothing, content that his service pleases God. On the other hand, he who is not at one with God, or doubts, hunts and worries in what way he may do enough and with many works move God. (Luther, *Treatise on Good Works*, WML I, p. 191)

Pastoral preaching holds up before the believer the pattern of Christian freedom—God's own freedom to love:

Although the Christian is thus free from all works, he ought in this liberty to empty himself, to take upon himself the form of a servant, to be made in the likeness of men, to be found in fashion as a man, and to serve, help and in every way deal with his neighbor as he sees that God through Christ has dealt and still deals with himself. (Luther, *Treatise on Christian Liberty*, WML II, p. 337)

Luther unpacked stunning metaphors of faith's kingship and priesthood in his preaching of Christian liberty:

This priesthood and kingship we explain as follows: first, as to the kingship, every Christian is by faith so exalted above all things that by a spiritual power he is lord of all things without exception, so that nothing can do him any harm whatever, nay, all things are made subject to him and compelled to serve him to his salvation. Thus Paul says in Rom. 8:28, "All things work together for good to them who are called." And, in 1 Cor. 3:22, "All things are yours, whether. . . . life or death, or things present or things to come, and ye are Christ's." Not as if every Christian were set over all things, to possess and control them by physical power,—a madness with which some churchmen are afflicted,—for such power belongs to kings, princes and men on earth. Our ordinary experience in life shows us that we are subjected to all, suffer many things and even die; nay, the more Christian a man is, the more evils, sufferings and deaths is he made subject to, as we see in Christ the first-born Prince Himself, and in all His brethren, the saints. The power of which we speak is spiritual; it rules in the midst of enemies, and is mighty in the midst of oppression, which means nothing else than that strength is made perfect in weakness, and that in all things I can find profit unto salvation, so that the cross and death itself are compelled to serve me and to work together with me for my salvation. This is a splendid pre-rogative and hard to attain, and a true omnipotent power, a spir-itual dominion, in which there is nothing so good and nothing so evil, but that it shall work together for good to me, if only I be-lieve. And yet, since faith alone suffices for salvation, I have need of nothing, except that faith exercise the power and dominion of its own liberty. Lo, this is the inestimable power and liberty of Christians.

Not only are we the freest of kings, we are also priests forever, which is far more excellent than being kings, because as priests we are worthy to appear before God to pray for others and to teach one another the things of God. For these are the functions of priests, and cannot be granted to any unbeliever. . . . Who then can comprehend the lofty dignity of the Christian? Through his kingly power he rules over all things, death, life and sin, and through his priestly glory is all powerful with God, because God does the things which he asks and desires, as it is written, "He will fulfil the desire of them that fear Him; He also will hear their cry, and will save them" (Ps. 145:19). To this glory a man attains, surely not by any works of his, but by faith alone. (Luther, *Treatise on Christian Liberty*, WML II, pp. 324-325)

IX ❧ PREACHING THE WORKS OF LOVE

Any pastor who seeks by preaching to enable Christian freedom must also speak often of its corollary, responsible love of the neighbor. With-out love, freedom will turn to license. Attentive pastoral preaching seeks to guard against antinomian distortions of Christian freedom. For good works can no more be disjoined from faith than fruit from roots.

He who has right faith yet continues to sin is like a man whose face has no eyes. But he who has no faith, even though he may do some good, is like a man who draws water and pours it into a barrel with holes in it. (John Climacus, *Ladder of Divine Ascent,* Step 26, sec. 51, p. 195)

Opportunities for good works once offered may not be repeated:

Cato says: *"Fronte capillata post est occasio calva."* In front opportunity has hair but it is bald behind. And the statement of Bonaventura is excellent: *"Qui deserit occasionem deseretur ab occasione."* He who neglects an opportunity will be neglected by the opportunity. (Luther, WA 43, p. 348f, WLS 1, #1142, p. 389)

The persistent delay of good works—procrastination—has remained a serious concern of pastoral care and a proper subject of pastoral preaching. Each individual is responsible for the planning and proper use of his or her limited time.

Let him who is still willing to take advice and assistance diligently listen to the helpful counsel of St. Paul that he may yet redeem the time and not sleep away this rich and golden year of God's grace; as also Christ earnestly warns in the parable of the five foolish virgins (Matt. 25:10-11). These, too, might have made their purchase in time, before the coming of the Bridegroom. But since they waited until it was time to meet the Bridegroom, they missed both the market and the wedding.

The poets and sages of old amused themselves with the story about the crickets or grasshoppers. During the winter, when these had nothing more to eat, they went to the ants and besought them to give them something of what they had gathered; and when the ants asked: What did you do in the summer that you did not lay in a supply against the winter? The crickets replied: We sang. Then they had to hear this answer: If you sang away the summer, you must now dance in the winter. (Luther, WA 22, p. 331; WLS 1, #1144, p. 390)

Luther cautioned the faithful about simplistically relying upon God so as to do nothing:

All this is said against those who tempt God, who want to do nothing, and who imagine that God should give and do whatever they desire, without their labor and industry. To them this proverb is proper advice: *"Verlasse dich drauf und backe nicht"* (Rely on it [God's help], and do not bake); again: *"Harre, bis dir ein gebraten Huhn ins Maul fliege"* (Wait until a fried chicken flies into your mouth). . . . The right middle way is not to be lazy and indolent or to rely on one's own work and doing but to work and act and yet expect all success from God alone. (Luther, WA 31 I, p. 436f.; WLS 3, #4830, p. 1495)

Selections in Part Two have focussed upon pastoral care through preaching, and the special forms of pastoral counsel given through public teaching from scriptures. The authority and authenticity of preaching is insured from generation to generation by accountability to the apostolic tradition. The preacher must enter deeply and congruently into his own feeling and experience if he is to drive home a point profoundly in the hearts of others. Although preaching is done by means of human language, under the address of scripture it becomes God's own address. The pastoral preacher seeks to make plausible the word of God's own care for humanity. Christian preaching holds up before the believer the pattern of Christian freedom—God's own freedom to love.

3 Pastoral Care Through Prayer

SOUL CARE OCCURS within a caring community whose primary corporate act is the praise of God's care. It is not incidental that the same pastor who meets persons in one-on-one conversation concerning the health of their souls, also leads the service of worship where life is received with thanksgiving, sins are confessed, divine pardon received, and life consecrated to God. Since the life of prayer holds up before God all dimensions of the nurture of the soul, it is a crucial activity of care of souls. Guidance of the service of common prayer is an indispensable aspect of pastoral guidance.

I ❦ WORSHIP AND THE CARE OF SOULS

In the divine presence one must be prepared to "ransack the heart," according to Joseph Hall, the Anglican divine. Aided by common prayer, scripture and sacrament, the service of worship invites and allows the self to descend into the depths of self-examination. Cleansing prepares for the welcome guest, God himself. One whose heart is cluttered and enmeshed inwardly in ambiguity and sin has little room for the divine guest:

> There are three main businesses wherein God accounts His service here below to consist. The first is our address to the Throne of Grace and the pouring out of our souls before Him in our Prayers; the second is, the reading and hearing His most Holy Word; the third is, the receipt of His Blessed Sacraments; in all of which there is place and use for a settled devotion. . . . What do we in our prayers but converse with the Almighty, and either carry our souls up to Him or bring Him down to us? . . . Descend into thyself therefore, and ransack thy heart, whoever would be a true client of devotion. Search all the close windings of it with the torches of the Law of God, and if there be any iniquity found lurking in the secret corners, drag it out and

abandon it. . . . As the soul must be clean from sin, so it must be clear and free from distractions. The intent of our devotion is to welcome God to our hearts; now where shall we entertain Him if the rooms be full, thronged with cares and turbulent passions? (Joseph Hall, The Devout Soul, 1643, Works, VI, pp. 477-79, 485-489; *Angl.*, pp. 618-619)*

Tertullian's early description of what was occurring in Christian worship included corrective pastoral admonition as well as scriptural exposition and intercession for the society:

We are a society with a common religious feeling, unity of discipline, a common bond of hope. We meet in gathering and congregation to approach God in prayer. . . . We pray also for Emperors, for their ministers and those in authority, for the security of the world, for peace on earth, for postponement of the end. We meet to read the books of God—if anything in the nature of the times bids us look to the future or open our eyes to facts. In any case, with those holy words we feed our faith, we lift up our hope, we confirm our confidence; and no less we reinforce our teaching by inculcation of God's precepts. There is, besides, exhortation in our gatherings, rebuke, divine censure. For judgement is passed, and it carries great weight, as it must among those certain that God sees them; and it is a notable foretaste of judgement to come, if anyone has so sinned as to be banished from all share in our prayer, our assembly, and all holy intercourse. Our presidents are elders of proved character, who have reached this honour not for a price, but by character; for nothing that is God's goes for a price. (Tertullian, *Apology*, 39.1-6; NE, sec. 147, p. 174; cf. ANF III, p. 46)*

The soul is nurtured in worship through praise, timely admonition, earnest petition for peace and justice, preaching of the gospel and law, and scriptural study correlated with the emerging needs of the times. The chief means of pastoral care is the living bread that feeds the soul. It was not offered to individuals in isolation, apart from the sacramental community at prayer.

Let no one deceive himself [cf. 1 Cor. 6:9]: unless a man is within the sanctuary, he lacks the bread of God [cf. John 6:33; 1 Cor. 9:13; 10:18]. If the prayer of one or two has such power [cf. Matt. 18:19, 20], how much more does that of the bishop and the whole church? (Ignatius of Antioch, *Letter to Ephesians*, sec. 5, AF, p. 79)

There can be no pastoral care without prayer. The assumption appeared early that communion is received only after confession. The second century Didache stated clearly the connection between penitence, reparation, and the service of Eucharist.

Assemble on the Lord's Day, and break bread and offer the Eucharist; but first make confession of your faults, so that your sacrifice may be a pure one. Anyone who has a difference with his fellow is not to take part with you until they have been reconciled, so as to avoid any profanation of your sacrifice. (*Didache*, sec. 14, ECW, p. 234)

Luther spoke of two elements that cannot be omitted in any service of Christian worship:

A Christian congregation should never gather together without the preaching of God's Word and prayer, no matter how briefly. (Luther, "Concerning the Order of Public Worship, 1523," LW 53, p. 11)

Another perennial pastoral function connected with the life of prayer is the pastoral blessing, not only after the worship service, but in and through ordinary conversations. George Herbert set forth reasons why the pastoral blessing was to be viewed as a standard function of pastoral activity. The pastor looks for ways of expressing pastoral blessings at timely moments of personal interaction:

Now a blessing differs from prayer in assurance; because it is not performed by way of request, but of confidence and power, effectually applying God's favor to the blessed, by yielding interest on that dignity in which God has invested the priest, and by the engaging of God's own power and institution for a blessing. The neglect of this duty in ministers themselves has made the people also neglect it. Now they are so far from craving this benefit from their spiritual father that they often go out of church before he has blessed them. Once the priest's *Benedicite* and his holy water were over-highly valued. Now we are fallen to the clean contrary, from superstition toward coldness and atheism. But the parson first values the gift in himself, and then teaches his parish to value it. And it is observable, that if a minister talks with a great man in the ordinary course of complimenting language, he shall be esteemed as an ordinary complimenter. But if he often interposes a blessing, when the other gives him just opportunity by speaking any good, this unusual form begets a reverence, and makes him esteemed according to his profession. The same is to be observed in writing letters also. To conclude: if all men are to bless upon occasion as it says in Rom 12:14, how much more those who are spiritual fathers. (George Herbert, *CP*, Ch. XXXVI, CWS, p. 111)*

The pendulum had swung in Herbert's time from overestimating to underestimating the role of the pastoral blessing. The pastor whose conversation is willing to settle for routine exchanges and compliments receives its reward. The pastor who finds opportunity to express sincere and heart-felt pastoral blessings finds himself viewed in terms of his calling, not merely in terms of routine sociability.

Thomas Aquinas viewed the sacraments as a series of pastoral remedies for crises, human struggles, and behavioral deficits:

The sacraments of the Church were instituted for two reasons: to perfect man in those things concerned with God's worship in accord with the religion of Christian life, and to be a cure for the evils caused by sin. For both these reasons, seven sacraments are suitable. . . .

The number of sacraments can be gleaned also from their institution as a remedy against the evil caused by sin. For Baptism is intended to remedy the absence of spiritual life; Confirmation remedies the weakness of the recently born soul; the Eucharist remedies the soul's tendency to sin; Penance remedies the actual sin committed after Baptism; Sacrament of the Sick remedies the remainders of sins—of those sins not altogether removed by Penance, whether on account of negligence or ignorance; Order remedies divisions in the community; Matrimony remedies concupiscence in the individual and the numerical deficit brought about by death.

Other people see in the number of sacraments a certain harmony with virtues and evils and punishments for sin. They assert that Baptism harmonizes with faith and is directed to the cure of original sin; Sacrament of the Sick, to hope directed against venial sin; the Eucharist, to charity, directed against the punishment of malice; Order, to prudence directed against ignorance; Penance, to justice, directed against mortal sin; Matrimony to temperance, directed against concupiscence; Confirmation, to fortitude, directed against weakness. (Thomas Aquinas, *Summa Theologica*, IIIa, Q. 65, Art. 1, Vol. III, p. 2375)*

Each sacrament, virtue and vice is treated more fully in the *Summa Theologica*. The sacraments are a complete armamentarium against sin on behalf of the growth of virtue. Accordingly, the pastoral office is primarily concerned with activating the sacramental life through a sacramental ministry. The three theological virtues, faith, hope, and charity, correlate with baptism, unction, and Eucharist. The four primary moral virtues (prudence, justice, temperance, and fortitude) correlate with ordination, penance, matrimony, and confirmation, as follows:

SACRAMENT	REMEDIES VICE	THROUGH VIRTUE
Baptism	original sin	faith
Unction	venial sin	hope
Eucharist	malice	charity
Ordination	ignorance	prudence
Penance	mortal sin	justice
Matrimony	concupiscence	temperance
Confirmation	weakness	fortitude

II ❧ ON PREPARING THE SOUL FOR THE PRAISE OF GOD

The Christian service of worship is a public event, led by the same pastor who quietly and individually cares for each hurt or endangered member of the flock. It requires the forethought, planning, decorum, and organization necessary for a public occasion that bespeaks its importance and its meaning.

If the prayer, praise, proclamation, and sacramental action that occur in Christian worship are as crucial to the health of the soul as the classic pastoral writers allege, then it is to be expected that they will be prepared for carefully. The first element in the preparation of the community for public worship is the pastor's own inward preparation. The Apostolic Constitutions employed the metaphor of the ship's captain readying himself, and the crew and passengers for hazardous voyage:

> Be a builder up, a converter, apt to teach, forbearing of evil, of a gentle mind, meek, long-suffering, ready to exhort, ready to comfort, as one of God. When you call together an assembly of the Church, it is as if you were the commander of a great ship. Set up the enterprise to be accomplished with all possible skill, charging the deacons as mariners to prepare places for the brethren as for passengers, with all due care and decency. (*Constitutions of the Holy Apostles*, Bk. II, Sec. VII, ANF VII, p. 421)*

Luther compared worship preparation to a scaffolding for the construcion of a house. The scaffolding is not an end in itself, but a means:

> We have stuck to founding, building, singing, ringing, to vestments, incense burning, and to all the additional preparations for

divine worship up to the point that we consider this preparation the real, main divine worship and do not know how to speak of any other. And we are acting as wisely as the man who wants to build a house and spends all his goods on the scaffolding and never, as long as he lives, gets far enough along to lay one stone of his house. Guess where that man intends to live when the scaffolding is torn down? (Luther, WA 8, 378; W_S 1, p. 302)

The best preparation for worship is a life singlemindedly filled with goodness. If one brings to worship a divided heart, it becomes an obstacle to prayer:

For at the beginning God accepted the gifts of Abel, because he offered with singlemindedness and righteousness; but He did not accept the offering of Cain, because his heart was divided with envy and malice, which he cherished against his brother, as God says when reproving his hidden thoughts: "If you do well, you are accepted; if not, sin is a demon crouching at the door. It shall be eager for you, and you will be mastered by it" (Gen. 4:7). God is not appeased by sacrifice. For if any one shall endeavour to offer a sacrifice merely on the strength of outward appearance, albeit discretely, in due order, and according to appointment, while in his soul he does not have that fellowship with his neighbor that is right and proper, nor does he stand in awe of God;—he who thus cherishes secret sin does not deceive God by that sacrifice which is offered correctly as to outward appearance. Such an oblation will profit him nothing; rather only the giving up of that evil which has been conceived within him, so that sin may not the more, by means of the hypocritical action, render him the destroyer of himself. (Irenaeus, *Against Heresies*, Bk. IV, Ch. xviii, sec. 3, ANF I, p. 485)*

God is not fooled by our hypocrisies. External correctness is not noted in God's eyes so much as the correspondence between the inward condition of the heart and the outward justice shown toward the neighbor. The decisive preparation for worship happens inwardly, strictly in the presence of God. No pastoral writer has captured this inwardness more profoundly than the medieval mystic, Ramon Lull, who taught that when one is with God, one is not alone, and that paradoxically when others intrude into the God-and-person dialogue, oddly enough an unexpected aloneness may emerge.

The Lover was all alone in the shade of a fair tree. Men passed by that place and they asked him why he was alone. And the

Lover answered, "I am alone now that I have seen you and heard you. Until now I was in the company of my Beloved." (Ramon Lull, *The Book of the Lover and the Beloved*, sec. 47, p. 24)

Maximus cautioned that if moral self-examination is not stringently honest, it may become an obstacle to prayer:

Examine your conscience with the greatest accuracy, lest because of you your brother may not be reconciled. Do not cheat it, since it knows the hidden things of your heart, accuses you at the time of your passing, and becomes an obstacle in time of prayer. (Maximus the Confessor, *The Four Centuries of Charity*, Ch. 4, sec. 33, ACW, p. 197)

Not everyone is authorized to approach the altar. The *Athanasian Canons* set forth reasons why those whom God has not called and set apart are not to engage in sacred ministry:

The Lord said to Moses: "No mortal man may see me and live" (Ex. 33:20). David knew this when he wrote: "Terrible art thou, O Lord; who can stand in thy presence when thou art angry?" (Ps. 76:7). And the prophet David never ventured to draw near to the Lord or, like a priest, to offer sacrifice, even though he longed so to do. For it is he who wrote: "How dear is thy dwelling-place, thou Lord of Hosts! I pine, I faint with longing for the courts of the Lord's temple" (Ps 84:1-2). His desire to approach the altar and to be a priest was far greater than his desire for the glory of his kingdom. For by no means do all have authority to approach the altar. Rather this is only for those whom the Lord has chosen for this duty. They must then perform his service in fear and trembling. For David had seen how Saul, who without right or authority made a priestly offering, received instead of a blessing a curse, and fell into great grief. For God took from him his glory when he ventured to approach the sanctuary, being not a priest, seeking to take upon himself the office of Samuel, the faithful priest. It was for this reason that God took from him his kingdom and gave it to David, because he approached the altar unfittingly. (*Athanasian Canons*, sec. 1, pp. 4-5)*

The temple into which the Christian worshipper enters is primarily a temple of repentance, faith, and grace, not a temple made by hands:

We come now to the matter of the Temple; and I will show you how mistaken these miserable folk were in pinning their hopes to the building itself, as if that were the home of God, instead of to

God their own Creator. Indeed, they were scarcely less misguided than the heathen in the way they ascribed Divine holiness to their Temple. . . . God is at this moment actually dwelling within us in that poor habitation of ours. How so? Why, the message of His Faith, and in the call of His promise; in the wisdom of His statutes, and the precepts of His teaching; in His own very Presence inwardly inspiring us, and dwelling within us; in His unlocking of the temple doors of our lips, and His gift to us of repentance. It is by these ways that He admits us, the bondsmen of mortality, into the Temple that is immortal. (*The Epistle of Barnabas,* sec. 16, ECW, p. 215)

A powerful approach to contemplative prayer is suggested by Ignatius Loyola. It is a step by step procedure that takes the worshipper through ten commandments, seven cardinal sins, three powers of the soul, and five senses of the body. It is remarkably comprehensive, yet condensed, way of entry into the life of prayer:

The first method of prayer is on the Ten Commandments, the seven capital sins, the three powers of the soul, and the five senses of the body. The purpose of this method of prayer is to provide a method of procedure, and some exercises in which the soul may prepare itself and make progress, thereby making its prayer more acceptable. . . .

1. The Ten Commandments
Method: For the first method of prayer, it is well to consider and to think over the first commandment, how I have kept it, and which I have failed. For this consideration, I will take, as a rule, the time required to recite three times the "Our Father" and the "Hail Mary." If in this time I discover faults I have committed, I will ask pardon and forgiveness for them, and say an "Our Father." I will follow this same method for each of the Ten Commandments. . . .

II. The Capital Sins
Method: Regarding the seven capital sins, after the additional direction, the preparatory prayer is to be made in the manner already prescribed, the only change is that the matter here is the sins which are to be avoided, whereas before it was the commandments to be observed. In like manner the procedure and the rule prescribed above are to be observed, together with the colloquy.

In order to know better the faults committed relating to the capital sins, let the contrary virtues be considered. Thus the better to avoid these sins, one should resolve and endeavor by devout exercises to acquire and retain the seven virtues contrary to them.

III. The Powers of the Soul

Method: The same method and rule that were followed for the commandments should be observed with regard to the three powers of the soul, [memory, understanding, will], with the addition, preparatory prayer, and colloquy.

IV. The Five Senses of the Body

Method: The same method will also be followed with regard to the five senses of the body, only the subject matter is changed. (Ignatius Loyola, *Spiritual Exercises*, pp. 105-6)

III ∮ THE PASTORAL ORDERING OF WORSHIP

It is a pastoral responsibility to seek to insure that the praise of God is fittingly provided for those entrusted to one's pastoral care. If soul care involves the guidance of the community at prayer, then the pastor must give deliberate attention to the right ordering of the service of worship. As early as Clement of Rome it was argued that worship services should proceed with some fixed order, and not in a purely spontaneous way:

There ought to be strict order and method in our performance of such acts as the Master has prescribed for certain times and seasons. Now, it was His command that the offering of gifts and the conduct of public services should not be haphazard or irregular, but should take place at fixed times and hours. (Clement of Rome, *To the Corinthians*, sec. 40, ECW, p. 44)

Luther thought that vigorous pastoral leadership was required to avoid either extremes of excessive piety or exuberance:

We pastors must see to it that ceremonies are made and observed in such a manner that people become neither too disorderly [*wild*] nor too sanctimonious [*zu gar heilig*]. (Luther, W-T 1, No. 882, WLS 1, #904, p. 308)

Paul's injunction to worship God "decently and in order" (1 Cor. 14:40) was taken seriously by the pastoral writers:

But, surely, I fear these men are not more faulty in the one extreme than many Christians are in the other, who place a kind of holiness in a slovenly neglect, and so order themselves as if they thought a nasty carelessness in God's services were most acceptable to Him. . . . For the rectifying of which misconceits and practices, let it be laid down as an undoubted rule,—that it is a thing well-pleasing to God that there should be all outward cleanliness, gravity, reverent and comely postures, meet furniture, utensils, places, used and observed in the service of the Almighty,—a truth, sufficiently grounded upon that irrefragable canon of the Apostle, "Let all things be done decently, and in order" (1 Cor. 14:40); whereof order refers to persons and actions, decency to the things done and the fashion of doing them. (Joseph Hall, Holy Decency in the Worship of God, Works, VI, p. 464; *Angl.*, p. 543)

The *Athanasian Canons* urged pastors to seek to insure a context for worship characterized by quietude, composure, and awe in the presence of God's majesty. Responsibility for a fitting context falls squarely upon the presiding pastor (*presbuteros*):

Shouting children, those who are constantly talkative, those who deliberately refuse instruction, and those who behave themselves in an unseemly way, are not to be in the worship service. . . in order that the word of God may be glorified and the people hear in quietness, with silence in the whole church, until they finish the word of God with the benediction. If any talk with a loud voice, the blame falls upon the presbyter, in that the deacons have not trained the people. (*Athanasian Canons*, sec. 57, pp. 38-39)*

A gardening analogy—the function of leaves for fruit—was employed by Anglican divine John Bramhall to illumine the relation of religious ceremonies to pastoral care:

Ceremonies are advancements of order, decency, modesty, and gravity in the service of God, expressions of those heavenly desires and dispositions which we ought to bring along with us to God's House, helps of attention and devotion, furtherances of edification, visible instructors, helps of memory, exercises of faith, the shell that preserves the kernel of religion from contempt, the leaves that defend the blossoms and the fruit; but if they grow over thick and rank, they hinder the fruit from coming to maturity, and then the gardener plucks them off. (John Bramhall, *The Consecration and Succession of Protestant Bishops Justified*, Ch. XI, Works, III, p. 170; *Angl.*, pp. 544)*

IV ॐ Modes of Worship

Assuming the biblical mandate for "decency and order," there have nonetheless emerged over two millenia many liturgies, rites, language-frames, and approaches to worship. These arose as the church met one after another new cultural situation. Considerable tolerance has been shown toward these varieties of forms of worship that have been received as consistent with ancient ecumenical teaching. In different times and places the Christian community has experimented widely with modes of worship. According to the Greek church historian, Socrates Scholasticus (c. 380-450), so diverse were these worship practices by the fifth century that it would be impossible to enumerate them:

In the same city of Alexandria, readers and chanters are chosen indifferently from the catechumens and the faithful; whereas in all other churches the faithful only are promoted to these offices. . . . I have also known of another peculiarity in Thessaly, which is, that they baptize there on the days of Easter only. . . . At Antioch in Syria the site of the church is inverted; so that the altar does not face toward the east, but toward the west. . . . In short, it is impossible to find anywhere, among all the sects, two churches which agree exactly in their ritual respecting prayers. At Alexandria no presbyter is allowed to address the public: a regulation which was made after Arius had raised a disturbance in that church. At Rome they fast every Saturday. At Caesarea of Cappadocia they exclude from communion those who have sinned after baptism as the Novatians do. . . . The Novatians in Phrygia do not admit such as have twice married; but those of Constantinople neither admit nor reject them openly, while in the Western parts they are openly received. This diversity was occasioned, as I imagine, by the bishops who in their respective eras governed the churches; and those who received these several rites and usages, transmitted them as laws to their posterity. However, to give a complete catalogue of all the various customs and ceremonial observances in use throughout every city and country would be difficult—rather impossible. (Socrates Scholasticus, *Ecclesiastical History*, Bk. V, Ch. 22, NPNF 2, II, p. 132)

This yields the impression of liturgical diversity amid the fairly rigorous doctrinal cohesion that prevailed in the period of the ecumenical councils. There seemed to be room for a tolerable variety of acceptable liturgies. Another passage from Socrates on the "Indifferent Canon" illustrates the embrace of this diversity. It allowed different churches to keep the Easter feast at different times and in different ways according to local practices, without offense to church unity:

[There was a] disagreement that existed respecting the Feast of Easter. . . . They passed a canon respecting this feast, which they entitled "indifferent," declaring that "a disagreement on such a point was not a sufficient reason for separation from the church;

and that the council of Pazum had done nothing prejudicial to the catholic canon. That although the ancients who lived nearest to the times of the apostles differed about the observance of this festival, it did not prevent their communion with one another, nor create any dissension. Besides that the Novatians at imperial Rome had never followed the Jewish usage, but always kept Easter after the equinox; and yet they did not separate from those of their own faith, who celebrated it on a different day." From these and many such considerations, they made the "Indifferent" Canon, above-mentioned, concerning Easter, whereby every one was at liberty to keep the custom which he had by predilection in this matter, if he so pleased; and that it should make no difference as regards communion, but even though celebrating differently they should be in accord in the church. (Socrates Scholasticus, *Ecclesiastical History*, Bk. V., Ch. XXI, NPNF 2, II, p. 129)

Luther argued that worship may occur anywhere:

The worship of God (*Gottesdienst*) is the praise of God. This should be free at the table, in private rooms, downstairs, upstairs, at home, abroad, in all places, by all people, at all times. (Luther, WA 10 I, 2, 81; WLS 3, p. 1546)

An important summary of the Reformed Protestant understanding of worship practice is found in the Westminster Confession. Scripture instructs the worshipper more fully than nature. One prays in the name of the Son by the power of the Spirit. Preaching is complemented by hearing; the preached-heard Word is complemented by the Sacraments; and Word and Sacrament are complemented by family and private worship, which are complemented by common worship:

The light of nature shows that there is a God, who has lordship and sovereignty over all; is good, and does good unto all; and is therefore to be feared, loved, praised, called upon, trusted in, and served with all the heart, all the soul, and with all the might. But the acceptable way of worshiping the true God is instituted by himself, and so limited to his own revealed will, that he may not be worshiped according to the imaginations and devices of men, or the suggestions of Satan, under any visible representations or any other way not prescribed in the Holy Scripture. . . . Prayer with thanksgiving, being one special part of religious worship, is by God required of all; and that it may be accepted, it is to be made in the name of the Son, by the help of his Spirit, according to his will, with understanding, reverence, humility, fervency, faith, love, and perseverance; and, if vocal, in a known tongue; . . . the reading of the Scriptures with godly fear; the sound preaching; and conscionable hearing of the Word, in obedience unto God with understanding, faith, and reverence; singing of psalms with grace in the heart; as, also, the due administration and worthy receiving of the sacraments instituted by Christ; are all parts of the ordinary religious worship of God. . . . God is to be worshiped everywhere in spirit and truth; as in private families daily, and in secret each one by himself, so more solemnly in the public assemblies. (Westminister Confession, Ch. XXI, *CC*, pp. 216-217)

That the essence of worship is to be found everywhere in the human condition is noted by Luther in discussing Adam's simple pattern of worship:

God gave Adam Word, worship, and religion in its barest, purest, and simplest form, in which there was nothing laborious, nothing elaborate. For He does not prescribe the slaughter of oxen, the burning of incense, vows, fastings, and other tortures of the body. Only this he wants: that he praise God, that he thank Him, that he rejoice in the Lord, and that he obey Him by not eating from the forbidden tree. (Luther, "Lectures on Genesis Chapters One to Five, 1535-36," LW 1, p. 106)

The active life of fidelity in human relationships, honesty, responsible sexuality, and preserving of life—that sphere dealt with in the second table of the Decalogue—should not be thought of as separable from worship. For that is where the life of worship takes active shape. The life of worship is best expressed not by perennial withdrawal from the world but by a rhythm of withdrawal and engagement, as expressed by the two tables of law:

To be sure, it is true that the foremost and highest worship of God is preaching and hearing God's Word, administering the Sacraments, etc.,—performing the works of the First Table of the Ten commandments. Nevertheless, also the performance of all the works of the Second Table of the Ten Commandments, such as honoring father and mother, living a patient, chaste, and decent life, is worshiping God. For he who leads such a life is serving and honoring the same God. (Luther, "Sermon on the Gospel of John, Chapter Fifteen, 1537," WA 45, p. 682; WLS 3, p. 1547; cf. LW 24, p. 242)

V ❦ THE PASTOR AND THE SUNDAY SERVICE

Pastoral care through worship comes to its clearest expression for most parishioners in the weekly service on the Lord's Day. Early accounts reveal the essential content and understanding of the Sunday service. Justin, a second century Chrisian martyr, wrote one of the earliest accounts of the primitive Christian liturgy, combining lection, sermon, praise, congregational responsiveness, and Eucharist:

On the day called Sunday there is a meeting in one place of those who live in cities or the country, and the memoirs of the apostles or the writings of the prophets are read as long as time permits. When the reader has finished, the president in a discourse urges and invites [us] to the imitation of these noble things. Then we all stand up together and offer prayers. And, as said before, when we have finished the prayer, bread is brought, and wine and water, and the president similarly sends up prayers and thanksgivings to the best of his ability, and the congregation assents, saying the Amen; the distribution, and reception of the consecrated [elements] by each one, takes place and they are sent to the absent by the deacons. We all hold this common gathering on Sunday, since it is the first day, on which God transforming darkness and matter made the universe, and Jesus Christ our Saviour rose from the dead on the same day. For they crucified him on the day before Saturday, and on the day after Saturday, he appeared to his apostles. (Justin, *First Apology*, sec. 67, LCC I, p. 287)

The order of service was set forth in the Apostolic Constitutions, of Syrian origin:

When there have been two lessons severally read, let some other person sing the hymns of David, and let the people join at the conclusions of the verses. Afterwards let our Acts be read, and the Epistles of Paul our fellow-worker, which he sent to the churches under the conduct of the Holy Spirit, and afterwards let a deacon or a presbyter read the Gospels. . . . While the Gospel is read, let all the presbyters and deacons, and all the people, stand up in great silence. . . . After this, let all rise up with one consent, and looking towards the east, after the catechumens and penitents are gone out, pray to God. . . . As to the deacons, after the prayer is over, let some of them attend upon the oblation of the Eucharist, ministering to the Lord's body with fear. . . . Then let the men give the men, and the women give the women, the Lord's kiss. But let no one do it with deceit, as Judas betrayed the Lord with a kiss. After this let the deacon pray for the whole Church, for the whole world, and the several parts of it, and the fruits of it. . . . After this let the sacrifice follow, the people standing, and praying silently; and when the oblation has been made, let every rank by itself partake of the Lord's body and precious blood in order. (*Constitutions of the Holy Apostles*, Book II, Sec. VII, Ch. lvii, ANF VII, p. 421)

Bread, wine and water are brought in by the laity as fruits of their labors, and received with thanksgiving by the presbyter—essential elements to be consecrated for sacramental use in baptism and holy communion. The service was held on Sunday to celebrate the resurrection. The Christian liturgy is a resurrection liturgy:

On the day of the resurrection of the Lord, that is, the Lord's day, assemble yourselves together, without fail, giving thanks to God, and praising Him for those mercies God has bestowed upon you through Christ. (*Constitutions of the Holy Apostles*, Bk. VII, Sec. II, Ch. xxx, ANF VII, p. 471)

The pastor will be asked: Why shouldn't every day be a day of worship? Luther answered:

Every day should be "Sabbath" for us Christians; for we should hear God's Word every day and should lead our lives in accordance with it. At the same time Sunday has been arranged for the common people, so that everyone may on that day in particular hear and learn God's Word and live in accordance with it. For during the other days of the week the common man must tend to his work and earn a living. And God is content to have him do so, for He has commanded man to work. (Luther, WA 36, p. 331; WLS 3, p. 1331)

George Herbert knew how important to a congregation was the vital piety, demeanor, and sincerity of the chief liturgist, the pastor, whose liturgical duties he described:

No Sermon moves them so much to a reverence (which they forget again when they come to pray), as a devout behavior in the very act of praying. Accordingly his voice is humble, his words treatable, and slow; yet not so slow neither, as to let the fervency of the supplicant hang and die between speaking, but with a grave liveliness, between fear and zeal, pausing yet pressing, he performs his duty. Besides his example, he, having often instructed his people how to carry themselves in divine service, exacts of them all possible reverence, by no means enduring either talking or sleeping or gazing or leaning or half-kneeling or any undutiful behavior in them, but causing them, when they sit or stand or kneel, to do all in a straight and steady posture. . . . (George Herbert, *CP*, Ch. VI, CWS, pp. 60f.)

VI ❧ CONTINUITY IN LITURGICAL TRADITION

The pastoral writers were keenly aware of the dangers of constant changes in modes of worship, and sought to set reasonable bounds to the process of revision and reform.

I do not of my own accord like to introduce ceremonies and regulations; for once you begin to do this, there is no end to the practice. (Luther, *Table-Talk*, WA-T 5, #5212; WLS 1, p. 309; cf. LW 54, p. 397)

Since liturgical changes are likely to cause offense, they should be introduced only rarely and with adequate preparation:

Although I must acknowledge that you committed no sin when you touched the sacrament with your hands, nevertheless I must tell you that it was not a good work, because it caused offence everywhere. For the universal custom is, to receive the blessed sacrament directly from the hands of the priest. Why will you not herein also serve those who are weak in the faith and abstain from your liberty? It does not help you if you do it, nor harm you if you do it not.

Therefore no new practices should be introduced, unless the Gospel has first been thoroughly preached and understood, even as it has been with you. (Luther, The Eight Wittenberg Sermons, Fifth Sermon, WML II, p. 414)

There is a temptation to divisiveness in liturgical reforms, however well motivated. Jeremy Taylor thought it was better to educate laity to the received service than change it:

Let no minister of a parish introduce any ceremony, rites, or gestures, though with some seeming piety and devotion, but what are commanded by the Church, and established by law: and let these also be wisely and usefully explicated to the people, that they may understand the reasons and measures of obedience; but let there be no more introduced, lest the people be burdened unnecessarily, and tempted or divided. (Jeremy Taylor, *RAC*, Bk. III, sec. 39, *CS*, p. 14)

VII ❧ ELEMENTS OF PRAYER: ADORATION, THANKSGIVING, CONFESSION, PETITION, AND INTERCESSION

The early pastoral literature developed an analysis of the phases, types, and sequential elements of prayer. The pastor who understands the fundamental structure of prayer, its major modes, and timely ordering, will better lead the congregation in prayer.

Origen (c. 185-c. 254) was among the earliest to analyze this sequence of themes through which Christian prayer appropriately moves— praise, thanksgiving, confession, prayer for healing and pardon, petition, and intercession, concluding with doxology:

It seems to me there are four topics that need to be sketched out and that I have found scattered in the Scriptures, indicating that each one should organize one's prayer according to these topics. This is what they are: In the beginning and the preface of the prayer something having the force of praise should be said of God through Christ, who is praised with Him, and by the Holy Spirit, who is hymned with Him. After this each person should place general thanksgivings, bringing forward for thanksgiving the benefits given many people and those he has himself received from God. After thanksgiving it seems to me that he ought to blame himself bitterly before God for his own sins and then ask, first, for healing that he may be delivered from the habit that brings him to sin and, second, for forgiveness of the sins that have been committed. And after confession, the fourth topic that seems to me must be added is the request for great and heavenly things, both private and general, and concerning his household and his dearest. And, finally, the prayer should be concluded with a doxology of God through Christ in the Holy Spirit. . . . First, giving praise may be found in the following words from Psalm 104:1-3): "O Lord my God, thou art great indeed, clothed with majesty and splendour, and wrapped in a robe of light. Thou hast spread out the heavens like a tent and on their waters laid the beams of thy pavilion; who takest the clouds for thy chariot, riding on the wings of the wind". . . . As for thanksgiving. . . David is amazed at God's gifts and thanks Him for them in these words, "What am I, Lord God, and what is my family, that thou hast brought me thus far?" (2 Sam. 7:18). . . . An example of confession is: . . . . "My wounds fester and stink because of my folly. I am bowed down and utterly prostrate. All day long I go about as if in mourning" (Ps. 38:5-6).

An example of petition or request is found in Psalm 28:3: "Do not drag me away with the ungodly, with evildoers." Other examples are like this one.

And having begun with praise it is right to conclude the prayer by ending with praise, hymning and glorifying the Father of all through Jesus Christ in the Holy Spirit, to whom be glory forever (cf. Rom. 16:27; Heb. 13:21; Gal. 1:5; 2 Tim. 4:18). (Origen, *On Prayer*, Sec. XXXIII.1-6, CWS, pp. 169-170, NEB)*

John Climacus (c. 570-649) similarly followed this orderly sequence for Christian prayer:

Before all else, let us list sincere thanksgiving first on the scroll of our prayer. On the second line, we should put confession and heartfelt contrition of soul. Then let us present our petition to the King of all. This is the best way of prayer. (John Climacus, *Ladder of Divine Ascent*, Step 28, sec. 7, p. 213)

John of Damascus (c. 675-c. 749) summarized, in a way that has become familiar to subsequent pastoral writers, five phases of the service of worship (adoration, awe, thanksgiving, petition, and confession) as follows:

Worship is a sign of submission. Submission implies abasement and humiliation. There are many different kinds of worship.

The first kind of absolute worship is adoration, which we give to God alone. . . . The second kind of absolute worship is the awe and yearning we have for God because of the glory which is His by nature. He alone is worthy to be glorified, but no one can of himself glorify Him, because He himself is the source of all glory, all goodness, unapproachable light, incomparable sweetness, boundless perfection, an abyss of goodness, inscrutable wisdom, infinite power, who alone is worthy in Himself to be admired, worshipped, glorified and desired. The third kind of absolute worship is thanksgiving for all the good things He has created for us. . . . The fourth kind of absolute worship is inspired by our needs and hopes for His blessing. Since we realize that without His help we possess no goodness and are able to do nothing, we worship Him, beseeching Him to listen to each one of our needs and desires, that we may be delivered from evil and attain to goodness. The fifth kind of absolute worship is repentance and confession. As sinners we worship and prostrate ourselves before God, begging Him to forgive our sins, as is fitting for servants to do. (John of Damascus, *On Divine Images*, Third Apology, sec. 27-32, pp. 82-83)

Thomas Aquinas carefully delineated the conditions and parts of prayer:

Three conditions are requisite for prayer. First, that the person who prays should approach God Whom he prays: this is signified in the word prayer, because prayer is the raising up of one's mind to God. The second is that there should be a petition, and this is signified in the word intercession. In this case sometimes one asks for something definite, and then some say it is intercession properly so called, or we may ask for something indefinitely, for instance to be helped by God, or we may simply indicate a fact, as in Jo 11:3, "Behold, he whom Thou lovest is sick," and then they call it insinuation. The third condition is the reason for impetrating [beseeching] what we ask for: and this either on the part of God, or on the part of the person who asks. The reason of impetration on the part of God is His sanctity, on account of which we ask to be heard, according to Dan. 9:17,18, "For Thy own sake, incline, O God, Thy ear"; and to this pertains supplication (*obsecratio*), which means a pleading through sacred things, as when we say, "Through Thy nativity, deliver us, O Lord." The reason for impetration on the part of the person who asks is thanksgiving; since through giving thanks for benefits received we merit to receive yet greater benefits, as we say in the collect. Hence a gloss on 1 Tim 2:1 says that "in the Mass, the consecration is preceded by supplication," in which certain sacred things are called to mind; that prayers are in the consecration itself, in which especially the mind should be raised up to God; and that intercessions are in the petitions that follow, and thanksgivings at the end.

We may notice these four things in several of the Church's collects. Thus in the collect of Trinity Sunday the words, "Almighty eternal God" belong to the offering up of prayer to God; the words, "Who has given to Thy servants," etc. belong to thanksgiving; the words, "grant, we beseech Thee," belong to intercession; and the words at the end, "Through our Lord," etc. belong to supplication. (Thomas Aquinas, *Summa Theologica*, II-II, Q. 83, Art. 17, I, pp. 1551-1552)

Izaak Walton (1593-1683), the biographer of many Anglican pastoral writers, noted in his life of George Herbert how useful it is that the pastor make clear to communicants the structure and design of Christian worship:

And that they might pray with understanding, he did usually take occasion to explain not only the Collect for every particular Sunday, but the reasons of all the other Collects and Responses in our Church Service; and made it appear to them that the whole Service of the Church was a reasonable, and therefore an acceptable, sacrifice to God; as namely, that we begin with Confession of ourselves to be vile, miserable sinners; and that we begin so because till we have confessed ourselves to be such, weare not capable of that mercy which we acknowledge we need and pray for. But having in the Prayer of Our Lord begged pardon for those sins which we have confessed, and hoping that as the Priest hath declared our absolution, so by our public confession and real repentance, we have obtained that pardon, then we dare and do proceed to beg of the Lord, to open our lips, that our mouths may shew forth His praise; for, till then, we are neither able nor worthy to praise Him. But this being supposed, we are then fit to say, "Glory be to the Father, and to the Son, and to the Holy Ghost"; and fit to proceed to a further service of our God, in the Collects, and Psalms, and Lauds that follow in the Service. (Izaak Walton, *Life of Rev. George Herbert, 1670,* p. 295; *Angl.,* p. 730)

VIII ❧ PASTORAL SUPPLICATION

In petitioning, or asking prayer, the pastor holds up before God the needs of the people.

Clement of Rome provided one of the earliest models of how one might pray pastorally:

Open the eyes of our hearts to know thee, who alone art Highest, amid the highest, and ever abidest Holy amidst the holy. Thou dost bring down the haughtiness of the proud, and scatterest the devices of the people. Thou settest up the lowly on high, and the lofty thou dost cast down. Riches and poverty, death and life, are in thine hand; thou alone art the discerner of every spirit, and the God of all flesh. Thine eyes behold the depths and survey the works of man; thou art the aid of those in peril, the saviour of them that despair, the creator and overseer of everything that hath breath. . . . do thou deliver the afflicted, pity the lowly, raise the fallen, reveal thyself to the needy, heal the sick, and bring home thy wandering people. Feed thou the hungry, ransom the captive, support the weak, comfort the faint-hearted. Let all the nations of the earth know that thou art God alone, that Jesus Christ is thy child, and that we are thy people and the sheep of thy pasture. (Clement of Rome, *To the Corinthians*, sec. 59, ECW, pp. 54-55)

Thomas Traherne, the English metaphysical poet and clergyman, offered a moving example of a prayer for illumination and grace:

As my body without my soul is a carcass, so is my soul without Thy Spirit a Chaos, a dark, obscure heap of empty faculties; ignorant of itself, unsensible of Thy goodness, blind to Thy glory; dead in sins and trespasses. Having eyes I see not, having ears I hear not, having an heart I understand not the glory of Thy works and the glory of Thy Kingdom. O Thou Who art the root of my being and the Captain of my salvation, look upon me. Quicken me, O Thou life-giving and quickening seed. Visit me with Thy light and Thy truth; let them lead me to Thy Holy Hill and make me to see the greatness of Thy love in all its excellencies, effects, emanations, gifts, and operations. O my Wisdom! O my righteousness, Sanctification, and Redemption! Let Thy wisdom enlighten me, let Thy knowledge illuminate me, let Thy Blood redeem me, wash me and clean me, let Thy merits justify me, O Thou Who art equal unto God, and didst suffer for me. Let Thy righteousness clothe me. Let Thy Will imprint the form of itself upon mine; and let my will become conformable to Thine, that Thy Will and mine may be united, and made one for evermore. (Thomas Traherne, Centuries of Meditations, First Century, No. 93, pp. 68f; *Angl.*, p. 776)

From the early liturgies of the ante-Nicene period, we have this example of a supplication to God to accept offertory:

Accept the thank-offerings of those who have presented them this day, as Thou didst accept the gifts of Thy righteous Abel: . . . As Thou didst accept the sacrifice of our father Abraham, the incense of Zacharias, the alms of Cornelius, and the widow's two mites, accept also the thank-offerings of these, and give them for the things of time the things of eternity, and for the things of earth the things of heaven. . . . Be with us, O Lord, who minister unto Thy holy name. Bless our meetings, O Lord. Utterly uproot idolatry from the world. (*Early Liturgies*, ANF VII, pp. 556-557)

Again, a pre-Nicene model of a pastoral supplication:

Deliver the captive; rescue the distressed; feed the hungry; comfort the faint-hearted; convert the erring; enlighten the darkened; raise the fallen; confirm the wavering; heal the sick; and guide them all, good Lord, into the way of salvation, and into Thy sacred fold. Deliver us from our iniquities; protect and defend us at all times. (*Early Liturgies*, ANF VII, pp. 557)

Thomas Aquinas stated reasons why it is fitting to ask God for temporal things as means to lawful ends when we pray:

As Augustine says (*ad Probam, de orando Deum*, Ep. 130:12), "It is lawful to pray for what it is lawful to desire." Now it is lawful to desire temporal things, not indeed principally, by placing our end in them, but as helps whereby we are assisted in tending towards beatitude, in so far as they are the means of supporting the life of the body, and are of service to us as instruments in performing acts of virtue, as also the Philosopher states (Ethics 1:8). Augustine too says the same to Proba (ibid. 6,7) when he states that "it is not unbecoming for anyone to desire enough for a livelihood, and no more." (Thomas Aquinas, *Summa Theologica*, II-II, Q. 83, Art. 6, Vol. I, p. 1541)

Similarly, Thomas considered whether one ought to ask for something definite when one prays:

According to Valerius Maximus (*Fact. et Dict. Memor.* vii.2), Socrates deemed that we should ask the immortal gods for nothing else but that they should grant us good things, because they at any rate know what is good for each one, whereas when we pray we frequently ask for what it had been better for us not to obtain. This opinion is true to a certain extent, as to those things which may have an evil result, and which man may use ill or well, such as riches, by which, as stated by the same authority (ibid.), many have come to an evil end; honors, which have ruined many; power, of which we frequently witness the unhappy results; splendid marriages, which sometimes bring about the total wreck of a family. Nevertheless there are certain goods which man cannot ill use, because they cannot have an evil result. Such are those which are the object of beatitude and whereby wemerit it, and these the saints seek absolutely when they pray, as in Ps. 79:4, "Show us Thy face, and we shall be saved", and again in Ps. 118:35, "Lead me into the path of Thy commandments".... Although man cannot by himself know what he ought to pray for, the Spirit, as stated in the same passage, [Romans 8:26] helps our infirmity, since by inspiring us with holy desires, he makes us ask for what is right. (Thomas Aquinas, *Summa Theologica*, II-II, Q. 83, Art. 5, Vol. I, pp. 1540-1541)*

Here is an early pastoral absolution, praying for forgiveness of sin of the penitent:

O Lord Jesus Christ, Son of the living God, Lamb and Shepherd, who takest away the sin of the world, who didst freely forgive their debt to the two debtors, and gavest remission of her sins to the woman that was a sinner, who gavest healing to the paralytic, with the remission of his sins; forgive, remit, pardon, O God, our offences, voluntary and involuntary, in knowledge and in ignorance, by transgression and by disobedience, which Thy all-holy Spirit knows better than Thy servants do. (*Early Liturgies*, ANF VII, p. 550)

This pastoral benediction has survived from the early fourth century:

Going on from strength to strength, and having fulfilled all the divine service in Thy temple, even now we beseech Thee, O Lord our God, make us worthy of perfect loving-kindness; make straight our path: root us in Thy fear, and make us worthy of the heavenly kingdom, in Christ Jesus our Lord, with whom Thou art blessed, together with Thy all-holy, and good, and quickening Spirit, now and always, and for ever. (*Early Liturgies*, ANF VII, p. 550)

Luther commented on what we mean when we say "Amen":

God help us, without doubting, to obtain all these petitions, and suffer us not to doubt that Thou has heard us and wilt hear us in them all; that it is "Yea," not "Nay," and not "Perhaps." Therefore we say with joy, "Amen—it is true and certain." Amen. (Luther, *A Brief Explanation*, WML II, p. 384)

IX ⚘ PASTORAL INTERCESSION

While the distinctive stress in supplication is upon the humble entreaty (with the earnestness of an unworthy one who would rightly come before the holy God with a request), the more distinctive stress in intercession is upon entreaty on behalf of others. To intercede is to ask for another. Intercession carries the connotation of acting between two parties so as to reconcile differences. Intercession is thus a pastoral attempt at peacemaking between sinners and God, asking for the benefits of Christ's mediation to be manifested toward particular persons. In pastoral intercession those interceded for may be personally named.

Thomas Aquinas thoughtfully clarified how one might best pray for others:

When we pray we ought to ask for what we ought to desire. Now we ought to desire good things not only for ourselves, but also for others.... Hence Chrysostom (Hom. 14, in Matth.): "Necessity binds us to pray for ourselves, fraternal charity urges us to pray for others: and the prayer that fraternal charity proffers is sweeter to God than that which is the outcome of necessity."

Reply Obj. 1. As Cyprian says (*De Orat. Dom.*), "We say 'Our Father' and not 'my Father,' 'Give us' and not 'Give me,' because the Master of unity did not wish us to pray privately, that is for ourselves alone, for He wished each one to pray for all, even as He Himself bore all in one." (Thomas Aquinas, *Summa Theologica*, II-II, Q. 83, Art. 7, Vol. II, p. 1542)

Origen argued that it is finally the Spirit who intercedes, not ourselves. We are called to pray for the Spirit's own intercession:

[Intercession occurs] in the writings of the Apostle, where he quite reasonably assigns prayer to our control, but intercession to that of the Spirit, since He is better and has boldness with the One to whom He makes intercession. What he says is, "For what we should pray for as we ought we do not know, but the Spirit Himself makes special intercession for us to God with sighs too deep for words. And He who searches the hearts knows what is the mind of the Spirit, because the Spirit intercedes for the saints according to the will of God" (Rom. 8:26-27). For the Spirit "makes special intercession" and "intercedes," but we pray. (Origen, *On Prayer*, sec. 4-5, CWS, p. 111)

Augustine recognized a subtle dialectic in prayer—we do not know exactly what we are praying for, since it is not present to us, but we nonetheless pray for the good we cannot rightly envision:

This blessing is nothing else than the "peace which passeth all understanding" (Phil. 4:7), even when we are asking it in our prayers, we know not what to pray for as we ought. For inasmuch as we cannot present it to our minds as it really is, we do not know it, but whatever image of it may be presented to our minds we reject, disown, and condemn; we know it is not what we are seeking, although we do not yet know enough to be able to define what we seek.

There is therefore in us a certain learned ignorance so to speak—an ignorance which we learn from that Spirit of God who helps our infirmities. For after the apostle said, "If we hope for what we see not, then do we with patience wait for it," he added in the same passage, "Likewise the Spirit also helpeth our infirmities: for we know not what we should pray for as we ought, but the Spirit itself maketh intercession for us, with groanings which cannot be uttered. And He that searcheth the hearts knoweth what is in the mind of the Spirit, because He maketh intercession for the saints according to the will of God." (Rom. 8:25-27). . . . He therefore makes the saints intercede with groanings which cannot be uttered, when He inspires them with longings for that great blessing, as yet unknown, for which we patiently wait. For how is that which is desired set forth in language if it be unknown, for if it were utterly unknown it would not be desired; and on the other hand, if it were seen, it would not be desired. (Augustine, *Letters*, LXXX, To Proba, NPNF 1, I, p. 468)

John Cosin, the Anglican divine, showed why pastoral intercession for the people is a constant and central pastoral function:

God is more respective to the prayers which they make for the people than ever the people are to the sermons which they make to them. And in this respect are the Priests called God's remembrancers, because they put God in mind of His people, desiring Him to keep and bless them daily with things needful both for their bodies and their souls. . . . It was the office that was appointed the priests in the Law, "He shall make an atonement for the people," not so much to teach and preach to the people (as men now-a-days think all the office lays in doing that), but "to offer sacrifice and incense unto the Lord," which was but a figure of that which the ministers of Christ were to do in the Gospel. Therefore Samuel professes it openly, to the shame of all others, that he should sin no less in neglecting to pray for the people, than he should in leaving off to teach them the right way of God's commandments; both which are needful, but to them that are already converted prayer is more necessary than preaching. . . .

David's diligence in performing his duty for the good of the people was such, as he professes it, "At midnight I will rise up to give thanks unto Thee"; so Paul and Silas rose at midnight to sing praises unto God. It were, therefore well to be wished that the like order were taken in the Church now, and that the Sacrifice of Prayer might be continually offered up unto God among Christians, as well as it was in the synagogues of the Jews. (John Cosin, Works, LACT V, p. 9-11; *Angl.*, p. 629)

The pastor may be asked: If God knows all already, then why are we commanded to let our requests be made known to God?

When the same apostle says, "Let your requests be made known unto God" (Phil. 4:6), this is not to be understood as if thereby they become known of God, who certainly knew them before they were uttered, but in this sense, that they are to be made known to ourselves in the presence of God by patient waiting upon Him, not in the presence of men by ostentatious worship. (Augustine, *Letters*, CXXX, To Proba, Ch. 9, NPNF 1, I, p. 465)

X ❧ EFFECTUAL PRAYER

Instruction in the effective practice of prayer has been a recurrent task of pastoral counsel in the classical tradition. Here is an example of such instruction by Origen:

The person who is about to come to prayer should withdraw for a little and prepare himself, and so become more attentive and active for the whole of his prayer. He should cast away all temptation and troubling thoughts and remind himself, so far as he is able, of the majesty whom he approaches, and that it is impious to approach Him carelessly, sluggishly, and disdainfully; and he should put away all extraneous things. This is how he should come to prayer, stretching out his soul, as it were, instead of his hands, straining his mind toward God instead of his eyes. (Origen, *On Prayer*, Ch. XXXI, sec. 2, CWS, p. 164)

Origen explained why Christian prayer is to the Father through the Son by the power of the Spirit:

Now if we are to take prayer in its most exact sense, perhaps we should not pray to anyone begotten, not even to Christ Himself, but only to the God and Father of all, to whom even our Savior Himself prayed, as we have explained, and to whom he taught us to pray. For when He heard "teach us to pray," He did not teach us to pray to Himself, but to the Father by saying "Our Father in heaven, and so forth" (Lk. 11:1ff; Mt. 6:5ff). . . . We should pray only to the God and Father of all, yet not without the High Priest. . . . And so, when the saints give thanks to God in their prayers, they acknowledge through Christ Jesus the favors He has done. . . . For you must not pray to the High Priest appointed on your behalf by the Father (cf. Heb. 8:3) or to the Advocate who is charged by the Father with praying for you (cf. 1 John 2:1). Rather you must pray through the High Priest and Advocate, who is able to sympathize with your weaknesses, since He has been tempted in every respect as you are, and yet tempted without sin (Heb. 4:15). (Origen, *On Prayer*, Ch. XV, sec. 1-4, CWS, pp. 112-114)

Effectual prayer cannot be separated from effective reconcilation with the neighbor:

For what sort of deed is it to approach the peace of God without peace? the remission of debts while you retain them? How will he appease his Father who is angry with his brother. . . . Even if we must be angry, our anger must not be maintained beyond sunset, as the apostle admonishes. . . . Nor merely from anger, but altogether from all perturbation of mind, ought the exercise of prayer to be free, uttered from a spirit such as the Spirit unto whom it is sent. For a defiled spirit cannot be acknowledged by a holy Spirit, nor a sad by a joyful, nor a fettered by a free. (Tertullian, *On Prayer*, Ch. XI, ANF III, p. 685)

The very disposition of prayer is itself productive of other goods. The prayer that comes cleanly and honestly out of unsullied motivation is bound to be beneficial in some way:

I believe that profit often meets and joins the person who prays as he ought or who makes every effort to do so as far as he is able. First, the person who composes his mind for prayer is inevitably profited in some way. Through his very disposition for prayer he adorns himself as to present himself to God and to speak to Him in person as to someone who looks upon him and is present. (Origen, *On Prayer*, Ch. VIII, sec. 2, CWS, p. 97)

Augustine counseled Proba to pray for only one thing:

Whoever desires from the Lord that "one thing," and seeks after it, asks in certainty and in confidence, and has no fear lest when obtained it be injurious to him, seeing that, without it, anything else which he may have obtained by asking in a right way is of no advantage to him. The thing referred to is the one true and only happy life, in which, immortal and incorruptible in body and spirit, we may contemplate the joy of the Lord for ever. All other things are desired, and are without impropriety prayed for, with a view to this one thing. For whosoever has it shall have all that he wishes, and cannot possibly wish to have anything along with it which would be unbecoming. (Augustine, *Letters*, CXXX, To Proba, NPNF 1, I, pp. 467-468)

The power of prayer was attested by Tertullian:

Prayer amplifies grace by virtue, that faith may know what she obtains from the Lord, so as better to understand what she is for God's sake suffering. . . . Prayer has been known to recall the souls of the departed from the very path of death, to transform the weak, to restore the sick, to purge the possessed, to open prison-bars, to loose the bonds of the innocent. Likewise it washes away faults, repels temptations, extinguishes persecutions, consoles the faintspirited, cheers the high-spirited, escorts travellers, appeases waves, makes robbers stand aghast, nourishes the poor, governs the rich, upraises the fallen, arrests the falling, confirms the standing. (Tertullian, *On Prayer*, Ch. XXIX, ANF III, pp. 690-691)*

Augustine examined the paradoxical sense in which we are to pray without ceasing:

It may seem surprising that, although He has forbidden "much speaking," He who knoweth before we ask Him what things we need has nevertheless given us exhortation to prayer in such words as these: "Men ought always to pray and not to faint" (Lk. 18:1); setting before us the case of a widow, who, desiring to have justice done to her against her adversary, did by her persevering entreaties persuade an unjust judge to listen to her, not moved by a regard either to justice or to mercy, but overcome by her wearisome importunity; in order that we might be admonished how much more certainly the Lord God, who is merciful and just, gives ear to us praying continually to Him, when this widow, by her unremitting supplication, prevailed over the indifference of an unjust and wicked judge, and how willingly and benignantly He fulfils the good desires of those whom He knows to have forgiven others their trespasses, when this suppliant, though seeking vengeance upon her adversary, obtained her desire. . . . When we cherish uninterrupted desire along with the exercise of faith and hope and charity, we "pray always." But at certain stated hours and seasons we also use words in prayer to God, that by these signs of things we may admonish ourselves, and may acquaint ourselves with the measure of progress which we have made in this desire, and may more warmly excit ourselves to obtain an increase of its strength. For the effect following upon prayer will be excellent in proportion to the fervour of the desire which precedes its utterance. And therefore, what else is intended by the words of the apostle: "Pray without ceasing," than, "Desire without intermission from Him who alone can give it, a happy life, which no life can be but that which is eternal" . . . Far be it from us either to use "much speaking" in prayer or to refrain from prolonged prayer, if fervent attention of the soul continue. (Augustine, *Letters*, CXXX, To Proba, NPNF 1, I, pp. 464-465)

John Climacus used courtroom and medical analogies to press the awesomeness of prayer:

If you have ever been under trial before an earthly judge, you will not need any other pattern for your attitude in prayer. But if you have never stood before a judge yourself and have not seen others being cross-questioned, then learn at least from the way the sick implore the surgeons when they are about to be operated on or cauterized. (John Climacus, *Ladder of Divine Ascent*, Step 28, sec. 8, p. 213)

XI ❦ The Language and Forms of Pastoral Prayer

The pastor is specifically charged to pray for the flock. Pastoral prayer is prayer representatively held up before God on behalf of the people. Corporate or common prayer is therefore distinguished from individual prayer by the fact that a congregation is present and the whole body is being represented in prayer by the pastor. This requires befitting language that appropriately forms the confessions, thanksgivings and petitions of the community into a vocal, corporate act at a particular time and place.

Prayer is two-fold, common and individual. Common prayer is that which is offered to God by the ministers of the church representing the body of the faithful: wherefore such like prayer should come to the knowledge of the whole people for whom it is offered: and this would not be possible unless it were vocal prayer. . . . On the other hand individual prayer is that which is offered by any single person, whether he pray for himself or for others; and it is not essential to such a prayer as this that it be vocal. . . . Vocal prayer is employed not in order to tell God something He does not know, but in order to lift up the mind of the person praying or of other persons to God. (Thomas Aquinas, *Summa Theologica*, II-II, Q. 83, Art. 12, Vol. II, p. 1547)

The gift of pastoral prayer is not reducible to rhetoric, linguistic construction, persuasion, or elocution. One of the most moving descriptions of the qualities needed in representative prayer was offered by Anglican Bishop Joseph Hall:

Some think that a man has the gift of prayer who can utter the thoughts of his heart roundly to God, express himself smoothly in the phrase of the Holy Ghost, and press God with most proper words and passionate vehemence. Surely this is a commendable faculty wherever it is. But this is not the gift of prayer. One might better call it, if you will, the gift of elocution. Do we say that one has the gift of pleading who can talk eloquently at the court of law, who can in good terms loudly and earnestly importune the judge for his client, and not rather he that brings the strongest reason, and quotes his books and precedents with most truth and clearest evidence, so as may convince the jury and persuade the judge? Similarly, do we say one has the gift of preaching who can deliver himself in a flowing manner of speech to his hearers, cite Scriptures or Fathers, please his audience with the flowers of rhetoric? Or rather, does he have the gift of preaching who can divide the word aright, interpret it soundly, apply it judiciously, send it home to the conscience, speaking in the evidence of the Spirit, powerfully convincing the disputants, comforting the dejected, and drawing every soul nearer to heaven? We must say the same thing about prayer. He of whom it may be truly said that he has the gift of prayer is not the one who has the most running tongue, for prayer is not so much a matter of the lips as of the heart. Rather is it he who has the most illuminated apprehension of the God to Whom he speaks, the deepest sense of his own wants, the most eager longings after grace, the most fervent desire of supply from heaven, and in a word, whose heart sends up the strongest groans and cries to the Father of Mercies. (Joseph Hall, The Devout Soul, Works, VI, pp. 477-79; *Angl.*, p. 616)*

Athanasius argued that traditionally received prayers are to be specially revered by the remembering community:

For as much better as the life of the saints is than that of other people, by so much also are their expressions superior to those we construct and, if one were to speak the truth, more powerful as well. For they greatly pleased God in these, and when saying them, as the Apostle put it, "they conquered kingdoms, enforced justice, received promises, stopped the mouths of lions, quenched raging fire, escaped the edge of the sword, won strength out of weakness, became mighty in war, put foreign armies to flight, and women received their dead by resurrection" (Hebr. 11:33-34). (Athanasius, Letter to Marcellinus, sec. 31, ACW 10, p. 127)

It has not ordinarily been left exclusively to the privatized imagination or individual creativity of each pastor to invent the order, design and language of worship in each parish. The repetitive, intergenerational character of common prayer has an educative, upbuilding effect on the soul that is difficult otherwise to achieve. The pastor need not avoid, but should use repetition and form. All divine services need not be alike, but all ought to reflect the apostolic faith:

The prescribing a form in general is more for our edifying, than to leave everyone to do what seems Good in his own eyes, we have the concurrent testimony, experience, and practice of the Universal Church; for we never read or heard of any Church in the world, from the Apostles' days to ours, but what took this course. Though all have not used the same, yet no Church but have used some form or other. And, therefore, for any man to say that it is not lawful, or not expedient, or not to edifying, to use a form of prayer in the public worship of God, is to contradict the general sense of Christianity, to condemn the Holy Catholic Church, and to make himself wiser than all Christians that ever were before him. . . . For we cannot but all find by our own experience how difficult it is to fasten anything that is truly good, either upon ourselves or others; and that it is rarely, if ever, effected without frequent repetitions of it. Whatsoever good things we hear only once, or now and then, though, perhaps, upon the hearing of them, they may swim for awhile in our brains, yet they seldom sink down into our hearts, so as to move and sway the affections, as it is necessary they should do, in order to our being edified by them. (William Beveridge, *A Sermon on the Excellency and Usefulness of the Common Prayer*, Works, Vol. VI, pp. 370-373; *Angl.*, pp. 624-626)

It has been much debated whether public prayer should be in Latin or in a language understood by the people. The case for the vernacular is based on the nature of prayer as an act of the understanding:

It is repugnant to the nature and end of vocal prayer that the same should be exercised in a form of words which people that pray together understand not. For prayer is an ascending of the mind to God; and according to Aquinas and other Schoolmen it is an action of the understanding faculty. (Francis White, A Reply to Jesuit Fisher's Answer to Certain Questions Propounded by His Most Gracious Majesty, King James, 1624, pp. 367f; *Angl.*, p. 634)

XII ❧ THE LORD'S PRAYER AS PATTERN

In the Lord's Prayer, a model is offered for the guidance of all Christian prayer, including pastoral prayer. Believers whose lives are hid in Christ, who live in a new age, under a new law, have been given a new way of praying. In extremely brief scope the Lord's Prayer expresses, as Tertullian argued, the "epitome of the whole gospel":

The Spirit of God and the Word of God, and the Reason of God—Word of Reason, and Reason and Spirit of Word—Jesus Christ our Lord, namely, who is both the one and the other,—has determined for us, the disciples of the New Testament, a new form of prayer; for in this particular also it was needful that new wine should be laid up in new skins, and a new breadth be sewn to a new garment. Besides, whatever had been in bygone days, has either been quite changed, as circumcision; or else supplemented, as the rest of the Law; or else fulfilled, as Prophecy; or else perfected, as faith itself. . . . In the Prayer is comprised an epitome of the whole Gospel. . . . In summaries of so few words, how many utterances of the prophets, the Gospels, the apostles— how many discourses, examples, parables of the Lord, are touched on! . . . . The honour of God in the "Father;" the testimony of faith in the "Name;" the offering of obedience in the "Will;" the commemoration of hope in the "Kingdom;" the petition for life in the "Bread;" the full acknowledgment of debts in the prayer for their "Forgiveness;" the anxious dread of temptation in the request for "Protection." (Tertullian, *On Prayer*, Ch. 1, and Ch. 9, ANF III, pp. 681ff.)

In his treatise on Prayer, Origen set forth an insight that has recently been rediscovered by twentieth century New Testament critics—that prayer to the Father, Abba, was not common in the Old Testament, and may be highly distinctive of the ministry of Jesus. For classical trinitarian thought, this reinforces the notion of the unique and intimate Sonship of Jesus to God the Father:

"Our Father in heaven." It is right to examine what is said in the Old Testament quite carefully to see whether any prayer may be found in it calling God "Father." Up till now, though I have looked as carefully as I can, I have not found one. I do not mean that God was not called Father or that those who are supposed to have believed in God were not called sons of God; but nowhere have I found in a prayer the boldness proclaimed by the Savior in calling God Father. (Origen, *On Prayer*, Ch. XXII, sec. 1, CWS, p. 123)

The Apostolic Constitutions commended saying the Lord's Prayer three times a day:

Pray thus thrice in a day, preparing yourselves beforehand, that ye may be worthy of the adoption of the Father; lest, when you call Him Father unworthily, you be reproached by Him. (*Constitutions of the Holy Apostles*, Bk. VII, Sec. II, ANF VII, p. 470)

Every good prayer is anticipated by the insurmountably good way of praying taught by Jesus, according to Augustine:

If we pray rightly, and as becomes our wants, we say nothing but what is already contained in the Lord's Prayer. And whoever says in prayer anything which cannot find its place in that gospel prayer, is praying in a way which, if it be not unlawful, is at least not spiritual; and I know not how carnal prayers can be lawful, since it becomes those who are born again by the Spirit to pray in no other way than spiritually. For example, when one prays: "Be Thou glorified among all nations as Thou art glorified among us" (Ecclus. 36:4,18), and "Let Thy prophets be found faithful," what else does he ask than, "Hallowed be Thy name"? . . . . When one says: "Order my steps in Thy word, and let not any iniquity have dominion over me" (Ps. 119:133), what else is he saying than, "Thy will be done on earth as it is in heaven"? When one says: "Give me neither poverty nor riches" (Prov. 30:8), what else is this than, "Give us this day our daily bread"? When one says: "Lord, remember David, and all his compassion" (Ps. 132:1 LXX), or, "O Lord, if I have done this, if there be iniquity in my hands, if I have rewarded evil to them that did evil to me" (Ps.

7:3-4), what else is this than, "Forgive us our debts as we forgive our debtors"? When one says: "Take away from me the lusts of the appetite, and let not sensual desire take hold on me" (Ecclus. 23:6), what else is this than, "Lead us not into temptation"? When one says: "Deliver me from mine enemies, O my God; defend me from them that rise up against me" (Ps. 58:1), what else is this than, "Deliver me from evil"? And if you go over all the words of holy prayers, you will, I believe, find nothing which cannot be comprised and summed up in the petitions of the Lord's Prayer. Wherefore, in praying, we are free to use different words to any extent, but we must ask the same things. (Augustine, *Letters*, CXXX, To Proba, Ch. 22, NPNF 1, I, p. 466)

By meditating upon each phrase of the Lord's prayer, Ignatius Loyola proposed an extended spiritual exercise in contemplative prayer:

He should then say, "Father," and reflect upon this word as long as he find meanings, comparisons, relish, and consolation in the consideration of it. He should then continue the same method with each word of the "Our Father," or of any other prayer that he may wish to contemplate in this manner. . . . .

During the contemplation on the "Our Father," if he finds in one or two words good matter for thought, relish, and consolation, he should not be anxious to pass on, even though he spend the entire hour on what he has found. When the hour is over, he will say the rest of the "Our Father" in the usual way. . . . .

The third method of prayer is a rhythmical recitation. . . . . At each breath or respiration, he is to pray mentally, as he says one word of the "Our Father," or any other prayer that is being recited, so that between one breath and another a single word is said. During this same space of time, he is to give his full attention to the meaning of the word, or to the person whom he is addressing, or to his own unworthiness, or to the difference between the greatness of this Person and his own lowliness. He will continue, observing the same procedure and rule, through the other words of the "Our Father" and the other prayers, namely, the "Hail Mary," the "Anima Christi," the "Creed," and the "Hail Holy Queen." (Ignatius Loyola, *Spiritual Exercises*, pp. 107-108)

XIII ❧ PUBLIC PRAYER

The root meaning of the term "parson" is person, in the special sense that an individual has become "the person" of the community representatively in prayer before God. There is a sense in which the parson embodies or "personates" the community, becomes representatively the unified voice of the community at prayer.

So recurrent and crucial is this pastoral act that the pastoral writers have sought to provide reliable guidelines for the public prayer of the pastor. Thus public prayer cannot be separated from the task of soul care. Bishop Gilbert Burnet's guidelines for public pastoral prayer focus upon the heartfelt entry of the pastor into the language of prayer:

He must bring his Mind to an inward and feeling Sense of those things that are prayed for in our Offices: That will make him pronounce them with an equal measure of Gravity and Affection, and with a due Slowness and Emphasis. I do not love the Theatrical way. . . . And a hasty running through the Prayers, are things highly unbecoming; they do very much lessen the Majesty of our Worship, and give our Enemies advantage to call it dead and formal, when they see plainly, that he who officiates is dead and formal in it. A deep Sense of the things prayed for, a true Recollection and Attention of Spirit, and a holy Earnestness of Soul, will give a Composure to the Looks, and a weight to the Pronunciation, that will be tempered between affectation on the one hand, and Levity on the other. (Burnet, *Of the Pastoral Care*, Ch. VII; *CS*, p. 87)

Philip Doddridge provided this summary instruction for assisting young pastors in improving the gift of prayer:

Converse much with your own hearts, get well acquainted with the state of your souls, attend to your spiritual wants and weaknesses, frequently recollect the mercies you receive from God, and inquire what returns you have made. . . . In all your prayers avoid the extremes of too mean and too pompous a style. A pompous style shows a mind too full of self, and too little affected with a sense of divine things. . . . Aim at nothing but pouring out the soul before God in the most genuine language. . . . The principal parts of prayer are Invocation with Adoration, Confession, Petition, Intercession with Thanksgiving. . . . Be not too solicitous to introduce novelties into your prayers. Desire not to pray as nobody ever prayed before, or will probably ever pray again. Novelties may sometimes amuse, but in prayer they more frequently disgust. Besides, they have the appearance of too much art, and as new things are generally the product of the imagination, they are not so proper for prayer as preaching, and even in that they must be moderate.

Remember it is the peculiar office of the Spirit of God to help us in prayer. Engage in it, therefore in dependence upon him; and maintain a continual dependence on the intercession and influence of Christ.

I shall now give you some directions which relate more immediately to public prayer.

Begin with a solemn recollection of spirit. Think seriously of the majesty of that Being to whom you are addressing yourselves, and of the importance of the business in which you are engaging. . . . Endeavour to have a unity of design running through your scheme of prayer, and let one petition be connected with another by natural but never laboured transition. . . . Remember the particular cases of your hearers, and the immediate concerns of the congregation. . . . Let the last prayer be agreeable to the sermon; introduce the principal thoughts and heads, but do not turn it into a preaching prayer, nor repeat any peculiarly fine passages of the sermon, lest you should seem too fond of them. (Doddridge, *Lectures on Preaching*, XIII sec. 2-20, pp. 71-76)*

Since truth is one, true prayer seeks simplicity of expression. Origen developed this penetrating argument for short prayers, along with a psychological explanation of our tendency to multiply words:

According to the text of the Gospel only "the Gentiles" heap up empty phrases, since they have no impression of the great and heavenly requests and offer every prayer for bodily and outward things. . . . Truth is one, but lies are many; and true righteousness is one, but there are many ways of counterfeiting it; and the wisdom of God is one, but many are the wisdoms—doomed to pass away—of this age and of the rulers of this age (1 Cor. 2:6); and the word of God is one, but many are the words foreign to God. Therefore, no one will escape sin when words are many; and no one who thinks he will be heard, when words are many, can be heard (cf. Prov. 10:19). (Origen, *On Prayer*, Ch. XXI, sec. 1-2, CWS, p. 122)

The simplicity of this argument makes it easy to miss its profundity: Since there are many ways of lying, there are likewise many ways to dissemble in prayer. Since the truth is one, there is only one way to speak the truth in prayer, and that is with direct, candid simplicity that does not hide behind many words. Thomas Aquinas developed much the same thought in dependence upon Augustine:

Augustine says (*ad Probam Ep. 130*): "It is said that the brethren in Egypt make frequent but very short prayers, rapid ejaculations, as it were, lest that vigilant and erect attention which is so necessary in prayer slacken and languish." . . . As Augustine says (*ad Probam loc. cit.*), "to pray with many words is not the same as to pray long; to speak long is one thing, to be devout long is another. For it is written that our Lord passed the whole night in prayer (Lk. 6:12), and that He 'prayed the longer' in order to set us an example." Further on he says: "When praying say little, yet pray much so long as your attention is fervent. For to say much in prayer is to discuss your need in too many words: whereas to pray much is to knock at the door of Him to whom we pray, by the continuous and devout clamor of the heart. Indeed this business is frequently done with groans rather than with words, with tears rather than with speech." (Thomas Aquinas, *Summa Theologica*, II-II, Q. 83, Art. 14, Vol. I, p. 1549)*

Pray often, not long:

Pray frequently and effectually; I had rather your prayers should be often than long. It was well said of Petrarch. . . . "When you speak to your superior, you ought to have a bridle on your tongue"; much more when you speak to God. (Jeremy Taylor, A Letter to a Person Newly Converted to the Church of England, Works, XI, pp. 206f; *Angl.*, p. 615)

XIV ❧ THE SPATIAL ORDERING OF THE COMMUNITY AT PRAYER

Since prayer is a public act of soul care—a representative ministry of the most recurrent sort—the pastoral writers discussed many special questions concerning its rightful enactment. Among these are whether there are special dispositions and postures for prayer, particular places for particular prayers, and how the life of prayer is to be placed in time and space.

Our concern here is how care of souls through common prayer seeks to order itself spatially, seeking the appropriate physical place or locus for its fitting enactment. Although this may seem trivial to modern readers, it was taken with great seriousness by the classical pastoral writers. Prayer has been thought to be especially fitting in certain *loci* of time and space. Pastoral care requires reflection on the due placement of common prayer.

Origen offered an ingenious explanation for what he regarded as the most fitting posture for prayer:

The question of disposition must be referred to the soul, that of the posture to the body. Thus, Paul . . . describes the disposition and says that we must pray "without anger or quarreling"; and he describes the posture by the phrase "lifting holy hands" (1 Tim. 2:8). . . . The position with the hands outstretched and the eyes lifted up is to be preferred before all others, because it bears in prayer the image of characteristics befitting the soul and applies it to the body . . . .

Kneeling is necessary when someone is going to speak against his own sins before God, since he is making supplication for their healing and their forgiveness. We must understand that it symbolizes someone who has fallen down and become obedient. . . .

Since there are four directions, north, south, west, and east, who would not immediately acknowledge that it is perfectly clear we should make our prayers facing east, since this is a symbolic expression of the soul's looking for the rising of the true Light. (Origen, *On Prayer*, Ch. XXXI-XXXII, CWS, pp. 164-168)

Only God is to be worshipped, but God may be worshipped through visible images and representations. John of Damascus stated the classic case for a holy place of worship in which visual representations of the holy life (mosaics, paintings, and icons, for example, of the cross) assist the believer toward penitence and faith. While only God is to be worshipped, God may be worshipped relatively or relationally through appointed creaturely means. Seven types are noted:

How many things in Scripture can we find that were worshipped in a relative sense? What are the different ways we offer this relative worship to created things?

First of all, those places where God, who alone is holy, has rested. . . . [Since the saints] partake of the divine nature, they are to be venerated, not because they deserve it on their own account, but because they bear in themselves Him who is by nature worshipful. . . . The second kind of relative worship we give to created things concerns those places and things by which God has accomplished our salvation, whether before the coming of the Lord, or since the dispensation of His incarnation, such as Mount Sinai, and Nazareth, the cave and manger of Bethlehem, the holy mountain of Golgotha. . . . The third kind of relative worship we give to objects dedicated to God, such as the holy Gospel and other books, for they have been written for our instruction. . . . The fourth kind of relative worship is given to those images which were seen by the prophets (for they saw God in the images of their visions). . . . Thus, we venerate the honorable figure of the cross, or the likeness of the physical features of our God, or of her who gave birth to Him in the flesh, and everyone who is part of Him. The fifth kind of relative worship is our veneration of each other, since we are God's inheritance, and were made according to His image, and so we are subject to each other, thus fulfilling the law of love. The sixth kind of relative worship is given to those who have been given authority to rule over us. The apostle says, "pay all of them their due, . . . honor to whom honor is due" (Rom. 13:7). . . . The seventh kind of relative worship is given to masters by their servants, and to benefactors who grant the requests of their petitioners, as was the case when Abraham did reverence to the Hittites, when he bought the cave of Machpelah from Ephron.

It is needless to say that fear, desire, and honor all are signs of worship, as are submission and abnegation. But no one should worship anyone as God. Worship as God only Him who is God by nature. (John of Damascus, *On the Divine Images*, Third Apology, sec. 33-40, NPNF 2, IX, pp. 84-88)

An early interpretation of the positioning of clergy and laity in the bascilica was set forth in the Apostolic Constitutions:

Let the building be long, with its head to the east, with its vestries on both sides at the east end, and so it will be like a ship. In the middle let the bishop's throne be placed, and on each side of him let the presbytery sit down; and let the deacons stand near at hand, in close and small girt garments, for they are like the mariners and managers of the ship: with regard to these, let the laity sit on the other side, with all quietness and good order. (*Constitutions of the Holy Apostles*, Book II, Sec. VII, ch. lvii, ANF VII, p. 421)

XV   ❧   THE TEMPORAL ORDERING OF PRAYER

The life of prayer not only exhibits a fit ordering in space, but also a way of ordering time. The pastor is expected to guide the community of faith into an appropriate order of prayer for each day, each week, and each year. Although views differ considerably as to how these are to be ordered, depending upon historical and cultural perspective, it has always seemed important that some order be sought. The Anglican divine, John Cosin, for example, provided a sixteenth century list of regular devotional acts through which laity were guided through time by the pastor. This ordering of time was considered intrinsic to the care of souls:

To observe the Festivals and Holy Days appointed. To keep the Fasting Days with devotion and abstinence. To observe the Ecclesiastical Customs and Ceremonies established, and that without obstinacy or contradiction. To repair unto the public service of the Church for Matins and Evensong, with other Holy Offices at times appointed, unless there be a just and an unfeigned cause to the contrary. To receive the Blessed Sacrament of the Body and Blood of Christ with frequent devotion, and three times a year at least, of which times Easter to be always one. And for better preparation thereunto, as occasion is, to unburden and quit our consciences of those sins that may grieve us, or scruples that may trouble us, to a learned and discreet Priest, and from him to receive advice, and the benefit of Absolution. (John Cosin, *A Collection of Private Devotions*, 1560, Works, LACT II, p. 121; *Angl.*, p. 612)*

The Apostolic Constitutions provided this daily ordering of prayer:

Offer up your prayers in the morning at the third hour, the sixth, the ninth, the evening, and at cock-crowing: in the morning, returning thanks that the Lord has sent you light, that He has brought you past the night, and brought on the day; at the third hour, because at that hour the Lord received the sentence of condemnation from Pilate; at the sixth, because at that hour He was crucified; at the ninth, because all things were in commotion at the crucifixion of the Lord. . . . In the evening, giving thanks that He has given you the night to rest from the daily labours; at cock-crowing, because that hour brings the good news of the coming on of the day. . . . If it be not possible to assemble either in the church or in a house, let every one by himself sing, and read, and pray, or two or three together. (*Constitutions of the Holy Apostles*, Bk. VIII, sec. IV, Ch. xxxiv, ANF VII, p. 496)

Biblical grounds for the three-fold pattern of daily prayer were set forth by Tertullian. He thought that such a daily order would assist in tearing us away from temporal engagements to strengthen communion with God:

The first infusion of the Holy Spirit into the congregated disciples took place at "the third hour." Peter, on the day on which he experienced the vision of Universal Community exhibited in that small vessel, had ascended into the upper parts of the house, for prayer's sake "at the sixth hour" (Acts 10:9). He was going into the temple with John "at the ninth hour" (Acts 3:1) when he restored the paralytic to his health. Even though these practices stand simply without any precept for their observance, still it may be granted that they establish a definite presumption, which may both add stringency to the admonition to pray, and may, as if by command, tear us out from our businesses to such a duty. So we too pray at least three times a day, debtors as we are to Three— Father, Son, and Holy Spirit. So did Daniel pray in accordance with Israel's discipline. (Tertullian, *On Prayer*, Ch. XXV, ANF III, p. 690)*

A model for morning prayer was provided in the Apostolic Constitutions:

O God, the God of spirits and of all flesh, who art beyond compare, and standest in need of nothing, who hast given the sun to have rule over the day, and the moon and the stars to have rule over the night, do Thou now also look down upon us with gracious eyes, and receive our morning thanksgivings. Have mercy upon us. For we have not "spread out our hands unto a strange God" (Ps. 44:20). For there is not among us any new God, but Thou, the eternal God who art without end, who hast given us being through Christ, and given us our wellbeing through Him. Grant us, we pray, eternal life through Him; with whom glory, and honour, and worship be to Thee and to the Holy Spirit for ever. Amen. (*Constitutions of the Holy Apostles*, Bk. IV, sec. IV, Ch. xxxviii, ANF VII, p. 497)*

John Climacus thought that the beginning of the day required a significant spiritual discipline, so as to begin the redeeming and transforming of the rest of the day:

There is an evil spirit, called the forerunner, who assails us as soon as we awake from sleep and defiles our first thought. Devote the first-fruits of your day to the Lord, because the whole day will belong to whomever gets the first start. It is worth hearing what an expert told me: "From my morning," he said, "I know the course of the whole day." (John Climacus, *Ladder of Divine Ascent*, Step 26, sec. 104, p. 177)

Origen reflected on spiritual refreshment through prayer at midday:

Midday denotes those secret places of the heart in which the soul pursues the clearer light of knowledge from the Word of

God; for midday is the time when the sun is at the zenith of its course. . . . God appeared to [Abraham] at the oak of Mambre, as he was sitting at the door of his tent at midday. . . . He will have this midday time within himself; and, being set as it were in the noon through this purity of heart, he will see God as he sits by the oak of Mambre, which means From Seeing.

With regard to the time of vision, then, he "sits at midday" who puts himself at leisure in order to see God. (Origen, *The Song of Songs*, CWS, pp. 225-26)

The Apostolic Constitutions provided a pattern for offering thanks in the evening:

O God, who art without beginning and without end, the Maker of the whole world by Christ, and the Provider for it, but before all His God and Father, the Lord of the Spirit, and the King of intelligible and sensible beings; who hast made the day for the works of light, and the night for the refreshment of our infirmity,—for "the day is Thine, the night also is Thine: Thou has prepared the light and the sun" (Ps. 74:16)—do Thou now, O Lord, Thou lover of mankind, and Fountain of all good, mercifully accept of this our evening thanksgiving. Thou who has brought us through the length of the day, and hast brought us to the beginnings of the night, preserve us by Thy Christ, afford us a peaceable evening, and a night free from sin, and vouchsafe us everlasting life by Thy Christ, through whom glory, honour, and worship be to Thee in the Holy Spirit for ever. Amen. (*Constitutions of the Holy Apostles*, Bk. VIII, sec. IV, Ch. xxxvii, ANF VII, p. 496)

It is fitting that preaching be correlated with the seasons of the Christian year:

Let every preacher in his parish take care to explicate to the people the mysteries of the great festivals, as of Christmas, Easter, Ascension-day, Whitsunday, Trinity Sunday, the Annunciation of the blessed Virgin Mary; because these feasts, containing in them the great fundamentals of our faith, will, with most advantage, convey the mysteries to the people, and fix them in the memories, by the solemnity and circumstances of the day. (Jeremy Taylor, *RAC*, Bk. IV, sec. 61; *CS*, p. 20)

It is a pastoral responsibility to clarify the sequence of events and celebrations of the Christian year. Izaac Walton recalled that George Herbert did this exceptionally well in his exemplary ministry:

He instructed them also what benefit they had by the Church's appointing the celebration of Holy-days, and the excellent use of them; namely, that they were set apart for particular commemorations of particular mercies received from Almighty God; and (as Reverend Mr. Hooker says) to be the landmarks to distinguish times. For by them we are taught to take notice how time passes by us. . . . Namely, at our Christmas, a day in which we commemorate His Birth, with joy and praise; and that eight days after this happy Birth, we celebrate His Circumcision; namely, in that which we call New-year's Day. And that upon that day which we call Twelfth-Day, we commemorate the manifestation of the unsearchable riches of Jesus to the Gentiles. . . . By the Lent-Fast we imitate and commemorate our Saviour's humiliation in fasting forty days; and, that we ought to endeavour to be like Him in purity. And, that on Good-Friday we commemorate and condole His Crucifixion. And at Easter, commemorate His glorious Resurrection. And he taught them, that after Jesus had manifested Himself to His Disciples to be that Christ that was crucified, dead and buried; and by His appearing and conversing with His Disciples for the space of forty days after His Resurrection, He then, and not till then, ascended into Heaven, in the sight of those Disciples,—namely, on that day which we call the Ascension, or Holy Thursday. And that we then celebrate the performance of the promise which He made to His Disciples, at or before His Ascension,—namely, that though He left them, yet He would send them the Holy Ghost to be their Comforter; and that he did so on that day which the Church calls Whitsunday. Thus the Church keeps an historical and circular commemoration of times, as they pass by us, of such times as ought to incline us to occasional praises, for the particular blessings which we do, or might, receive by those holy Commemorations. (Isaac Walton, *Life of Rev. George Herbert*, pp. 295-303; *Angl.*, p. 732)

This sabbath prayer of early Christian communities shows how profoundly the Christian tradition had reappropriated and transmuted the Jewish sabbath:

O Lord Almighty, Thou hast created the world by Christ, and hast appointed the Sabbath in memory thereof, because that on that day Thou hast made us rest from our works, for the meditation upon Thy laws. Thou hast also appointed festivals for the rejoicing of our souls that we might come into the remembrance of that wisdom which is created by Thee. . . . Thou didst enjoin the observation of the Sabbath, not affording them an occasion of idleness, but an opportunity of piety, for their knowledge of Thy power, and the prohibition of evils; having limited them as within an holy circuit for the sake of doctrine, for the rejoicing upon the seventh period. On this account was there appointed one week, and seven weeks, and the seventh month, and the seventh year, and the revolution of these, the jubilee, which is the fiftieth year for remission, that men might have no occasion to pretend ignorance. On this account He permitted men every Sabbath to rest, that so no one might be willing to send one word out of his mouth in anger on the day of the Sabbath. For the Sabbath is the ceasing of the creation, the completion of the world, the inquiry after laws, and the grateful praise to God for the blessings He has bestowed upon men. (*Constitutions of the Holy Apostles*, Bk. VII, sec. I, Ch. xxxvi, ANF VII, p. 474)

Care of souls permits the rest of souls. We rest that God may better work in us:

On the seventh day God rested and ceased from all His works, which He had made. . . . This Sabbath has now for us been changed into the Sunday, and the other days are called work-days; the Sunday is called rest-day or holiday or holy day. . . . This rest or ceasing from labors is of two kinds, bodily and spiritual. . . . The bodily rest is that of which we have spoken above, namely, that we omit our business and work, in order that we may gather in the church, see mass, hear God's Word and make common prayer. . . . For, as we see, the priests and clergy celebrate mass every day, pray at all hours and train themselves in God's Word by study, reading and hearing. For this reason also they are freed from work before others, supported by tithes and have holy-day every day, and every day do the works of the holy-day, and have no work-day, but for them one day is as the other. And if we were all perfect, and knew the Gospel, we might work every day if we wished, or rest if we could. For a day of rest is at present not necessary nor commanded except only for the teaching of God's Word and prayer.

This spiritual rest, which God particularly intends in this Commandment, is this: that we not only cease from our labor and trade, but much more, that we let God alone work in us. (Luther, *Treatise on Good Works*, WML I, pp. 240-241)

XVI ❧ ON MUSIC AND THE CARE OF SOULS

The work of pastoral care through worship has depended significantly upon the gift of music. No period of Christian care of souls has proceeded without music.

Athanasius brilliantly described how music affects the soul. As the ideas of the soul are known through words, the feelings of the soul are expressed through music. The soul becomes united through music. The soul may be moved by the Spirit analogous to a musical instrument being plucked by a musician.

As in music the pluck is used to strike the string, so the human soul may in music become like a stringed instrument completely devoted to the Spirit, so that in all one's members and emotions one is thoroughly responsive to the will of God. The harmonious reading of the Psalms is a figure and type of such undisturbed and calm equanimity of our thoughts. For just as we discover the ideas of the soul and communicate them through the words we put forth, so also the Lord, wishing the melody of the words to be a symbol of the spiritual harmony in a soul, has provided that the odes may be chanted tunefully, and the Psalms recited with song. The desire of the soul is this—to be beautifully disposed, as it is written: "Is anyone among you cheerful? Let him sing praise" (Jas. 5:13). In this way that which is disturbing and rough and disorderly in it is smoothed away, and that which causes grief is healed when we sing psalms. . . .

The melody of the phrases is brought forth from the soul's good order and from the concord with the Spirit. The singers who sing not only with words, but also with understanding may greatly benefit not only themselves but those who hear them. Blessed David, making music in this way for Saul, was himself well pleasing to God. He drove away from Saul the troubled and frenzied disposition, making his soul calm. Similarly, liturgists who are able to sing in this way are summoning the souls of the people into tranquility, and calling them into harmonious accord with those who form the heavenly chorus. Psalms are not recited with melodies merely to make pleasant sounds. Rather, this is a sure sign of the harmony of the soul's reflections. Indeed, the melodic psalmody is a symbol of the mind's well-ordered and undisturbed condition. The praising of God in well-tuned cymbals and harp and ten-stringed instrument was again a figure and sign of the parts of the body coming into natural concord like harp strings. When this happens, the thoughts of the soul become like cymbals. Body and soul then live and move and have their being in unity together through this grand sound, as if through the command of the Spirit, so, as it is written, one overcomes the dying of the body through life in the Spirit. One who sings praise beautifully brings rhythm to the soul. By this means one leads the soul from disproportion to proportion. The result is that the encouraged soul loses fear, thinks on good things, and embraces the future. Gaining composure by the singing of praises, the soul transcends the life of passions, and joyfully beholds according to the mind of Christ the most excellent thoughts. (Athanasius, A Letter To Marcellinus, ACW 10, pp. 124-126)*

By the fourth century, the praise of God was being chanted, and music regarded as a model of proportionality, resonance, harmony, and unity for the soul. The passionate discord of the body is brought into unity through music. The congregation was eschatologically viewed as singing in harmony with the angelic hosts.

There were at least two hypotheses about why music serves the care of souls. One was a purely aesthetic explanation, and the other, preferred by Athanasius, combined an aesthetic with a theological explanation on the relation of the soul and the passions. Athanasius was asking why scriptures are chanted and sung rather than merely read:

It is important not to pass over the question of why words of this kind are chanted with melodies and strains. For some of the simple among us, although they believe indeed that the phrases are divinely inspired, imagine also, on account of the sweetness of sound, that the psalms are rendered musically for the sake of the ear's delight. But this is not so. For Scripture did not seek out that which is pleasant and winning as an end in itself, but this also has been fashioned for the benefit of the soul, for many reasons, but especially two: First, because it is fitting for the Divine Scripture to praise God not in compressed speech alone, but also in the voice that is richly broadened.... The second reason is that, just as harmony that unites flutes effects a single sound, so also, seeing that different movements appear in the soul—including the power of reasoning, eager appetite, high-spirited passion, and the motivations that shape the active parts of the body—the reason intends man neither to be discordant in himself, nor to be at variance with himself.... In order that such confusion not occur in us, the reason intends the soul that possesses the mind of Christ, as the Apostle said, to use music as a guide (1 Cor. 14:15), and by it both to be a master of its passions and to govern the body's members, so as to comply with reason. (Athanasius, A Letter to Marcellinus, ACW 10, pp. 123-124)*

The notion that music has therapeutic value was strongly advanced by Luther. Music fights mightily against the demons of the heart:

Experience testifies that, after the Word of God, music alone deserves to be celebrated as mistress and queen of the emotions of the human heart (of animals nothing is to be said at present). And by these emotions men are controlled and often swept away as by their lords. A greater praise of music than this we cannot conceive. For if you want to revive the sad, startle the jovial, encourage the despairing, humble the conceited, pacify the raving, mollify the hate-filled—and who is able to enumerate all the lords of the human heart, I mean the emotions of the heart and the urges which incite a man to all virtues and vices?—what can you find that is more efficacious than music? (Luther, WA 50, p. 371f; WLS 2, pp. 982-983)

This is why it is pertinent for the pastor to encourage the nurture of souls through music. Izaac Walton wrote of the Anglican pastor and poet, George Herbert:

His chiefest recreation was music, in which heavenly art he was a most excellent master and did himself compose many Divine Hymns and Anthems, which he set and sung to his lute or viol; and, though he was a lover of retiredness, yet his love to music was such that he went usually twice every week on certain appointed days to the Cathedral Church in Salisbury; and at his return would say that his time spent in prayer and Cathedral music elevated his soul, and was his Heaven upon earth. But before his return thence to Bemerton, he would usually sing and play his part at an appointed private music-meeting; and, to justify this practice, he would often say, Religion does not banish mirth, but only moderates and sets rules to it. (Isaac Walton, *Life of Rev. George Herbert*, p. 303; *Angl.*, p. 735)

Since music speaks to human afflictions, it is especially pertinent to pastoral care:

How sweetly doth this music sound, in this dead season! In the day-time, it would not, it could not, so much affect the ear. All harmonious sounds are advanced by a silent darkness.
Thus is it with the glad tidings of salvation. The Gospel never sounds so sweet, as in the night of persecution or of our own

private affliction. It is ever the same. The difference is, in our disposition to receive it.

O God, Whose praise it is to give songs in the night, make my prosperity conscionable and my crosses cheerful. (Joseph Hall, *Occasional Meditations*, 44, Works, XI, p. 94; *Angl.*, p. 763)

Methodius invited all Christians to enter fully into song and music and hear God's own speech through them:

Let every one come, then, and hear the divine song [of the prophets] without any fear. . . . For it is worthy of us to hear such a song as this; and to hear such singers as these seems to me to be a thing to be prayed for. But if one wishes to hear the choir of the apostles as well, he will find the same harmony of song. For the others sang beforehand the divine plan in a mystical manner; but these sing an interpretation of what has been mystically announced by the former. Oh, concordant harmony, composed by the Divine Spirit! Oh, the comeliness of those who sing the mysteries of God! Oh, that I also may join in these songs in my prayer. Let us then also sing the like song, and raise the hymn to the Holy Father, glorifying in the Spirit Jesus, who is in His bosom. Shun not, man, a spiritual hymn, nor be ill disposed to listen to it. (Methodius, *Concerning Free-Will*, ANF VI, p. 356)

Athanasius offered this counsel for singers, a simple but significant contribution to the interpretation of song: Sing out of the depths of oneself, not as though these words addressed to another, but personally to you.

After the prophecies about the Savior and the nations, he who recites the Psalms is uttering the rest as his own words, and each sings them as if they were written concerning him, and he accepts them and recites them not as if another were speaking, nor as if speaking about someone else. But he handles them as if he is speaking about himself. And the things spoken are such that he lifts them up to God as himself acting and speaking them from himself. (Athanasius, A Letter to Marcellinus, ACW 10, sec. 11, p. 110)

Luther speculated on why the prophets practiced music more than any other form of art:

I firmly believe, nor am I ashamed to assert, that next to theology no art is equal to music; for it is the only one, except theology, which is able to give a quiet and happy mind. This is manifestly proved by the fact that the devil, the author of depressing care and distressing disturbances, almost flees from the sound of music as he does from the word of theology. This is the reason why the prophets practiced music more than any art and did not put their theology into geometry, into arithmetic, or into astronomy, but into music, intimately uniting theology and music, telling the truth in psalms and songs. (Luther, "Letters of 1528-1530," WA-Br 5, p. 639; WLS 2, p. 983; cf. LW 49, p. 428)

Can music-haters be trusted?

I am not satisfied with him who despises music, as all fanatics do; for music is an endowment and a gift of God, not a gift of men. It also drives away the devil and makes people cheerful; one forgets all anger, unchasteness, pride, and other vices. I place music next to theology and give it the highest praise. (Luther, W-T 6, #7034; WLS 2, #3091, p. 980)

The Synod of Quinisext was concerned with the quality and kind of music that was employed within the church:

We will that those whose office it is to sing in the churches do not use undisciplined vociferations, nor force nature to shouting, nor adopt any of those modes which are incongruous and unsuitable for the church. (Synod of Quinisext, A.D. 692, Canon LXXV, The Seven Ecumenical Councils, NPNF 2, XIV, p. 398)

Selections in Part Three have focussed upon pastoral care through prayer. Soul care occurs within a caring community whose primary corporate act is the praise of God's care. Guidance of the service of prayer is an indispensable aspect of pastoral guidance. The soul is nurtured in worship through praise, thanksgiving, confession, timely admonition, earnest petition for peace and justice, intercession, preaching of the gospel and law, and scriptural study correlated with the needs of the times. Public worship requires forethought, decorum, and organization necessary for a public occasion that bespeaks its importance and its meaning. Pastoral prayer holds up before God the needs of the people. Instruction in the practice of prayer is a pastoral responsibility, the Lord's Prayer being a primary pattern. The ordering of worship in time and space requires pastoral responsibility in guiding the worshipping community through the seasons of the Christian year, and the maintenance of a proper space for worship. Music is an inestimable dimension of the care of souls.

4 Pastoral Care Through Baptism: The Ministry of Beginnings

CARE OF SOULS precedes baptism in one sense, for much that the pastor does leads up to baptism. Yet in another sense, the care of souls within the Christian community begins with baptism. For in baptism new life in the caring community is visibly manifested. Baptism marks a starting point in the care of a particular person within the community of faith. The personal name traditionally given in baptism marks the receiving of an identity within the healing, redemptive family of God.

Whether pastoral care precedes or follows baptism, there can be no doubt that the ministry of baptism is a central act of pastoral service, a crucial moment in the care of souls. The classical pastoral writers thought carefully about baptism as an act of pastoral care. They understood why the care-giving counselor is also baptizer, and why these two acts belong together. They reflected deliberately about how the pastor is to prepare recipients for baptism, what baptism is, why baptism is essentially a pastoral act, the effects of baptism, and the meaning of confirmation of one's baptism.

I ⚲ CARE-GIVER AS BAPTIZER

It is not an incidental point that the same one who offers counsel to troubled souls also serves as liturgical agent to bring, by means of the rite of baptism, souls into the fellowship of believers. The care-giver is baptizer.

Luther thought frequently of his baptism, derived great comfort from it, and commended to others the recollection of their baptism as a central consolation of life in Christ:

It will, therefore, be no small gain for a penitent to lay hold before all else on the memory of his baptism, confidently to call to mind the promise of God. ... His soul will find wondrous comfort, and will be encouraged to hope for mercy, when he considers that the divine promise which God made to him and which cannot possibly lie, still stands unbroken and unchanged, yea, unchangeable by any sins; as Paul says in 2 Timothy 2:13, "If we are faithless, he keeps faith, for he cannot deny himself." Ay, this truth of God will sustain him, so that if all else should sink in ruins, this truth, if he believe it, will not fail him. For in it he has a shield against all assaults of the enemy, an answer to the sins that disturb his conscience, an antidote for the dread of death and judgment, and a comfort in every temptation,—namely, this one truth,—and he can say, "God is faithful that promised, Whose sign I have received in my baptism. If God be for me, who is against me?" (cf. Rom. 6-8).

The children of Israel, whenever they repented of their sins, turned their thoughts first of all to the exodus from Egypt, and, remembering this, returned to God Who had brought them out. This memory and this refuge were many times impressed upon them by Moses, and afterward repeated by David. How much rather ought we to call to mind our exodus from Egypt, and, remembering, turn back again to Him Who led us forth through the washing of regeneration, which we are bidden remember for this very purpose. (Luther, *The Babylonian Captivity*, WML II, pp. 221-222, NEB)*

If baptism has this high order of importance in the comfort of the soul amid affliction, then the teaching of its recollection surely is a significant task of the pastoral teaching office. Yet what exactly is to be learned from baptism? It is fundamentally such a simple act. Tertullian examined the question of whether the very simplicity of baptism was potentially somewhat misleading:

There is absolutely nothing which makes men's minds more obdurate than the simplicity of the divine works which are visible in the act, when compared with the grandeur which is promised thereto in the effect; so that from the very fact, that with so great simplicity, without pomp, without any considerable novelty of preparation, finally, without expense, a man is dipped in water, and amid the utterance of some few words, is sprinkled, and then rises again, not much (or not at all) the cleaner, the consequent attainment of eternity is esteemed the more incredible.... Is it not wonderful, too, that death should be washed away by bathing? But it is the more to be believed if the wonderfulness be the reason why it is not believed.... Incredulity, on the other hand, wonders, but does not believe. For the simple acts it wonders at, it views as if they were vain; the grand results, as if they were impossible. And grant that it be just as you think, sufficient to meet each point is the divine declaration which precedes it: "Yet to shame the wise, God has chosen what the world counts folly" (1 Cor. 1:27), and, "What is impossible for men is possible for God" (Luke 18:27). (Tertullian, *On Baptism*, Ch. II, ANF III, p. 669, NEB)*

Faith celebrates the simplicity of baptism as consistent with God's own wisdom. The pastoral writers who have in fact been grasped by the simple mystery of baptism have pondered why something so common as water has become the central sign of entry and initiation into the believing community. Gregory of Nyssa, in defining baptism as cleansing from sin, described the renewal of spirit that accompanies it. He employed a medicinal metaphor, viewing baptism as a two-fold remedy for body and soul:

Baptism is a purification of sins, a remission of transgressions, a cause of renovation and regeneration. By regeneration you must understand a regeneration perceived by thought, not observed by the eyes. . . . For just as the new-born infant is free from accusations and penalties, so too the child of regeneration has no charges to answer, being released from accountability by kingly bounty. It is not the water that bestows this bounty (for then it would be exalted above all creation), but the commandment of God and the intervention of the Spirit, which comes sacramentally to give us liberty. But water has a part to play, by giving an outward sign of the purification. For when our body has been soiled by dirt and mud it is our practice to make it clean by washing in water. We therefore use water in the sacramental action also, signifying, by something perceived by the senses, a shining cleanliness which is not a bodily cleanliness. . . . Man, as we very well know, is composite, not simple: and therefore, for the healing of this twofold and conjunct being, medicines are assigned which suit and resemble his double nature. For his visible body, the sensible water; for his invisible soul, the unseen Spirit, invoked by faith, which comes in a fashion we cannot describe. (Gregory of Nyssa, LCF, p. 161)

Since the human malaise pervades both body and soul, the remedy, baptism, is applied by analogy at two levels, being signified by water, a visible, physical entity, yet what is signified is the renewing activity of the Holy Spirit who enlivens the soul with eternal life. In the Westminster Confession we find a concise Protestant summary of the ministry of baptism. It affirms its divine institution, its elements, meaning, modes, necessity, and effects:

Baptism is a sacrament of the New Testament, ordained by Jesus Christ, not only for the solemn admission of the party baptized into the visible Church, but also to be unto him a sign and seal of the covenant of grace, of his ingrafting into Christ, of regeneration, of remission of sins, and of his giving up unto God, through Jesus Christ, to walk in newness of life: which sacrament is, by Christ's own appointment, to be continued in his Church until the end of the world.

The outward element to be used in this sacrament is water, wherewith the party is to be baptized in the name of the Father, and of the Son, and of the Holy Ghost, by a minister of the gospel lawfully called thereunto.

Dipping of the person into the water is not necessary; but baptism is rightly administered by pouring or sprinkling water upon the person.

Not only those that do actually profess faith in and obedience unto Christ, but also the infants of one or both believing parents are to be baptized.

Although it be a great sin to condemn or neglect this ordinance, yet grace and salvation are not so inseparably annexed unto it, as that no person can be regenerated or saved without it, or that all that are baptized are undoubtedly regenerated.

The efficacy of baptism is not tied to that moment of time wherein it is administered; yet, notwithstanding, by the right use of this ordinance the grace promised is not only offered, but really exhibited and conferred by the Holy Ghost, to such (whether of age or infants) as that grace belongeth unto, according to the counsel of God's own will, in his appointed time.

The sacrament of baptism is but once to be administered to any person. (Westminister Confession, Ch. XXVIII, sec. i-vii, *C*, p. 225)

As the doctrine of the triune God is a summary of Christian teaching, so baptism epitomizes and displays the sum of ecumenical faith. For baptism from its beginnings has been conferred in the name of the Father, the Son, and the Holy Spirit. Early Christian theologies were largely a commentary on the baptismal formula. It was not the other way around, that the theologies were first developed, and then the baptismal formula later summarized them. Rather one can rightly say that Christian theology fundamentally began as a lengthy set of footnotes on the baptismal formula which preceeded all deliberate Christian doctrinal formulation. All the heresies against which early pastoral care had to struggle were essentially offenses against the baptismal formula.

If any bishop or presbyter does not baptize according to the Lord's constitution, into the Father, the Son, and the Holy Ghost, but into three beings without beginning, or into three Sons, or three Comforters, let him be deprived. (*Constitutions of the Holy Apostles*, Ecclesiastical Canons, Bk. VIII, sec. v, Canon 49, ANF VII, p. 503)

Baptism is intrinsically connected with orthodox faith, and definitive of the apostolic witness, according to the Council of Chalcedon:

This is the orthodox faith; this we all believe: into this we were baptized; into this we baptize. (Chalcedon, A.D. 451, Extracts, Session II, The Seven Ecumenical Councils, NPNF 2, XIV, p. 249)

Even though baptism has always been regarded as a solemn event, it has always been equally viewed as an incomparably happy occasion:

Happy is our sacrament of water, in that, by washing away the sins of our early blindness, we are set free and admitted into eternal life! (Tertullian, *On Baptism*, Ch. I, ANF III, p. 669)

Cyril's Catechetical Lectures compared the happiness of baptism with that of a wedding:

Let those souls get themselves ready, that are about to be wed to their spiritual Bridegroom. For lo! "the voice of one crying in the wilderness, Make ready the way of the Lord" (Isa. 40:3). For this wedding is no light matter, nor the usual and undiscriminating union of bodies, but is the election by faith made by "the Spirit that searcheth all things" (1 Cor. 2:10). For the espousals and marriage-contracts of this world are not invariably well-judged, but where there is wealth or beauty there the suitor is quick to give his hand. But in this wedding, it is not physical beauty, but the blameless conscience of the soul that engages. (Cyril of Jerusalem, *The Catechetical Lectures*, Lect. III, sec. 2, LCC IV, p. 90)

Among church fathers who have discussed baptism as a pastoral act with far-reaching implications for soul care, few have been more astute than Tertullian, who astutely sought to avoid misunderstandings of the teaching. One such potential misunderstanding appeared implicit in Paul's writings: If Abraham had faith sufficient without baptism, why cannot we also?

Some say, "Baptism is not necessary for them to whom faith is sufficient. For did not Abraham please God by a sacrament of no water, but of faith?" (cf. Rom. 4:9). . . . Grant that, in days gone by, there was salvation by means of bare faith, before the passion and resurrection of the Lord. But now that faith has been enlarged, and is become a faith which believes in His nativity, passion, and resurrection, there has been an amplification added by means of the sealing act of baptism. It is in some sense like the clothing of the faith that before was bare, and which cannot exist now without its proper law. For the law of baptizing has been imposed, and the formula prescribed: "Go forth therefore," He said, "and make all nations my disciples; baptize men everywhere in the name of the Father and the Son and the Holy Spirit" (Matt. 28:19). (Tertullian, *On Baptism*, Ch. XIII, ANF III, p. 676, NEB)*

Later, Augustine refined the same question, whether baptism is all that is needed for salvation, and whether conversion of the heart nullifies the necessity of baptism:

This all shows that the sacrament of baptism is one thing, the conversion of the heart is another; but the salvation of man is effected by these two. If one is missing, we are not bound to suppose that the other is absent: in an infant, baptism can exist without conversion; in the penitent thief, conversion without baptism. (Augustine, *On Baptism*, Ch. 4, sec. 31, 32, LCF, p. 243; cf. NPNF 1, IV, pp. 461f.)

II ❧ THE RECIPIENTS OF BAPTISM

The pastoral writers have puzzled over the complex interfacing of the divine will and human willing in baptism. It is of great significance to the comfort of the soul, thought Luther, that baptism is primarily God's work, and the human side of the action is primarily receptivity to the divine activity:

It is a work of God, not of man, as Paul teaches. The other works He works through us and with our help, but this one He works in us and without our help.

From this we can clearly see the difference, in baptism, between man the minister and God the Doer. For man baptises and does not baptise: he baptises, for he performs the work, immersing the person to be baptised; he does not baptise, for in that act he officiates not by his own authority, but in the stead of God. . . . This the words themselves indicate, when the priest says: "I baptise thee in the Name of the Father, and of the Son, and of the

Holy Ghost. Amen"—and not: "I baptise thee in my own name." It is as though he said: "What I do, I do not by my own authority, but in the name and stead of God, so that you should regard it just as if our Lord Himself had done it in a visible manner. The Doer and the minister are different persons, but the work of both is the same work, or, rather, it is the work of the Doer alone, through my ministry." . . . There is much of comfort and a mighty aid to faith in the knowledge that one has been baptised not by man, but by the Triune God Himself through a man acting among us in His name. (Luther, *The Babylonian Captivity,* WML II, pp. 224-225)

Since Paul at one point stated that he had been sent to preach, not to baptize, the question emerged as to why other clergy should not do likewise. Tertullian provided a classical response:

But they roll back an objection from that apostle himself, in that he said, "Christ did not send me to baptize, but to proclaim the Gospel" (1 Cor. 1:17) as if by this argument baptism were done away with! For if so, why did he baptize Gaius, and Crispus, and the house of Stephanas? However, even if Christ had not sent him to baptize, yet He had given other apostles the command to baptize. But these words were written to the Corinthians in regard of the circumstances of that particular time, when schisms and dissensions were agitated among them, while one was attributing everything to Paul, another to Apollos. For this reason the "peacemaking" apostle, for fear he should seem to claim all gifts for himself, says that he had been sent "not to baptize, but to proclaim." For preaching is the prior thing, baptizing the posterior. Therefore the preaching came first, but there can be no doubt that baptism was also authorized to one to whom preaching was authorized. (Tertullian, *On Baptism,* Ch. XIV, ANF III, p. 676, NEB)*

The question of how early baptism may be administered has remained a point of dispute among various interpreters. That the baptism of infants was practiced is seen from the Apostolic Constitutions:

Baptize your infants, and bring them up in the nurture and admonition of God. For says He: "Suffer the little children to come unto me, and forbid them not" (Matt. 19:14). (*Constitutions of the Holy Apostles,* Bk. VI, sec. III, Ch. xv, ANF VII, p. 457)*

Assuming that faith is prior to baptism, Augustine attempted to solve the dilemma of infant baptism by pointing to surrogate faith in the parents:

At this point men are wont to ask what good the sacrament of Christ's Baptism can do to infants, seeing that many of them die after having been baptized but before they can know anything about it. In this case it is pious and right to believe that the infant is benefited by the faith of those who bring him to be consecrated. This is commended by the salutary authority of the Church, so that everyone may realize how beneficial to him is his faith, seeing that one man's faith can be made beneficial for another who has no faith of his own. The son of the widow of Nain could have had no advantage from any faith of his own, for, being dead, he had no faith. But his mother's faith procured him the benefit of being raised from the dead (Luke 7:11ff). (Augustine, *On Free Will*, Bk. III, Ch. xxiii.67, LCC VI, p. 211)

Luther agreed with Augustine. In addressing the issue of the baptism of children, Luther's stress is upon the sovereign power of God to carry out his intention:

In contradiction of what has been said, some will perhaps point to the baptism of infants, who do not grasp the promise of God and cannot have the faith of baptism; so that either faith is not necessary or else infant baptism is without effect. Here I say what all say: Infants are aided by the faith of others, namely, those who bring them to baptism. For the Word of God is powerful, when it is uttered, to change even a godless heart, which is no less deaf and helpless than any infant. Even so the infant is changed, cleansed and renewed by inpoured faith, through the prayer of the Church that presents it for baptism and believes, to which prayer all things are possible. (Luther, *The Babylonian Captivity*, WML II, pp. 236-237)

However simply baptism has sought to manifest the unity of the body of Christ, it has often become a point of sharp controversy. Through successive historical crises, the pastoral tradition sought to define consensually the proper administration of baptism. This passage from Tertullian shows evidence that as early as the second century intense debates about baptism were going on: Who shall be baptized? What is the proper time for baptism? Should baptism be long delayed by penitents?

But they whose office it is, know that baptism is not rashly to be administered. . . . This precept is rather to be looked at carefully: "Give not the holy thing to the dogs, nor cast your pearls before swine" (Matt. 7:6). . . . "But," some say, "Paul too was, in fact, 'speedily' baptized:" for Simon, [sic, Ananias] his host, speedily recognized him to be "an appointed vessel of election" (Acts 9:15). God's approbation sends sure premonitory tokens before it; every "petition" may both deceive and be deceived. And so, according to the circumstances and disposition, and even age, of each individual, the delay of baptism is preferable; principally, however, in the case of little children. . . . The Lord does indeed say, "Forbid them not to come unto me" (Matt 19:14). Let them "come," then, while they are growing up; let them become Christians when they have become able to know Christ. . . . If any understand the weighty import of baptism, they will fear its reception more than its delay. (Tertullian, *On Baptism*, Ch. XVIII, ANF III, p. 677)*

In speaking of Simon, Tertullian apparently confused him with the "Judas" with whom Saul stayed (Acts 9:11); but it was Ananias who recognized him as "an appointed vessel." Tertullian's view on this matter did not become consensually received, but it remained a significant minority view. He argued that, given the hazards of sin after baptism, it is better to delay than hasten baptism. Tertullian also concluded that under conditions of necessity, lay persons could confer baptism, but that it was more fittingly conferred by those duly ordained for its administration:

Even laymen have the right; for what is equally received can be equally given. Unless bishops, or priests, or deacons, be on the spot, other disciples are called, i.e., to the work. The word of the Lord ought not to be hidden by any: in like manner, too, baptism, which is equally God's property, can be administered by all. But how much more is the rule of reverence and modesty incumbent on laymen—seeing that these powers belong to their superiors. . . . "all things are lawful, but not all expedient" (1 Cor. 10:23). Let it suffice assuredly, in cases of necessity, to avail yourself (of that rule), if at any time circumstance either of place, or of time, or of person compels you (so to do); for then the steadfast courage of the succourer, when the situation of the endangered one is urgent, is exceptionally admissible. (Tertullian, *On Baptism*, Ch. XVII, ANF III, p. 677)

Suppose one has already been baptized, yet, having strayed from faith, wishes to be baptized again. How have the pastoral writers responded to the possibility of re-baptism? Tertullian summarized the prevailing view:

We enter, then, the font once: once are sins washed away, because they ought never to be repeated. (Tertullian, *On Baptism*, Ch. XV, ANF III, p. 676)

This question was framed by a Pre-Nicene anonymous writer:

I observe that it has been asked among the brethren what course ought specially to be adopted towards the persons of those who although baptized in heresy, have yet been baptized in the name of our Lord Jesus Christ, and subsequently departing from their heresy, and fleeing as supplicants to the Church of God, should repent with their whole hearts, and only now perceiving the condemnation of their error, implore from the Church the help of salvation. The point is whether, according to the most ancient custom and ecclesiastical tradition, it would suffice, after that baptism which they have received outside the Church indeed, but still in the name of Jesus Christ our Lord, that only hands should be laid upon them by the bishop for their reception of the Holy Spirit, and this imposition of hands would afford them the renewed and perfected seal of faith; or whether, indeed, a repetition of baptism would be necessary for them, as if they should receive nothing if they had not obtained baptism afresh, just as if they were never baptized in the name of Jesus Christ. (Anonymous, *A Treatise on Re-Baptism*, s c. I, ANF V, p. 667)

An ongoing controversy accompanied the question of rebaptism. The sharp distinction between person and office of the pastor helped Luther conceptually with the issue:

Do not rebaptize children, as, it is true, Cyprian did. He had the false idea that he could not consider the Baptism of heretics a valid Baptism. Therefore he rebaptized them. But this reasoning is wrong, for we must distinguish office from person. A public sinner is also not in the unity of the Christian Church, and yet the office he holds in the church is not to be despised on this account. The reason: The office is not his but the Lord Jesus Christ's. However, if he intended to break the command of Christ and wanted to baptize, preach, and administer the Sacrament in a way different from that commanded by Christ, then we would have reason to reject his Baptism, his preaching, and other activities. But if he changes nothing that Christ has ordained, the fact that he is personally wicked and sinful does not detract anything from the office. (Luther, WA 52, p. 310f; WLS 2, pp. 933-934)

III ❧ The Sign of Baptism

Some imagine a lack of sophistication concerning comparative cultural anthropology and the history of religions among classical pastoral writers. Yet there is considerable evidence that, within the boundaries of the knowledge available to them, they were thinking resourcefully and significantly about how common elements of nature and human culture become symbolically used in the history of revelation.

The symbolism of water is a case in point. Tertullian argued that we can easily see in the history of religions an abundant use of water as a cleansing or purifying analogy. He did not hesistate to view Christian baptism as standing in continuity with that history. This typological reflection is not unlike what Jung would later call an archetypal mode of consciousness. For Tertullian, water symbolized the primordial state of creation:

We proceed to treat the question: "How foolish and impossible it is to be formed anew by water. In what respect, we ask, has this material substance merited a role of such high dignity?" I suppose it useful to examine the symbolic authority of the liquid element. It is found in abundance, and has been from the very beginning. For water is one of those things which, before all the furnishing of the world, were quiescent with God in a yet unshapen state. "In the beginning of Creation," says the Scripture, "when God made heaven and earth, the earth was without form and void, with darkness over the face of the abyss, and a mighty wind that swept over the surface of the waters" (Gen. 1:1,2). The first thing, O mortal man, that you must respect is the age of the waters, in that their very substance is ancient. The second thing you must respect is their dignity, in that they were the seat of the Divine Spirit, more pleasing to Him, no doubt, than all the other then existing elements. . . . [Others may ask:] "But do not the nations who are strangers to all understanding of spiritual powers also ascribe to their idols the imbuing of waters with the self-same efficacy?" Indeed they do. . . . For washing is the channel through which they are initiated into sacred rites—of some notorious Isis or Mithras. The gods themselves they similarly honor by washings. (Tertullian, *On Baptism*, Ch. III, IV, V, ANF III, p. 670-671, NEB)*

However universal the mystical symbolism of water may be, Tertullian warned against focussing upon water as such in teaching about baptism:

If I go forward in recounting universally from that time forward, or at more length, the evidences of the "authority" of this element, adducing how great is its power or its grace, how many ingenious devices, how many functions, how useful an instrumentality, it affords the world, I fear I may seem to have collected rather the praises of water than the reasons of baptism. Nonetheless I would be thereby teaching all the more fully that it is not to be doubted that God has made the material substance which He has disposed throughout all His products and works obey Him also in His own peculiar sacraments; and that the material substance which governs terrestrial life acts as agent likewise in the celestial.

But it will suffice to have thus called at the outset those points in which that primary principle of baptism is recognized—which was foreordained by the very attitude assumed for a type of baptism,—that the Spirit of God, who hovered over (the waters) from the beginning, would continue to linger over the waters of the baptized. (Tertullian, *On Baptism*, Ch. III-IV, ANF III, p. 670)

Water is a recurrent, multivalent biblical symbol embracing such diverse themes as primordial creation, deliverance, and purification:

Now if anyone is eager to learn why baptismal grace is given by means of water, and not by any other of the elements, he will find the answer if he takes up the Scriptures. For water is a great subject and the fairest of the four visible elements of which the world is made. . . . As water was the foundation of the world, so Jordan was the foundation of the Gospel. Israel was set free from Pharaoh by means of the sea, and the world was freed from sins "with the washing of water by the (divine) word" (Eph. 5:26). . . . The high-priest first washes and then offers the incense, for Aaron first washed with water and after that was invested as high-priest. How indeed could he properly intercede for others if he had not first been cleansed with water? (Cyril of Jerusalem, *The Catechetical Lectures*, Lect. III, sec. 5, LCC IV, pp. 92-93)

The death and resurrection theme was central for Luther in his discussion of the sign of baptism, what it signifies, and the relation of faith and baptism as follows:

The second part of baptism is the sign, or sacrament, which is that immersion into water whence also it derives its name; for the Greek *baptizo* means I immerse, and *baptisma* means immersion. For, as has been said, signs are added to the divine promises to represent that which the words signify, or, as they now say, that which the sacrament "effectively signifies." We shall see how much of truth there is in this. The great majority have supposed that there is some hidden spiritual power in the word or in the water, which works the grace of God in the soul of the recipient. Others deny this and hold that there is no power in the sacraments, but that grace is given by God alone, Who according to His covenant aids the sacraments He has instituted. Yet all are agreed that the sacraments are effective signs of grace.... Even so it is not baptism that justifies or benefits anyone, but it is faith in the word of promise, to which baptism is added. This faith justifies, and fulfils that which baptism signifies. For faith is the submersion of the old man and the emerging of the new.... Baptism, then, signifies two things—death and resurrection; that is, full and complete justification. The minister's immersing the child in the water signifies death; his drawing it forth again signifies life. Thus Paul expounds it in Romans 6:4, "By baptism we were buried with him, and lay dead, in order that, as Christ was raised from the dead in the splendour of the Father, so also we might set our feet upon the new paths of life." This death and resurrection we call the new creation, regeneration, and the spiritual birth. (Luther, *The Babylonian Captivity*, WML II, pp. 226-230, NEB)*

The pastor may be asked whether it is water in itself that is the source of regeneration and renewal. Luther answered:

It is not the water indeed that does them, but the word of God which is in and with the water, and faith, which trusts such word of God in the water. For without the word of God the water is simple water and no Baptism. But with the word of God it is a Baptism, that is a gracious water of life and a washing of regeneration in the Holy Ghost.... What does such baptizing with water signify? Answer: It signifies that the old Adam in us should, by daily contrition and repentance, be drowned and die with all sins and evil lusts and, again, a new man daily come forth and arise, who shall live before God in righteousness and purity forever. (Luther, *Small Catechism*, Sec. III, IV, WA 30 I, p. 285f; WLS 1, pp. 43-44)

IV ❧ Preparation for Baptism

Those being prepared for baptism were called catechumens (those receiving rudimentary instruction). A program of instruction was provided by pastors, called *catechesis*, or catechetical instruction, from which derives our word catechism. *Catechesis* was regarded by classical pastoral writers as a regular pastoral duty.

Tertullian's description of preparation for baptism was written in a period in which martyrdom was often the price paid for one's baptism:

> They who are about to enter baptism ought to pray with repeated prayers, fasts, and bendings of the knee, and vigils all the night through, and with the confession of all bygone sins, that they may express the meaning even of the baptism of John: "They were baptized," says the Scripture, "confessing their own sins" (Matt. 3:6). To us it is matter for thankfulness if we do now publicly confess our iniquities or turpitudes. For by doing so we at the same time are making satisfaction for our former sins by mortification of our flesh and spirit, and secondly we are laying the foundation of defences against the temptations which will closely follow. . . . Together with your brethren, ask from the Father, ask from the Lord, that His own specialties of grace and distributions of gifts may be supplied you. "Ask," Jesus says, "and ye shall receive" (Matt. 7:7). Well, you have asked, and have received; you have knocked, and it has been opened to you. Only, I pray that, when you are asking, you be mindful likewise of Tertullian the sinner. (Tertullian, *On Baptism*, Ch. XX, ANF III, pp. 678-679)

Baptismal instruction may be of benefit not only to those considering baptism, but also to those whose baptismal faith has remained for some time unexamined.

> A treatise on this matter will not be superfluous. It should instruct not only those who are just becoming newly formed in the faith, but also those who have been resting contentedly with having simply believed, yet without having fully examined the grounds of the traditions, who are trying to carry on, yet somewhat ignorantly, in an untried though probable faith. (Tertullian, *On Baptism*, Ch. I, ANF III, p. 669)*

An elementary outline of a systematic theology was provided by the Apostolic Constitutions in the proposed list of issues for examination in baptismal instruction. Such instruction apparently touched upon creation, providence, anthropology, Christology, and eschatology:

> Let the catechumens learn the order of the several parts of the creation, the sequential acts of providence, and the different dis-

pensations of the laws. Let them be instructed on why the world was made, and why human beings were appointed to be citizens in it. Let them also know of their own human nature, of what sort it is. . . . And how God still took care of and did not reject humanity. . . . Let those who offer themselves to baptism learn these and similar things during the time that they are catechumens. . . . And after this thanksgiving, let him instruct them in the doctrines concerning our Lord's incarnation, and in those concerning His passion, his resurrection from the dead, and his assumption. (*Constitutions of the Holy Apostles*, Bk. VII, sec. III, Ch. xxxix, ANF VII, pp. 475-476)*

Cyril of Jerusalem stressed the incomparable opportunity of early and sound catechetical teaching:

Think of this as being the season for planting young trees. If we do not now dig and set them deep in the earth, when can we find another opportunity for planting well what has been once planted badly? (Cyril of Jerusalem, *The Catechetical Lectures*, Procatechesis, sec. 11, LCC IV, p. 72)

The pastor is never to baptize without teaching. For the command to baptize and to teach are intrinsically welded together. Athanasius argued that bad theology has frequently emerged out of an inadequate understanding of baptism. Each heresy is, properly understood, a baptismal heresy. He illustrated this principle by viewing Arianism essentially as a baptismal heresy:

The Arians do not baptize into Father and Son, but into Creator and creature, and into Maker and work. And as a creature is other than the Son, so the Baptism, which is supposed to be given by them, is other than the truth, though they pretend to name the Name of the Father and the Son, because of the words of Scripture. For not he who simply says, "O Lord," gives Baptism; but he who with the Name has also the right faith. On this account therefore our Saviour also did not simply command to baptize, but first says, Teach; and then "Baptize into the Name of Father, and Son, and Holy Ghost" (Matt. 287:19); that the right faith might follow upon learning, and together with faith might come the consecration of Baptism. (Athanasius, *Discourses Against the Arians*, II, Ch. XVIII, sec. 17, NPNF 2, IV, p. 368)

The baptismal supplication found in the Apostolic Constitutions provides a glimpse of how the early church prayed for the Spirit to empower the act of baptism, so that the believer might through it share in the life, death and resurrection of Jesus:

Look down from heaven, and sanctify this water, and give it grace and power, so that he who is to be baptized, according to the command of Thy Christ, may be crucified with Him, and may die with Him, and may be buried with Him, and may rise with Him to the adoption which is in Him, that he may be dead to sin and live to righteousness. (*Constitutions of the Holy Apostles*, Bk. VII, sec. IV, Ch. xliii, ANF VII, p. 477)*

Should baptism be administered at certain seasons of the year?

The Passover affords a more than usually solemn day for baptism. For it was during the Passover that our Lord's Passion, into which we are baptized, was completed. . . . After that, Pentecost is a most joyous space for conferring baptisms. For it was at Pentecost that the resurrection of the Lord was repeatedly demonstrated among the disciples. . . . However, every day is the Lord's; every hour, every time, is apt for baptism. If there is a difference in the solemnity, there is no distinction in the grace. (Tertullian, *On Baptism*, Ch. XIX, ANF III, p. 678)*

V ❧ THE ACT OF BAPTISM

One of the earliest accounts of how the pastor confers baptism is found in the first century *Didache*. It is evident from this source that a number of issues were being debated very early that continued to be debated for many centuries: whether by immersion or sprinkling, whether by running or still water, whether fasting is presupposed:

The procedure for baptizing is as follows. After rehearsing all the preliminaries, immerse in running water "In the Name of the Father, and of the Son, and of the Holy Ghost." If no running water is available, immerse in ordinary water. This should be cold if possible; otherwise warm. If neither is practicable, then sprinkle water three times on the head "In the Name of the Father, and of the Son and of the Holy Ghost." Both baptizer and baptized ought to fast before the baptism, as well as any others who can do so; but the candidate himself should be told to keep a fast for a day or two beforehand. (*Didache*, Part 2, sec. 7, ECW, pp. 230-231)

Hippolytus (c. 170-c. 236) provided a fairly detailed account of the act of baptism:

And when they are chosen who are set apart to receive baptism let their life be examined, whether they lived piously while catechumens, whether "they honoured the widows" (1 Tim. 5:3), whether they visited the sick, whether they have fulfilled every good work.

If those who bring them bear witness to them that they have done thus, [then] let them hear the gospel. . . . [And] let those who are to be baptised be instructed to wash and cleanse themselves on the fifth day of the week. . . . Those who are to receive baptism shall fast on the Friday and on the Saturday. And on the Saturday the bishop shall assemble those who are to be baptised in one place, and shall bid them [all] to pray and bow the knee. . . . And they shall spend all the night in vigil, reading the scriptures [to them] and instructing them. . . . And at the hour when the cock crows they shall first [of all] pray over the water.

[When they come to the water, let the water be pure and flowing.]

And they shall put off their clothes.

And they shall baptise the little children first. And if they can answer for themselves, let them answer. But if they cannot, let their parents answer or someone from their family. . . . And when the presbyter takes hold of each one of those who are to be baptised, let him bid him renounce saying:

I renounce thee, Satan, and all thy service and all thy works.

And when he has said this let him anoint him with the Oil of Exorcism saying:

Let all evil spirits depart far from thee.

And also turning him to the East, let him say:

[I consent to Thee, O Father and Son and Holy Ghost, before whom all creation trembleth and is moved. Grant me to do all Thy wills without blame.]

Then after these things let him give him over to [the presbyter] who stands at the water [to baptise];

[And a presbyter takes his right hand and he turns his face to the East. Before he descends into the water, while he still turns his face to the East, standing above the water he says after receiving the Oil of Exorcism, thus: I believe and bow me unto Thee and all Thy service, O Father, Son and Holy Ghost. And so he descends into the water.]

And let them stand in the water naked. And let [a] deacon likewise go down with him into the water.

And let him say to him and instruct him: Dost thou believe in one God the Father Almighty, and His only-begotten Son Jesus Christ our Lord and our Saviour, and His Holy Spirit, Giver of life to all creatures, the Trinity of one Substance, one Godhead, one Lordship, one Kingdom, one Faith, one Baptism in the Holy Catholic Apostolic Church for life eternal [Amen]? And he who is baptised shall say [again] thus: verily, I believe.

And [when] he [who is to be baptised] goes down to the water, let him who baptises lay hand on him saying thus:

Dost thou believe in God the Father Almighty? And he who is being baptised shall say: I believe. Let him forthwith baptise him once, having his hand laid upon his head. And after [this] let him say: Dost thou believe in Christ Jesus, the Son of God, Who was born of Holy Spirit and the Virgin Mary, Who was crucified in the days of Pontius Pilate, And died, [and was buried] And rose the third day living from the dead And ascended into [the] heaven[s], And sat down at the right hand of the Father, And will come to judge the living and the dead? And when he says: I believe, let him [baptise him] the second time. And again let him say: Dost thou believe in [the] Holy Spirit in the Holy Church, And the resurrection of the flesh? And he who is being baptised shall say: I believe. And so let him [baptise him] the third time. And afterwards when he comes up [from the water] he shall be anointed by the presbyter with the Oil of Thanksgiving saying: I anoint thee with holy oil in the Name of Jesus Christ. And [so] each one drying himself [with a towel] they shall [now] put on their clothes, and after this let them be together in the assembly. (Hippolytus, *The Apostolic Tradition*, pp. 30-38)

This is among the most important documents of the pastoral tradition, showing the intricate confluence of liturgy, teaching, pastoral care, spiritual formation, and primitive systematic theology in the baptismal act. Instruction, fasting, cleansing and all night vigil preceeded baptism, an early morning rite, featuring the renunciation of Satan, anointment with oil, and the affirmation of the rule of faith.

Similar features were present in the baptismal order of the Apostolic Constitutions:

Let, therefore, the candidate for baptism declare thus in his renunciation:

I renounce Satan, and his works, and his pomps, and his worships, and his angels, and his inventions, and all things that are under him. And after his renunciation let him in his consociation say: And I associate myself to Christ, and believe, and am baptized into one unbegotten Being, the only true God Almighty, the Father of Christ, the Creator and Maker of all things, from whom are all things; and into the Lord Jesus Christ, His only begotten Son, the First born of the whole creation, who before the ages was begotten by the good pleasure of the Father, by whom all things were made, both those in heaven and those on earth, visible and invisible; who in the last days descended from heaven, and took flesh, and was born of the holy Virgin Mary, and did converse holily according to the laws of His God and Father, and was crucified under Pontius Pilate, and died for us, and rose again from the dead after His passion the third day, and ascended into the heavens, and sitteth at the right hand of the Father, and again is to come at the end of the world with glory to judge the quick and the dead, of whose kindgom there shall be no end. And I am baptized into the Holy Ghost, that is, the Comforter, who worked in all the saints from the beginning of the world, but was afterwards sent to the apostles by the Father, according to the promise of our Saviour and Lord, Jesus Christ; and after the apostles, to all those that believe in the Holy Catholic Church; into the resurrection of the flesh, and into the remission of sins, and into the kindgom of heaven, and into the life of the world to come. And after this vow, he comes in order to the anointing with oil. (*Constitutions of the Holy Apostles*, Bk. VII, sec. IV, sec. xl-xli, ANF VII, p. 476)*

The renunciation of Satan, three-fold baptism in the name of the tri-une God, and the sharing in Christ's death, burial and resurrection, were also major features of Ambrose's account of the baptismal rite:

He asked you, "Do you renounce the devil and his works?" What did you reply? "I renounce." "Do you renounce the world and its pleasures?" What did you reply? "I renounce." Remember what you said, and never let the terms of your bond slip from your mind. . . ." You were asked: "Do you believe in God the Father Almighty?" You said: "I believe," and you dipped; that is, you were buried. Again you were asked: "Do you believe in our Lord Jesus Christ, and in his cross?" You said: "I believe," and you dipped, therefore you were "buried with Christ". . . . A third time you were asked: "Do you believe also in the holy Spirit?" You said: "I believe," and you dipped for the third time, so that the threefold confession might cancel the fall of your earlier life. (Ambrose, *The Sacraments*, LCF, pp. 182-183)

Although Luther argued that immersion was the preferable mode, he did not insist upon it as a required mode for valid baptism:

Baptism (*Die Taufe*) is *baptismos* in Greek, and *mersio* in Latin, and means to plunge something completely into water, so that the water covers it. Although in many places it is no longer customary to thrust and dip infants into the font, but only with the hand to pour the baptismal water upon them out of the font, nevertheless the former is what should be done. (Luther, *The Holy and Blessed Sacrament of Baptism*, 1519, LW 35, p. 29)

Again, in *The Babylonian Captivity*:

I would have those who are to be baptized completely immersed in the water. . . . Not that I hold this to be necessary (*non quod necessarium arbitrer*). But it were well to give to so perfect and complete a matter a perfect and complete sign. (Luther, *The Babylonian Captivity*, WA 6, p. 534; WLS 1, p. 58)

This solemn prayer for the efficacy of baptism followed the ante-Nicene rite:

And after this, when he has baptized him in the name of the Father, and of the Son, and of the Holy Ghost, he shall anoint him with ointment, and shall add as follows:—

O Lord God, who art without generation, and without a superior, the Lord of the whole world, who hast scattered the sweet odour of the knowledge of the Gospel among all nations, do Thou grant at this time that this ointment may be efficacious upon him that is baptized, so that the sweet odour of Thy Christ may continue upon him firm and fixed; and that now he has died with Him, he may arise and live with Him. . . . After this let him stand up and pray that prayer which the Lord taught us. . . .

[Then the newly baptized shall] pray thus after the foregoing prayer, and say: O God Almighty, the Father of Thy Christ, Thy only begotten Son, give me a body undefiled, a heart pure, a mind watchful, an unerring knowledge, the influence of the Holy Ghost for the obtaining and assured enjoying of the truth, through Thy Christ, by whom glory be to Thee, in the Holy Spirit, forever. Amen. (*Constitutions of the Holy Apostles*, Bk. VII, sec. IV, Ch. xliv-xlv, ANF VII, p. 477)

VI ❧ The Effects of Baptism

For almost two millenia, pastors have been baptizing persons into the unity of faith. The act of baptism seeks to manifest that triune-grounded unity. Despite this, baptism remains a point of deep division in Christianity. There remain many questions about the effects of baptism, what actually occurs in baptism, whether it can be judged by its effects, and about the relation of new birth and baptism.

For example, does spiritual illumination accompany baptism? Justin Martyr's description indicates that such was an early Christian belief:

We learned from the apostles this reason for this [rite]. At our first birth we were born of necessity without our knowledge, from moist seed, by the intercourse of our parents with each other, and grew up in bad habits and wicked behavior. So that we should not remain children of necessity and ignorance, but [become sons] of free choice and knowledge, and obtain remission of the sins we have already committed, there is named at the water, over him who has chosen to be born again and has repented of his sinful acts, the name of God the Father and Master of all. . . . This washing is called illumination, since those who learn these things are illumined within. The illuminand is also washed in the name of Jesus Christ. . . . We, however, after thus washing the one who has been convinced and signified his assent, lead him to those who are called brethren, where they are assembled. They then earnestly offer common prayers for themselves and the one who has been illuminated and all others everywhere, that we may be made worthy, having learned the truth, to be found in deed good citizens and keepers of what is commanded, so that we may be saved with eternal salvation. (Justin Martyr, *First Apology*, sec. 61-65, LCC I, pp. 282-285)

Similarly Clement of Alexandria spoke of the expectation of a gift of new vision, an illumination accompanying baptism:

When we are baptized, we are enlightened; being enlightened, we become adopted sons; becoming adopted sons, we are made perfect; and becoming perfect, we are made divine. . . . Like those suffering from some blinding eye-disease who meanwhile receive no light from the outside and have none themselves, but must first remove the impediment from their eyes before they can have clear vision. In the same way, those who are baptized are cleansed of the sins which like a mist overcloud their divine spirit and then acquire a spiritual sight which is clear and unimpeded and lightsome, the sort of sight which alone enables us to behold divinity, with the help of the Holy Spirit who is poured forth from heaven upon us. (Clement of Alexandria, *Christ the Educator*, Bk. I, Ch. 6.26-28, FC 23, p. 26-28)

Sin after baptism was held to be unthinkable by many pastoral writers of the pre-Nicene period:

Beloved, be it known to you that those who are baptized into the death of our Lord Jesus are obliged to go on no longer in sin; for as those who are dead cannot work wickedness any longer, so those who are dead with Christ cannot practise wickedness. We do not therefore believe, brethren, that any one who has received the washing of life continues in the practice of the licentious acts of transgressors. (*Constitutions of the Holy Apostles*, Bk. II, sec. III, sec. vii, ANF VII, p. 398)

Luther employed a stunning political metaphor to speak of the invalidation of sin through baptism:

The jurisdiction, authority, and rights of a prince are not impaired because he has many faithless and disobedient subjects in his principality. Even so in Baptism: Once we have received it, we are included and received by it into the number of those who shall be saved, and God makes an eternal covenant of grace with us. That we thereafter often stumble and fall does not render this blessed Baptism futile. (Luther, WA 37, p. 668; WLS 1, p. 58)

What if baptism should result in no behavioral change?

If the "birth from above" is a refashioning of man's nature, we must ask what change is made to bring the grace of regeneration to perfection. . . . If the life after initiation is of the same quality as the uninitiated life, then, though it may be a bold thing to say, I will say it without flinching; in the case of such people the water is merely water, for the gift of the Holy Spirit in no way shows itself in what takes place. (Gregory of Nyssa, LCF, p. 160)

It is an ancient practice associated with Christian baptism that its recipient receives a name, and thus symbolically receives an identity in the family of God:

The Educator and Teacher is there naming us little ones, meaning that we are more ready for salvation than the worldly wise who, believing themselves wise, have blinded their own eyes. (Clement of Alexandria, *Christ the Educator*, Bk. I, Ch. 2.32, FC 23, p. 31)

One's baptism is not made less real by one's neglect of it, according to Luther's metaphor of the gift refused:

It is terrible to hear that people venture to slander God's work by saying: The trouble is that if he who receives Baptism does not believe, the Baptism is no good. If a person were given a hundred gulden but refused to take them, the hundred gulden would certainly retain their value, would they not? The fact that the fellow does not want the money does not in any way harm the gold. The same principle applies in the case of Baptism. (Luther, WA 46, p. 154; WLS 1, p. 55)

VII ❦ Does a Bad Pastor Nullify a Good Sacrament?

The Donatist controversy forced Augustine to sharpen a careful distinction between the sacrament itself and its effects, which has been widely received by subsequent pastoral writers. This distinction helped solve the question of whether an unworthy minister may confer a worthy sacrament, and whether the very validity of a sacrament is finally determined by its behavioral results:

The reason why the blessed Cyprian and other eminent Christians . . . decided that Christ's baptism could not exist among heretics or schismatics was that they failed to distinguish between the sacrament and the efficacy or working out of a sacrament. Because the efficacy and working out of baptism, in freedom from sins and in integrity of heart, was not found among heretics, it was supposed that the sacrament itself did not exist there. But if we turn our eyes to the multitude within the fold, it is clear that those within the unity of the church who are perverse and lead wicked lives can neither give nor have the remission of sins. Nevertheless the pastors of the Catholic Church spread through the whole world were quite clear that such men had the sacrament of baptism and could confer it; and through them the original custom was afterwards established by the authority of a plenary council. Even when a wandering sheep has received the Lord's brand-mark at the hands of dishonest robbers, and then comes into the security of Christian unity, it is restored, freed, and healed; but the Lord's brand-mark is recognized, not disallowed. . . . The recipient of a schismatic's baptism may receive it to his salvation, if he himself is not in schism. (Augustine, *On Baptism*, Ch. IV, sec. 1, LCF, p. 241; cf. NPNF 1, IV, pp. 446ff.)

This maxim, that one schismatically baptized may not be in schism, has profound modern ecumenical significance. It helps those who understand themselves not to be in schism with ancient apostolic ecumenical faith to experience their link with orthodox and catholic traditions that would regard their baptism as schismatic. Augustine was not the first, but among the most influential, to argue that baptism is not polluted by being administered by polluted ministers:

The water over which the name of God is invoked is not profane and polluted, even if that name is invoked by profane and polluted men; for neither God's creation nor God's name can be polluted. The baptism which is consecrated by the words of Christ in the Gospels is holy, even when conferred by the polluted, and on the polluted, however shameless and unclean they may be. This holiness is itself incapable of contamination, and the power of God supports his sacrament, whether for the salvation of those who use it aright, or the doom of those who employ it wrongly. The light of the sun, or of a lamp, is not defiled by contact with the filthy on which it shines: so how can Christ's baptism be defiled by the wickedness of any man? (Augustine, *On Baptism*, Ch. III, sec. 15, LCF, p. 242; cf. NPNF 1, IV, p. 441)

Nor does unworthily partaking nullify the validity of the sacrament:

Judas, to whom the Lord gave the piece of bread, gave the devil his chance to enter him, not by receiving something evil, but by receiving something in an evil way. So when a man receives the sacrament of the Lord unworthily the result is not that the sacrament is evil because he is evil, not that he has received nothing at all because he has not received it for his salvation. It is just as much the Lord's body and blood when a man "eats and drinks judgement to himself" (1 Cor. 11:29) by partaking unworthily. (Augustine, *On Baptism*, Ch. V, sec. 9, LCF, p. 246; cf. NPNF 1, IV, p. 467)

Centuries later the Anglican Thirty-nine Articles affirmed that the sacrament remains good even when administered by evil men:

Although in the visible Church the evil be ever mingled with the good, and sometimes the evil have chief authority in the Ministration of the Word and Sacraments, yet forasmuch as they do not the same in their own name, but in Christ's, and do minister by his commission and authority, we may use their Ministry, both in hearing the Word of God, and in receiving the Sacraments. Neither is the effect of Christ's ordinance taken away by their wickedness, nor the grace of God's gifts diminished from such as by faith, and rightly, do receive the Sacraments ministered unto them; which be effectual, because of Christ's institution and promise, although they be ministered by evil men. (Anglican Thirty-nine Articles of Religion, Ch. XXVI, CC, p. 275)

Calvin pressed the point even further:

If some Epicurean, inwardly grinning at the whole perfor-mance, were to administer the Supper to me according to the command of Christ and the rule given by him, and in due form, I would not doubt that the bread and the cup held forth by his hand are pledges to me of the body and the blood of Christ. (Calvin, *Antidote to Council of Trent*, SW, p. 216)

VIII ⚭ CONFIRMATION OF ONE'S BAPTISM

If baptism is the seal of God's promise, confirmation celebrates that promise as having been consciously and deliberately received. In confir-mation, one receives that grace which confirms, consummates and com-pletes the sacrament of baptism, and one thereby assumes personal responsibility for one's baptismal vows. In the service of confirmation, the church prays that confirmands will be empowered by the Spirit to service, and that grace shall increase in them all the days of their lives. Only the baptized can be confirmed, and only then at the age of suffi-cient accountability to understanding fully the implications of their bap-tism. Hence this pastoral act is an important part of soul care of young people and of persons newly entering into full and deliberate participa-tion in the Christian community.

That confirmation of baptism was a very ancient rite is clear from this prayer from Hippolytus (c. 170-235):

The bishop shall lay his hand upon them invoking and saying;
O Lord God, who did count these Thy servants worthy of the forgiveness of sins by the washing of regeneration, make them worthy to be filled with Thy Holy Spirit and send upon them Thy grace, that they may serve Thee according to Thy will. For to Thee is the glory, to the Father and to the Son with the Holy Ghost in the holy Church, both now and ever and world without end. Amen.

After this, pouring the consecrated oil from his hand and lay-ing his hand on his head, he shall say:
I anoint thee with holy oil in God the Father Almighty and Christ Jesus and the Holy Ghost.

And sealing him on the forehead, he shall give him the kiss of peace and say:

The Lord be with you.

And he who has been sealed shall say: And with thy spirit. And so he shall do to each one severally. (Hippolytus, *The Apostolic Tradition*, Ch. xxii, "Confirmation," sec. 1-4, pp. 38-39)*

Young persons are not to come to communion without instruction—a pre-Reformation maxim sustained by the Reformation:

When a child has been well enough instructed to pass the Catechism, he is to recite solemnly the sum of what it contains, and also to make profession of his Christianity in the presence of the Church.

Before this is done, no child is to be admitted to receive the Supper; and parents are to be informed not to bring them before this time. For it is a very perilous thing, for children as for parents, to introduce them without good and adequate instruction. (John Calvin, *Draft Ecclesiastical Ordinances*, 1541, SW, p. 240)

It is the nature of confirmation to confirm one's baptism, hence to learn what baptism means, and to enter into its covenant voluntarily. The Anglican pastor, John Cosin, provided this definition:

The ancient custom of the church of Christ was, after that persons were once baptized, to add unto their Baptism Imposition of hands, with earnest prayer for the gifts of God's graces to be bestowed upon them, whereby they might be confirmed and strengthened in that holy profession which, in the Sacrament of Baptism, they had first begun to make. (John Cosin, Correspondence, Part II, pp. 69-72; *Angl.*, p. 443)

The purpose of confirmation is distortable in the form of superstitious excess or the opposite defect of negligence:

Besides that extraordinary act of laying on the hand for curing of diseases and infirmities, practised by Our Blessed Saviour and His Apostles and for conveying the Holy Ghost in a miraculous way, in the Primitive Times there were three occasions and usages of Imposition of Hands,—in cases of 1. Confirmation; 2. of Ordination; 3. of Absolution and Readmission of Penitents. . . . It has been the lot of this sacred rite [i.e. of Confirmation] to fall into ill hands and to be foully wronged by a double extreme; the one, of Excess, the other, of Defect. The Excess, in a superstitious over-doing and over-valuing it; the Defect, in a neglective disestimation. (Joseph Hall, Apostolic Institution of Imposition of

Hands for Confirmation Revived, Sec. 2-5, Works, X, pp. 442-447; *Angl.*, p. 445)*

Baxter described how the practice of confirmation had fallen into abuse in his boyhood, lacking serious instruction:

When I was a schoolboy about fifteen years of age, the Bishop coming into the country, many went to him to be confirmed. We that were boys ran out to see the bishop among the rest, not knowing anything of the meaning of the business. When we came there, we met about thirty or forty in all, of our own stature and temper, that had come for to be "bishopped," as then it was called. The Bishop examined us not at all in one article of the Faith; but in a churchyard in haste we were set in a rank, and he passed hastily over us, laying his hands on our head, and saying a few words, which neither I nor any that I spoke with, understood; so hastily were they uttered, and a very short prayer recited, and there was an end. But whether we were Christians or infidels, or knew so much as that there was a God, the Bishop little knew nor inquired. And yet he was esteemed one of the best Bishops in England. And though the Canons require that the Curate or Minister send a certificate that children have learned the Catechism, yet there was no such thing done, but we ran of our own accord to see the Bishop only; and almost all the rest of the country had not this much. This was the old, careless practice of this excellent duty of Confirmation. (Richard Baxter, *Confirmation and Restauration*, Works, XIV, pp. 481f; *Angl.*, p. 449-450)

George Herbert argued against a specific age for receiving confirmation and first Eucharist. One is ready to receive when one understands the difference between Bread and bread:

The time of everyone's first receiving is not so much by years, as by understanding; particularly the rule may be this: When any one can distinguish the Sacramental from common bread, knowing the Institution, and the difference, he ought to receive, of what age soever. (George Herbert, *CP*, Ch. XXII, CWS, p. 86)

Selections in Part Four have focussed upon pastoral care through baptism, the ministry of beginnings—how baptism is understood and defined, to whom administered, its elements, modes, necessity, enactment, and effects, whether a bad pastor can nullify a good sacrament, and how it is confirmed.

5 Confession and Communion Counsel

Two subjects are joined in Part Five which have in the modern period become separated: confessional preparation for holy communion on the one hand, and on the other the ministry of holy communion as the pastoral act *par excellence*. The modernization, secularization, and psychologization of pastoral care has resulted in a form of confession that appears to bear little relationship to classical confessional prior to communion. But upon closer inspection, it may be that the form of communication in modern "pastoral psychotherapy" is a partial, unconscious reappropriation of classical communion counsel, largely unaware of its roots.

I ❧ The Hard Remedy of Confession

Our first step is to clarify the meaning of penitential confession generally, its intrinsic connection with Christian pastoral care, its trenchant challenge to the human spirit, its leading to pardon, and the role of restitution in serious confession. Only then will we be ready to move more directly into the subject of the ministry of holy communion as the epitome of pastoral care.

Anglican bishop Francis White concisely stated the four purposes of confession: instructing, admonishing, comforting, and readying for communion.

> The true ends of private Confession are these which follow: First, to inform, instruct, and counsel Christian people in their particular actions. Secondly, if they be delinquents, to reprove them and make them understand the danger of their sin. Thirdly, to comfort those that are afflicted, and truly penitent, and to assure them of remission of sins by the word of Absolution. Fourthly, to prepare people to the worthy receiving of the Holy Communion. (Francis White, A Reply to Jesuit Fisher's Answer to Certain Questions Propounded by His Most Gracious Majesty,

King James, 1624, pp. 187-189; *Angl.*, p. 515)

Despite the abuses that Martin Luther felt were distorting auricular confession in his time, he strongly commended to Christian laity the continued practice of private confession to a trusted pastor. The human need is great for talking through the struggles of conscience. From the pastor's side, the door to confession must always be open:

Private confession should be retained in the church, for in it consciences afflicted and crushed by the terrors of sin lay themselves bare and receive consolation which they could not acquire in public preaching. We want to open up confession as a port and refuge for those whose consciences the devil holds enmeshed in his snares and whom he completely bewitches and torments in such a way that they cannot free or extricate themselves and feel and see nothing else but that they must perish. For there is no other greater misery in this life than the pains and perplexities of a heart that is destitute of guidance and solace. To such, then, an approach to confession should be opened up so that they may seek and find consolation among the ministers of the church. (Luther, "Lectures on Genesis Chapters 31 to 37, 1544," LW 6, pp. 297-298; cf. WA 44, 221)

Yet the human heart is prone to resist asking forgiveness or receiving counsel. Where is the courage to confess secret sins to be found?

This cannot be done without discovering the nakedness and blemishes of the soul, and there is shame in that, and therefore men are unwilling to do it. But, to that I answer, that it is very unreasonable that should be a hindrance. . . . Indeed there were shame in it, yet as long as it may be a means to cure both your trouble and your sin too (certainly godly and faithful counsel may tend much to both) that shame ought to be despised; and it is sure it would, if we loved our souls as well as our bodies. For in bodily diseases, be they never so foul or shameful, we count him a fool who would rather miss the cure than discover it; and then it must here be so much a greater folly, by how much the soul is more precious than the body. (Anonymous, *The Whole Duty of Man*, 1684, Sunday III, sec. 23, p. 90; *Angl.*, p. 514)

Persons today often resist therapy because they do not want to be viewed or known as sick. In earlier times of pastoral care, parishioners resisted confession because they did not want to be viewed by themselves or others as sinners. These resistances are distinguishable. The metaphor of sickness does not take fully into account the distorted will, as does the basic idea of sin. In confession of sin, one deliberately takes responsibility for one's own distortions, and asks for divine forgiveness. The pastor's purpose is not only to hear confession, but to provide counsel for understanding the dynamics of whatever is welling up within it so as to direct one toward reparation, and at the crucial time to pronounce the word of divine pardon.

Confession can occur non-verbally, as in the case of Peter:

It was true of Peter, whose tears over his denial we know, although we do not read of other satisfaction or of confession. Whence Ambrose on Luke (22:62) says of this very denial by Peter and of his weeping: "I do not find what he said; I find that he wept. I read of his tears; I do not read of his satisfaction. Tears wipe away a wrong which it is disgraceful to confess with one's voice and weeping guarantees pardon and shame. Tears declare the fault without dread, they confess without prejudicing shame. Tears do not request pardon but deserve it. I find why Peter was silent, namely lest by asking for pardon so soon he should offend more." (Peter Abelard, *Ethics*, p. 101; cf. Ambrose, Exposition on Luke, x.88, CCL 45, p. 371; cf. MPL 15. 1825B-1826A)*

As nature provides animals with remedies for injury, so does grace provide the wounded human soul the remedy of confession (*exomologesis*) and communion:

Since you know that in *exomologesis* you have a second safeguard against hell which backs up that first line of defense, the Lord's Baptism, why do you abandon the means of salvation which is yours? Why are you slow to take hold of something which will restore you to health? Even dumb, irrational animals recognize, in due season, remedies supplied to them by God. When a stag is transfixed by an arrow, it knows that it must eat dittany in order to expel the arrowhead with its barbs projecting backwards from the wound. If a swallow blinds her young, she has learned to restore their sight with her own peculiar herb, the celandine. (Tertullian, *On Penitence*, ACW 28, p. 36)

Tertullian anticipated the psychoanalytic principle that repression drives psychological dysfunction ever more deeply into unawareness:

Confession lightens an offense as much as concealment aggravates it, for confession is counseled by satisfaction and concealment by impenitence. (Tertullian, *On Penitence*, ACW 28, p. 31)

Baxter concisely defined the therapeutic function of confession:

Unpardoned sin will never let us rest or prosper, though we be at ever so much care and cost to cover it: our sin will surely find us out, though we find not it out. The work of confession is purposely to make known our sin. . . . (Baxter, *RP*, p. 39)

The Benedictine rule urged full confession:

Confess to the abbot every unlawful thought as it arises in the heart, and the hidden sins we have committed. The Scripture advises this, saying: "Reveal your way to God and hope in him" (cf. Ps. 37:5): and again: "Confess to God because he is good: for his mercy endureth for ever" (cf. Ps. 106:1). And in the prophet: "I have made known my sin to thee, and have not covered my iniquities. I have said, I will declare to God my own iniquities against myself: and thou hast forgiven the wickedness of my heart" (Ps. 32:5). (Benedict of Nursia, Rule, LCC, IX, p. 303)

It may seem awkward in terms of our present communion practices for pastors to think of making themselves available on the days before communion for private confession to prepare parishioners for communion. It is not clear precisely how the ancient practice of communion confession might be practically restored. It does seem clear, however, that there was a crucial connection between confession and communion in the earliest centuries of pastoral care. We have lived through a century of evolutionary optimism that has taught us that humanity is good and history is getting better and better. These phrases have washed over us so many times that it is difficult to take the confession of sin seriously. But modern collective consciousness at a hidden level remains deeply and wretchedly concerned with the analysis and thwarted confession of sin, though it is seldom called by that name. Nonetheless, what takes place in much good secular psychotherapy is structurally similar to that close examination of conscience of classical communion counsel lacking its moral and sacramental dimensions.

As early as the *Didache*, a close relationship was assumed between confession and a right spirit in prayer:

In church, make confession of your faults, and do not come to your prayers with a bad conscience. That is the Way of Life. (*Didache*, sec. 4, ECW, p. 229)

Ambrose understood that a special opportunity for soul care is offered when one is in despair, "bottoming out" from a life wretchedly lived. He described that soul who is most ready for confession:

It is the soul who hears that she will not gather the fruit of her seeds, and, in losing the harvest, will find no strength for herself;

who hears that she will press the olive but will not find the oil of gladness or drink the wine of pleasure. It is the soul who finds that the deeds of the flesh are full of violence, full of deception, cheating, and fraud, empty shows of affection and calculated guile, and all those of her own house her enemies. (Ambrose, *Letters*, 45, To Horontianus, FC 26, pp. 238-239)*

Luther recognized, out of his own personal struggle, how difficult it is to comfort the terrorized conscience:

The man who has been humbled by God cannot forget the wound and the pain, for a hurt lingers in the memory far longer than a benefaction. Children illustrate this truth. Although a tender mother tries to quiet a child which she has chastised with the rod by giving it toys and other allurements, yet the pain so lingers in the memory that the child cannot hold back frequent sighs and bitter sobs. (Luther, "Lectures on Genesis Chapters Six to Fourteen, 1536," WA 42, 364; WLS 1, p. 322; cf. LW 2, p. 145)

Early Anglican writers followed the scholastic demarcation between venial sins (offenses against God not serious enough to cause the loss of sanctifying grace), and mortal (deadly) sins which trouble conscience so deeply that they require confession and absolution:

Venial sins that separate not from the grace of God need not so much to trouble a man's conscience; if he hath committed any mortal sin, then we require Confession of it to a Priest, who may give him, upon his true contrition and repentance, the benefit of Absolution. (John Cosin, Works, LACT, V, p. 163f; *Angl.*, p. 516)

II ❧ COMMUNION COUNSEL: PREPARING FOR THE LORD'S TABLE

The point seems to have been mislaid by modern pastoral writers that the context in which pastoral counsel is most pertinent, most valued, and most profoundly called for, is shortly before holy communion. Protestants sometimes imagine that this is a medieval scholastic idea. But the following texts show that this was a theme shared by patristic and Reformation writers. Here is a widely-read seventeenth century Anglican statement of the need to search out a discreet and godly minister to receive spiritual counsel before communion:

I shall add but one thing more concerning the things which are to be done before the Sacrament [i.e., Holy Communion], and that is an advice, that if any person upon a serious view of himself cannot satisfy his own soul of his sincerity, and so doubts whether he may come to the Sacrament, he does well not to rest wholly on his own judgement in the case. . . . In the midst of so many dangers which attend one's mistaking of himself, I would, as I said before, exhort him not to trust to his own judgement, but to make known his case to some discreet and godly Minister, and rather be guided by his judgement, who will probably (if the case be duly and without any disguise discovered to him) be better able to judge of him than he of himself. This is the counsel the Church gives in the Exhortation before the Communion, where it is advised that if any by other means already mentioned "cannot quiet his own conscience, but require further counsel and comfort, then let him go to some discreet and learned Minister of God's Word and open his grief, that he may receive such spiritual counsel, advice, and comfort that his conscience may be relieved, etc." (Anonymous, *The Whole Duty of Man*, 1658, Sunday III, sec. 21-23, pp. 87-90; *Angl.*, p. 513)*

An Anglican promulgation, the Irish Canons of 1634, set forth the desired procedure for inviting and hearing confession prior to communion:

The minister of every parish, and in Cathedral and Collegiate Churches some public minister of the Church, shall the afternoon before the said administration give warning by the tolling of the bell or otherwise, to the intent that if any have any scruple of conscience, or desire the special ministry of reconciliation, he may afford it to those that need it. And to this end the people are often to be exhorted to enter into a special examination of the state of their own souls. Those who find themselves either extremely dull or much troubled in mind, may resort to God's ministers to receive from them advice and counsel for the quickening of their dead hearts and the subduing of those corruptions to which they have become subject, as well as the benefit of Absolution likewise for the quieting of their consciences, by the power of the keys which Christ has committed to His ministers for that purpose. (The Irish Canons of 1634, Canon XIX, *Concilia Magnae Britanniae et Hiberniae*, Vol. IV, p. 501; cf. *Angl.*, pp. 516-517)*

Luther strongly commended private confession as an unparalleled remedy for the distressed conscience:

There is no doubt that confession is necessary and commanded of God. Thus we read in Matthew 3:6, "They were baptised of John in Jordan, confessing their sins." And in 1 John 1:9-10: "If we confess our sins, he is faithful and just to forgive us our sins. If we say that we have not sinned, we make him a liar, and his word is not in us." If the saints may not deny their sin, how much more ought those who are guilty of open and great sins to make confession! But most effectively of all does Matthew 18:15-17 prove the institution of confession, in which passage Christ teaches that a sinning brother should be rebuked, haled before the Church, accused and, if he will not hear, excommunicated. But he hears when, heeding the rebuke, he acknowledges and confesses his sin.

Of private confession, which is now observed, I am heartily in favor, even though it cannot be proved from the Scriptures; it is useful and necessary, nor would I have it abolished—nay, I rejoice that it exists in the Church of Christ, for it is a cure without an equal for distressed consciences. For when we have laid bare our conscience to our brother and privately made known to him the evil that lurked within, we receive from our brother's lips the word of comfort spoken by God Himself; and, if we accept it in faith, we find peace in the mercy of God speaking to us through our brother. (Luther, *The Babylonian Captivity*, WML II, p. 249-252)

Clement of Rome in the late first century had urged that faults be openly confessed:

So let us beg forgiveness for all our misdoings. . . . If men are really living in the fear and love of God, they would sooner endure affliction themselves than see their neighbours suffer, and would prefer reproach to fall on them rather than on the tradition of peaceful harmony which has been so proudly and loyally handed down to us. It is better for a man to admit his faults frankly than to harden his heart. (Clement of Rome, *To the Corinthians*, sec. 51, ECW, p. 50)

Yet, despite its benefits, confession remains for most people extremely difficult. Why?

All people are so minded that they do not want themselves and their dealings to become publicly known. All can bear to have us say that God is benevolent, and who in the world would deny that

God is just and always right when we judge Him? Yet people cannot bear to be rebuked. No one wants to be a homicide, thief, or miser before the world, nor be stained with gross vices. Who, then, is the man who hates the light? All of us! For not one of you would want his story written on his forehead. All of us still gladly hear people praise and honor us. No one thinks: Ah, God be gracious to me; for if the sins of which I am conscious in my heart were evident to the world, I should deserve to be hanged. To be sure, the world honors me; but if it knew who I am, it would spit at me.—But if we realized this, it would serve to humble us before God. . . . The proverbial saying is not meaningless: More souls go to heaven from the gallows than from the cemetery.—For those hanged on the gallows are forced to confess their sins and say: Lord, I am a wicked fellow, Thou art just.—Another man, however, dies on his bed but covers up his sin. . . . Everyone is so constituted that he does not want the sin he commits to be considered sin. He wants it to be called righteousness before the world and before God. However, it is also true that no one should betray and expose himself before the world, but everyone should cover his sins and ask God to forgive them; and you should be reconciled with those whom you have injured. (Luther, "Sermons on the Gospel of John Chapters Three and Four, 1529," WA 47, pp. 122f., WLS 1, pp. 327-328; cf. LW 22, pp. 403-404)

Luther argued that believers other than clergy may *in extremis* hear confession and point to God's pardon:

And so I advise these children, brethren and sisters: If your superiors are unwilling to grant you permission to confess your secret sins to whomever you wish, then take them to whatever brother or sister you will and confess them, receive absolution, and then go and do whatever you wish and ought to do; only believe firmly that you are absolved, and nothing more is needed. (Luther, *An Open Letter to the Christian Nobility*, WML II, p. 124)

The state does not have any just or legitimated power to ask a pastor to tell what was heard in confession:

Within the church's sphere of authority we deal in secret with the conscience and do not take its jurisdiction from the civil estate. Therefore people should leave us undisturbed in our sphere of authority and should not drag into their jurisdiction what we do in secret. (Luther, WA-T 4, #5179; WLS 1, p. 333)

III ❦ Soul Care to Penitents

Repentance may be immediately preceded by an experience of despair over oneself, bemoaning the recent course of one's life, accompanied by a new hunger for gracious empowerment and resolution to begin afresh. These processes of intense behavioral reversal, which have intrigued contemporary psychologists, have been of perennial interest to the writers of the pastoral tradition. Long before William James, classical writers studied carefully the dynamics of penitence, the psychology of *metanoia*—turning one's personal direction around, breaking through inner imprisonment, starting on the road to healing. These and other dynamics must be dealt with in soul care of the penitent.

Tertullian strongly commended the cartharic values of a searching, highly personal, *exomologesis* (confession). The future health of the soul depends upon making open what had been emotively concealed:

Exomologesis, then, is a discipline which leads a man to prostrate and humble himself. . . . Therefore, in humbling a man it exalts him. When it defiles him, he is cleansed. In accusing, it excuses. In condemning, it absolves. In proportion as you have had no mercy on yourself, believe me, in just this same measure God will have mercy upon you. Most men, however, shun this duty as involving the public exposure of themselves, or they put it off from day to day, thinking more about their shame, it seems to me, than about their salvation. They are like men who have contracted some disease in the private parts of the body, who conceal this from the knowledge of the physicians and thus preserve their modesty but lose their lives. (Tertullian, *Exomologesis*, sec. 9-10, ACW 28, pp. 31-32)

With characteristic realism, Luther described the crunch of the heart that yearns for divine mercy:

To repent means to feel the wrath of God in earnest because of one's sin, so that the sinner experiences anguish of heart and is filled with a painful longing for the salvation and the mercy of God. (Luther, "Lectures on Genesis Chapters 26 to 30, 1542," WA 43, p. 534; WLS 3, p. 1210; cf. LW, 5, p. 154)

Repentance begins in guilt and ends in hope of reconciliation:

Repentance is begun when we acknowledge our sins and are sincerely sorry for them; it is completed when trust in the mercy of God comes to this sorrow and hearts are converted to God and long for the forgiveness of sins. (Luther, Erlangen edition, Vol. 24, p. 482; WLS 3, p. 1210)

Shall confession occur only in the presence of the pastor, or before the congregation, or in solitude before God, or with a Christian brother or sister? Luther proposed a way of looking at all these levels of confession:

In the first place, There is a confession which is founded on the Scriptures; namely, when some one commits a sin publicly, or with other men's knowledge, and is accused before the congregation. If he abandons his sin, they intercede for him with God. . . . Secondly, A confession is necessary for us, when we go away in a corner by ourselves, and confess to God Himself and pour out before Him all our faults. . . . Thirdly, There is also a confession when one takes another aside, and tells him what troubles him, so that he may hear from him a word of comfort. . . . I will let no man take private confession away from me, and I would not give it up for all the treasures in the world, since I know what comfort and strength it has given me. No one knows what it can do for him except one who has struggled much with the devil. Yea, the devil would have slain me long ago, if the confession had not sustained me. For there are many doubts which a man cannot resolve by himself, and so he takes a brother aside and tells him his trouble. (Luther, The Eight Wittenberg Sermons, Eighth Sermon, WML II, pp. 422-424)

The Reformed tradition viewed penitence as a highly personalized act, in addition to stressing the value of public penitence and common prayer:

Repentance unto life is an evangelical grace, the doctrine whereof is to be preached by every minister of the gospel, as well as that of faith in Christ. . . . Although repentance be not to be rested in as any satisfaction for sin, or any cause of the pardon thereof, which is the act of God's free grace in Christ; yet is it of such necessity to all sinners that none may expect pardon without it. As there is no sin so small but it deserves damnation, so there is no sin so great that it can bring damnation upon those who truly repent.

Men ought not to content themselves with a general repentance, but it is every man's duty to endeavor to repent of his particular sins particularly. As every man is bound to make private confession of his sins to God, praying for the pardon thereof, upon which, and the forsaking them, he shall find mercy; so he that scandalizeth his brother, or the Church of Christ, ought to be willing, by a private or public confession and sorrow for his sin, to declare his repentance to those that are offended, who are thereupon to be reconciled to him, and in love to receive him. (Westminister Confession, Ch. XV, sec. 1-6, *CC* p. 209-210)

Bonaventure described three steps of penance: contrition, confession and satisfaction:

The integral parts of this sacrament are: contrition in the soul, oral confession, and actual satisfaction. Out of these penance is integrated when the sinner, after having perpetrated mortal sin, asserts the same by deed, accuses himself by word, and detests his sin within his soul, proposing never to repeat the sin. After these things have been done in the required manner together with absolution given by one with orders, the key, and the jurisdiction, man is absolved from sin, reunited with the Church, and reconciled with Christ through the medium of the priestly key. (Bonaventure, *Breviloquium*, p. 201)

They are blessed who mourn their misdeeds, because they are visited richly and often with the spirit of divine consolation. Hence do not be surprised if you find the wise believer ever attentive to his or her own inward sins:

Although the wise man sometimes deserves consolation so as to be mindful no longer of his sorrows, those, that is, for which he receives consolation, yet in order to make room for fresh consolations he is always looking for fresh causes of sorrow in himself. He does not immediately flatter himself that he is just in all respects. But he more searchingly accuses and judges himself the more he has begun to be enlightened; the more strictly, the more he has begun to be justified. To such a man, if I am not mistaken, the Spirit of consolation comes often, for he already anticipates his own coming; that is, he comes to accord consolation but he anticipates by teaching to mourn.

Devout and religious mourning occupies the first place and is outstanding in usefulness in the spirit's teaching. It is the highest wisdom of the saints, the safeguard of the just, the sobriety of the moderate, the first virtue of beginners, the spur of the proficient, the crown of the perfect, the salvation of those who are perishing, the harbor of those in danger: in a word it promises consolations in the present and joys in the future. (Guerric of Igny, *Liturgical Sermons*, Vol. 2, CFS 32, Sermon 39, sec. 6, pp. 121-122)

After enduring an extended period of martyrdom, persecution, and schism, the Church of the late fourth century had the pastoral task of healing its wounds, and bringing back into the fold many of the wandering flock. Here is the report of the First Council of Constantinople on how that ministry of reconciliation was managed and understood:

Those who from heresy turn to orthodoxy, and to the portion of those who are being saved, we receive according to the following method and custom: Arians and Macedonians, and Sabbatians, and Novatians, who call themselves Cathari or Aristeri, and Quarto-decimans or Tetradites, and Apollinarians, we receive, upon their giving a written renunciation (of their errors) and anathematize every heresy which is not in accordance with the Holy, Catholic, and Apostolic Church of God. Thereupon, they are first sealed or anointed with the holy oil upon the forehead, eyes, nostrils, mouth, and ears; and when we seal them, we say, "The Seal of the gift of the Holy Ghost." ... On the first day we make them Christians; on the second, catechumens; on the third, we exorcise them by breathing thrice in their face and ears; and thus we instruct them and oblige them to spend some time in the Church, and to hear the Scriptures; and then we baptize them ...

Our persecutions are but of yesterday. The sound of them still rings in the ears alike of those who suffered them and of those whose love made the sufferers' pain their own. It was but a day or two ago, so to speak, that some released from chains in foreign lands returned to their own churches through manifold afflictions; of others who had died in exile the relics were brought home; others again, even after their return from exile, found the passion of the heretics still at the boiling heat, and, slain by them with stones, as was the blessed Stephen, met with a sadder fate in their own than in a stranger's land. Others, worn away with various cruelties, still bear in their bodies the scars of their wounds and the marks of Christ. Who could tell the tale of fines, of disfranchisements, of individual confiscations, of intrigues, of outrages, of prisons? In truth all kinds of tribulation were wrought out beyond number in us, perhaps because we were paying the penalty of sins, perhaps because the merciful God was trying us by means of the multitude of our sufferings. For these all thanks to God, who by means of such afflictions trained his servants and, according to the multitude of his mercies, brought us again to refreshment. We indeed needed long leisure, time, and toil to restore the church once more, that so, like physicians healing the body after long sickness and expelling its disease by gradual treatment, we might bring her back to her ancient health of true religion. (Council of Constantinople, A.D. 382, The Synodical Letter, The Seven Ecumenical Councils, NPNF 2, XIV, pp. 185, 188)

IV ❧ THE MINISTRY OF PARDON

God's pardon is promised to those who sincerely confess sin. The offering of absolution is a crucial moment of pastoral activity. This occurs in every well-ordered service of Christian worship. The pastor is not the only one who can point to divine forgiveness, but by the inner address of God and the outward appointment of the church through vocation, the pastor is called and appointed to represent the people liturgically before God in petition, and to represent the good news of God's pardoning care by means of absolution to penitents.

Although a general absolution is fitting for common prayer, the ministry of pardon becomes all the more personalized at times in pastoral conversation. Pardon need not always be overtly articulated, and may be effectively communicated non-verbally. As any experienced pastor can attest, it can be an incomparably powerful pastoral act.

In the early period of the church's history, the pardon of penitents was not taken lightly, as may be seen from this early Christian instruction:

> Our Saviour Himself earnestly petitioned His Father for those who had sinned, as it is written in the Gospel: "Father, forgive them; they do not know what they are doing" (Luke 23:34). When the penitent comes in, an examination shall be made as to the sincerity of penitence, and whether one is ready to be received again into the church, having fasted according to the degree of one's offense, whether two, three, five, or seven weeks. If so, set free his conscience. Say whatever is fitting to him by way of admonition, instruction, and exhortation to a sinner for his reformation, that so he may continue privately in his humility, and pray to God to be merciful to him, saying: "If Thou, O Lord, shouldest keep account of sins, who, O Lord, could hold up his head? But in thee is forgiveness, and therefore thou art revered" (Ps. 130:3, 4). (*Constitutions of the Holy Apostles*, Bk. II, sec. III, ANF VII, p. 402, NEB)*

When in common prayer the people confess and receive absolution together, does everyone receive forgiveness equally? Does absolution bear weight because the minister asks it, or the people so earnestly desire it, or because God wishes to make it effective in us? The Anglican *via media* took a centrist route through long-standing ecclesial controversies by combining aspects of all three of these views of absolution: that it assumes or requires the petition of the penitent, that it is a declaratory application of God's promise to the penitent, and that it derives its power from God yet utilizing the human voice and language of the representative minister:

There are three opinions concerning Absolution. The first, entertained by a few, conceive it optative, precarious, or by petition only, as praying for the pardon of the sins of the penitent. The second think it declaratory only, that it, pronouncing the penitent absolved, by applying God's promises to the signs of his contrition. Lastly, some contend that it is authoritative, as deriving power and commission from God, not to declare the party absolved, but for the priest to do it in words denoting the first person. All these three opinions our Church seems in part to favour. The first under these words, "Almighty God have mercy upon you, pardon and deliver you," etc. (Absolution for the Communion). The second under these words, "Hath given charge and command to His Ministers, to declare and pronounce to His people, being penitent, the absolution and remission of their sins." The last by these words, "I absolve thee." Such an authoritative Absolution is proper at this point. For where the priest absolves in his own person, his Absolution is not fitly applicable to any but such as have given him evident tokens of hearty sorrow for their sins, such as Divine chastisement usually elicits. Extendible it is not to whole congregations (as in the former instances) where the confession is too general to be conceived in all real; and a confession at large can at most but pretend to an Absolution at large, effectual only to such a truly and sincerely repent. (Hamon L'Estrange, *Alliance of Divine Offices*, LACT, pp. 448f.; *Angl.*, p. 520)*

John Climacus urged promptness of confession and untardy reparation, so as to move through penitence to a lively awareness of genuine pardon. Otherwise the scrupulosity of confession may become a poisonous syndrome of self-recrimination:

An anchorite who remembers wrongs is an adder hidden in a hole, which carries about within itself deadly poison. The remembrance of Jesus' sufferings cures remembrance of wrongs, which is mightily shamed by His forbearance. Worms grow in a rotten tree, and malice finds a place in falsely meek and silent people. He who has cast it out has found forgiveness, but he who clings to it is deprived of mercies. Some, for the sake of forgiveness, give themselves up to labours and struggles, but a man who is forgetful of wrongs excels them. If you forgive quickly, then you will be generously forgiven. The forgetting of wrongs is a sign of true repentance. But he who dwells on them and thinks that he is repenting is like a man who thinks he is running while he is really asleep. (John Climacus, *The Ladder of Divine Ascent*, Step 9, sec. 13-17, p. 88-89)

There is a time for pardon—not too early, not too late. Too early it may accelerate wrongdoing. Too late it may fester in self-pity. Numerous pitfalls and potential misunderstandings may accompany the untimely ministry of pardon. Augustine found that pardon sounds exactly like license to those who are wrongly predisposed to interpret it as such:

This happened to St. Augustine. He preached the article of the forgiveness of sins, highly extolled God's grace, and taught that a man is justified and saved out of the pure grace and mercy of God, promised and won through Christ, without any merit or worthiness of his own. . . . Then he had to hear the Pelagians accuse him of being a harmful teacher and preacher, who could do no more than make people lax and lazy and keep them from doing good works and attaining perfection. Then St. Augustine had to defend himself by writing against these slanderers. He pointed out that he was not hindering perfection although he was preaching the forgiveness of sin, but that the message of the forgiveness of sins and of grace was helping people to attain true perfection. . . . There are many among us who understand the message of the Gospel in such a way as to imagine that they now need do no good, suffer nothing, and give nothing. (Luther, *Ascension Day Sermon*, 1534, WA 37, pp. 393f.; WLS 2, pp. 741-742)

When the pastor pronounces pardon, it always runs the risk of antinomian misunderstanding. This is why the timing of pardon in pastoral conversation is critical. There is no formal answer to the question of seasonable pardon that can be passed on in a formula. What is required is wisdom and prudent judgment to know when to pardon in such a way as not to encourage license.

Luther wrote of the ecstatic joy he experienced after having heard the counsel of Staupitz on true penitence as the love of God's righteousness:

This word of thine stuck in me like a sharp arrow of the mighty, and from that time forth I began to compare it with the texts of Scripture which teach penitence. Lo, there began a joyous game! The words frollicked with me everywhere! They laughed and gamboled around this saying. Before that there was scarcely a word in all the Scriptures more bitter to me than "penitence," though I was busy making pretences to God and trying to produce a forced, feigned love; but now there is no word which has for me a sweeter or more pleasing sound than "penitence." (Luther, Letter to Staupitz, WML I, p. 40)

Luther, who had personally struggled mightily with the ambiguities of assurance of his own forgiveness, thought it possible to hear God's forgiveness spoken directly through the mouth of the confessor:

If any one is wrestling with his sins and wants to get rid of them and looks for some assurance from the Scriptures, let him go and confess to another in secret; and accept what is said to him there as if God himself had communicated it through the mouth of this person. (Luther, The Eight Wittenberg Sermons, Eighth Sermon, WML II, p. 424)*

V ⚘ ON CHEAP GRACE: FORGIVENESS WITHOUT RESPONSIVENESS

When Pastor Dietrich Bonhoeffer spoke amid the Nazi regime of "cheap grace" that was willing to receive God's pardon without significant behavioral transformation in response to it, he was reappropriating a familiar theme of the classical pastoral writers. It has long been recognized that confession and pardon are profound pastoral acts, but easily distortable toward license, apathy, or quietude. Gregory the Great thought carefully about proper pastoral counsel targeted to those who lament sins but do not abandon them:

When the sow takes a bath in its muddy wallow, it makes itself even filthier. So, too, he who bewails his sins but does not abandon them, subjects himself to punishment for a more grievous sin. For he despises the pardon which he could have obtained by his tears. . . . They who lament their sins but do not abandon them are to be admonished to consider carefully that, for the most part, evil men are moved in vain by compunction to righteousness, just as, for the most part, the good are tempted to sin without harm. (Gregory the Great, *Pastoral Care*, Part III, Ch. 30, ACW 11, pp. 204-205)

Forgiveness is not offered in order to open the door to new sin:

When God, through His grace, grants us forgiveness of sins without our merit, so that we need not purchase it or earn it ourselves, we are at once inclined to draw this reassuring conclusion and to say: Well, so we need no longer do good!—Therefore, in addition to teaching the doctrine of faith in His grace, God must constantly combat this notion and show that this is not at all His meaning. Sins are assuredly not forgiven in order that they should be committed, but in order that they should stop; otherwise it should more justly be called the permission of sins, not the remission of sins. (Luther, *Sermon on Romans, Chapter 8*, WA 22, p. 132; WLS I, p. 520)

The question of whether one could truly repent and still continue in sin was rigorously debated among the Ante-Nicene Fathers during the period of persecution:

Examine your own conscience, and, as far as you are able, heal your wounds. But you must not think, since your offenses are removed by God's grace, that a licence is given you for sinning. . . . To repent is nothing else than to profess and to affirm that one will sin no more. . . . No one can be without fault as long as he is burdened with a covering of flesh, the infirmity of which is subject to the dominion of sin in a threefold manner—in deeds, in words, and thoughts. (Lactantius, *The Divine Institutes*, Bk. VI, Ch. XIII, ANF VII, p. 178)*

Tertullian recognized that the opportunity of penitence once offered might not be offered again:

If the indulgence of the Lord favors you with what you need for the restoration of that which you lost, be grateful for His repeated, nay rather, for His increased beneficence. For to give back is a greater thing than to give. . . . When a disease recurs the medicine must be repeated. You will prove your gratitude to the Lord if you do not refuse what He offers you anew. (Tertullian, *On Penitence*, ACW 28, p. 29)

Yet to repent repeatedly for the same sin was tantamount to not repenting at all. One had better gain new footing in that case:

[The penance] which is required of us and which brings us back to favor with the Lord, must never, once we have known and embraced it, be violated thereafter by a return to sin. In this case, no plea of ignorance excuses you. . . . He repudiates the giver when he abandons the gift; he rejects the benefactor when he dishonors the benefaction. How can God Himself be pleasing to a man who takes no pleasure in His gift? . . .

The man who began to satisfy the Lord by repenting his sin will satisfy the devil by repenting his repentance, and he will be as hateful to the Lord as he is dear to his adversary.

Some say, however, that God is satisfied if He be honored in heart and mind, even though this be not done externally. Thus they sin, yet lose not reverential fear and faith. That is to say, they lose not chastity and commit adultery! They lose not filial piety and poison a parent! . . . A wonderful example of wrong-headedness. (Tertullian, *On Penitence*, ACW 28, p. 22, 23)

The soul guide must strive for balanced judgment between two extremes: inordinate laxity in response to God's grace; and being too hard on those who fall short. There are indeed examples of times when the community of faith has made excessive judgments on one side or the other. There is no better place to go for an example than the desert ascetics, among whom St. Anthony exercised moderating judgment:

It happened one day that one of the brethren in the monastery of Abba Elias was tempted. Cast out of the monastery, he went over the mountain to Abba Anthony. The brother lived near him for a while and then Anthony sent him back to the monastery from which he had been expelled. When the brothers saw him they cast him out yet again, and he went back to Abba Anthony saying, "My Father, they will not receive me." Then the old man sent them a message saying, "A boat was ship-wrecked at sea and lost its cargo; with great difficulty it reached the shore; but you want to throw into the sea that which has found a safe harbour on the shore." When the brothers understood that it was Abba Anthony who had sent them this monk, they received him at once. (Anthony the Great, sec. 21, *Sayings of the Desert Fathers*, pp. 4-5)

VI ❧ Restitution

One of the points at which behavior modification theories and "responsibility therapies" are most akin to the classical pastoral tradition is in their seriousness about attempts to restore damages done, to make reparation for misdeeds. In behavior change strategies that follow the modern pattern of Alcoholics Anonymous, for example, this reparative concern is integral to the process of reconciliation. It is one of the most familiar themes in classical pastoral care.

Gregory the Great chided those who would pretend to quit sin, but fail to make any concrete or meaningful reparation:

Those who desist from sinning but do not lament their sins are to be admonished not to suppose that their sins are forgiven on the mere plea that they have not been repeated, if they have not been cleansed by tears. A writer, for instance, who has given up writing, has not deleted what he has written, just because he has not added anything. So, too, one does not make reparation for insults offered, merely by holding one's peace, for, in truth, it is necessary that he abjure the words of his former pride by expressions of subsequent humility. Nor, again, is a debtor discharged, merely because he incurs no further debts, if he has not paid the debts already incurred. So, too, when we sin against God, we certainly do not make reparation merely by ceasing from evil. (Gregory the Great, *Pastoral Care*, Part III, Ch. 30, ACW 11, p. 206)

Thomas Aquinas used a legal analogy to define restitution:

Restitution is opposed to taking away. Now it is an act of commutative injustice to take away what belongs to another. Therefore to restore it is an act of that justice which directs commutations. . . . Even as the term commutation has passed from such like things to those actions and passions which confer reverence or injury, harm or profit on another person, so too the term restitution is applied, to things which though they be transitory in reality, yet remain in their effect; whether this touch his body, as when the body is hurt by being struck, or his reputation, as when a man remains defamed or dishonored by injurious words. (Thomas Aquinas, *Summa Theologica*, II-II, Q. 62, Art. 1, Vol. II, pp. 1455-1456)

The pastor is called to guide the process of restitution according to the rule of proportionality, i.e., restitution should be reasonably equal in value to whatever has been harmed, taken away, or injured, if possible. Restitution does not require more than compensation for damages. Thomas further developed this legal analogy:

Restitution re-establishes equality where an unjust taking has caused inequality. Now equality is restored by repaying the exact amount taken. Therefore there is no obligation to restore more than the exact amount taken. . . . The judge can exact more by way of damages. . . . Restitution belongs to justice, because it re-establishes equality. But if one were to restore what one did not take, there would not be equality. . . . Loss is so called from a man having less than his due. Therefore a man is bound to make restitution according to the loss he has brought upon another. . . .

Restitution must be made to the person from whom a thing has been taken.... If the person to whom restitution is due is unknown altogether, restitution must be made as far as possible, for instance by giving alms for his spiritual welfare (whether he be dead or living): but not without previously making a careful inquiry about his person. If the person to whom restitution is due be dead, restitution should be made to his heir, who is looked upon as one with him.... Whoever is cause of an unjust taking is bound to restitution. This happens in two ways, directly and indirectly. Directly, when a man induces another to take.... Indirectly, when a man does not prevent another from evil-doing (provided he is able and bound to prevent him), either by omitting the command or counsel which would hinder him from thieving or robbing, or by omitting to do what would have hindered him, or by sheltering him after the deed.... Not only is he bound to restitution who commits the sin, but also he who is in any way cause of the sin, whether by counselling, or by commanding, or in any other way whatever. (Thomas Aquinas, *Summa Theologica*, II-II, Q. 62, Art. 3-7, Vol. II, pp. 1457-1461)

Three levels of positive effects accompany acts of reparation:

Exterior penances are performed principally to produce three effects:

a. To satisfy for past sins.

b. To overcome ourselves, so that sensuality will be obedient to reason and our lower inclinations be subject to higher ones.

c. To seek and find some grace or gift that we wish to obtain, as for instance ... the solution of some doubt that is troubling us. (Ignatius Loyola, *Spiritual Exercises*, pp. 62-63)

Repentance becomes a hollow, feigned act, without restitution.

How very many indeed do we daily see dying, groaning deeply, reproaching themselves greatly for usuries, plunderings, oppressions of the poor, and all kinds of injuries which they have committed, and consulting a priest to free them from these faults. If, as is proper, the first advice given to them is this, that selling all they have, they restore to others what they have taken—in accordance with Augustine: "If something which belongs to another is not returned when it can be returned, repentance is not done but is feigned"—instantly by their reply they declare how hollow is their repentance for these things. (Abelard, *Ethics*, pp. 79, 81)

VII ❧ THE MINISTRY OF EUCHARIST

To shepherd is to feed the flock. The quintessential Christian pastoral act is one of feeding: eating and drinking, receiving spiritual nourishment for our souls. All that we have said thus far about confession is prologue to the ministry of Eucharist.

No pastoral act is more central to the care of souls than the Supper where the resurrected Christ himself is present at the table. If all acts of pastoral care were stopped except Eucharist, the work of pastoral care would remain vital and significant. Graham Greene's novel, *The Heart of the Matter*, has precisely that premise: an unworthy priest is being chased by a tyrannical government in the hills—the last priest who can offer holy communion to the people. Even though he can care for the flock only in one way and that rather poorly, nonetheless his ministry has moving significance to those who receive the living Christ in the bread and wine under conditions of tyranny.

What is this power of the Eucharist to care for souls? Why is the ministry of the Eucharist so central to pastoral care? How does God's own care meet us in the Eucharist? Christ's broken body becomes truly present to the community through the broken bread:

What the Lord did not endure on the cross [the breaking of his legs] he submits to now in his sacrifice for his love of you: he permits himself to be broken in pieces that all may be filled. (John Chrysostom, *Homilies on First Corinthians*, Homily 24, LCF, pp. 174-175)

The death and resurrection of Jesus is not only proclaimed through the sacramental act but is embodied to the believing community:

We proclaim the death, in the flesh, of the only-begotten Son of God, Jesus Christ, and acknowledge his return to life from the dead and his ascension into heaven, and as we do this we perform the bloodless sacrifice in the churches: and thus we approach the consecrated gifts of the sacrament, and are sanctified by partaking of the holy flesh and the precious blood of Christ, the Saviour of us all. (Cyril of Alexandria, *Epistles*, Epistle 17, To Nestorius, sec. 3, LCF, p. 267)

The benefits of Christ's death and resurrection are conveyed to the believer through the supper in a way analogous to food, providing nourishment for the soul:

Our Lord Jesus, in the night wherein he was betrayed, instituted the sacrament of his body and blood, called the Lord's Supper, to be observed in his Church, unto the end of the world; for the perpetual remembrance of the sacrifice of himself in his death, the sealing all benefits thereof unto true believers, their spiritual nourishment and growth in him, their further engagement in, and to all duties which they owe unto him; and to be a bond and pledge of their communion with him, and with each other, as members of his mystical body.... The Lord Jesus hath, in this ordinance, appointed his ministers to declare his word of institution to the people, to pray, and bless the elements of bread and wine, and thereby to set them apart from a common to an holy use; and to take and break the bread, to take the cup, and (they communicating also themselves) to give both to the communicants; but to none who are not then present in the congregation. (Westminister Confession, Ch. XXIX, sec. 1-3, *CC*, p. 225)

"Set-apart" ministry consecrates the set-apart elements of communion for holy use. The pastoral effect of the reception of the supper is to seal in our hearts the promise of the gospel:

Our Lord, therefore, instituted the Supper, first, in order to sign and seal in our consciences the promises contained in his gospel concerning our being made partakers of his body and blood, and to give us certainty and assurance that therein lies our true spiritual nourishment, and that having such an earnest, we may entertain a right reliance on salvation. (John Calvin, *Short Treatise on the Holy Supper of Our Lord Jesus Christ*, Sec. 6, SW, p. 510)

The whole body of Christ is communicated through the Eucharist, according to Catherine of Siena. She used the conflated metaphors of a broken mirror whose fragments reflect perfectly, a single light that illumines many, and candles of varied sizes lit from a single flame, to express the essential unity and paradoxical equality of all faithful recipients of communion:

When you break a mirror the reflection to be seen in it is not broken; similarly, when the host is divided God and man are not divided, but remain in each particle.... If you have a light, and the whole world should come to you in order to take light from it—the light itself does not diminish—and yet each person has it all.... Suppose that there are many who bring their candles, one weighing an ounce, others two or six ounces, or a pound, or even more, and light them in the flame, then in each candle, whether large or small, is the whole light, that is to say, the heat, the colour, and the flame; nevertheless you would not judge that he whose candle weighs an ounce has less of the light than he whose candle weighs a pound. Now the same thing happens to those who receive this Sacrament. Each one carries his own candle, that is the holy desire, with which he receives this Sacrament, which of itself is without light, and lights it by receiving this Sacrament. (Catherine of Siena, *A Treatise of Prayer*, pp. 230-231)*

The authenticity and apostolicity of the Eucharist must be guarded in order to maintain the unity of the body:

Make certain, therefore, that you all observe one common Eucharist; for there is but one Body of our Lord Jesus Christ, and but one cup to union with His Blood, and one single altar of sacrifice—even as also there is but one bishop, with his clergy and my own fellow-servitors the deacons. This will ensure that all your doings are in full accord with the will of God. (Ignatius of Antioch, *To the Philadelphians*, sec. 4, ECW, p. 112)

The sense in which Christ is mystically present in the Supper has been repeatedly discussed by the pastoral tradition, but there is little question that Christ is truly present. This centrist statement shows the difficulty of articulating the mystery of Christ's presence in the sacrament:

The opinion of Zwingli which the Divines of Zurich tenaciously maintained and defended, namely that "Christ is present in the Eucharist only by the contemplation of faith; that there is no place to be given here to a miracle, since we know in what way Christ is present to His Supper, namely, by the quickening Spirit, spiritually and efficaciously; that Sacramental union consists wholly in signification," etc., is by no means to be approved, since it is most clearly contrary to Scripture and the common opinion of all the Fathers. . . .
The holy Fathers . . . most firmly believed that he who worthily receives the mysteries of the Body and Blood of Christ really and actually receives into himself the Body and Blood of Christ, but in a certain spiritual, miraculous, and imperceptible way. . . .
The opinion of those Protestants and others seems to be most safe and most right who think, nay, who most firmly believe, that the Body and Blood of Christ are really and actually and substantially present and taken in the Eucharist, but in a way which the human mind cannot understand and much more beyond the power of man to express, which is known to God alone and is not revealed to us in the Scriptures,—a way indeed not by bodily or oral reception, but not only by the understanding and merely by

faith, but in another way known, as has been said, to God alone, and to be left to His omnipotence. (William Forbes, *Considerationes Modestae*, Bk. I, Ch. I.2ff.; *Angl.*, p. 471)

Luther argues that sacrament of holy communion profoundly personalizes pastoral care:

When I preach the death of Christ, I am delivering a public sermon in the congregation. In it I am not giving to any person in particular; he who grasps the saving truth grasps it. But when I administer the Sacrament, I am applying it to him in particular who is taking it; I am giving him Christ's body and blood that he (personally) may have the forgiveness of sins, purchased through Christ's death and preached in the congregation. This is something more than the ordinary sermon. (Luther, "The Sacrament of the Body and Blood of Christ Against the Fanatics, 1526," WA 19, p. 504; WLS 3, p. 1242; cf. LW 36, p. 348)

VIII ❧ THE INVITATION TO THE LORD'S TABLE

Who are the rightful recipients of holy communion, under what conditions are they invited to the Lord's table, and how are they to receive the curative sacrament?

In one sense *all* are invited, and the supper is for *all*, even though all may not faithfully receive it, as John Chrysostom sought to clarify:

"Thus Christ also was once offered" (Heb. 9:28). By whom? By himself, to be sure. Here the author shows that [Christ] is not only a priest, but also victim and sacrifice. Then he gives the reason for his being offered: "Offered once to bear the sins of many." Why "many" and not "all"? Because all did not believe. He, for his part, did indeed die for all, to save all; for his death was equivalent to the death of all. (Chrysostom, *Homilies on Hebrews*, Homily 17, LCF, p. 173)

The supper has relevance for all humanity, and is intended for all, as Christ's death and resurrection is for all; yet regrettably not all come to believe, partake and participate in Christ's death and resurrection.

Those are best prepared for holy communion who are instructed in its meaning and seek to live out its implications in their lives.

According to custom, urge that each one of the people individually should take his part. One's own conscience is best for choosing carefully or turning aside. It provides a firm foundation for the upright life, provided it has suitable instruction. But the imitation of those who have already been tested and who have led upright lives is most excellent for the understanding and practice of these commandments. "It follows that anyone who eats the bread or drinks the cup of the Lord unworthily will be guilty of desecrating the body and blood of the Lord. A man must test himself before eating his share of the bread and drinking from the cup" (1 Cor. 11:27-28). (Clement of Alexandria, *The Stromata, or Miscellanies*, Bk. I, Ch. I, ANF II, p. 300, NEB)*

Serious moral self-examination accompanies the preparation and approach to holy communion. The ill-prepared may be harmed by unworthy reception, according to Catherine of Siena:

It gives life and adorns the soul with every grace, in proportion to the disposition and affection of him who receives It; similarly It gives death to him who receives It unworthily. (Catherine of Siena, *A Treatise of Discretion*, p. 66)

It need not be assumed that we must present ourselves as morally perfected in order to merit the gift of communion with the Lord. Much more, according to Luther, should we be aware of our inability to merit that communion which the cross merits:

He who has not felt the battle within him, is not distressed by his sins nor has a daily quarrel with them, and wishes no protector, defender and shield to stand before him, is not yet ready for this food. This food demands a hungering and longing man, for it delights to enter a hungering soul, one that is in constant battle with its sins and eager to be rid of them. . . . This is what Christ did, when He prepared to institute the blessed sacrament. He brought anguish upon His disciples and trembling to their hearts when He said that He would go away from them, and again they were tormented when He said: One of you shall betray me. Think you not that that cut them to the heart? Truly, they received the word with all fear, and sat there as though they were all traitors to God. And after He had made them all tremble with fear and sorrow, then only did He institute the blessed sacrament as a comfort, and consoled them again. For this bread is a comfort for the sorrowing, a healing for the sick, a life for the dying, a food for all the hungry, and a rich treasure for all the poor and needy. (Luther, The Eight Wittenberg Sermons, Sixth Sermon, WML II, p. 418-419)

The pastor may be asked by those who feel unworthy to receive the sacrament whether they do best to stay away until they feel worthy. Isaac Barrow answered:

What unworthiness should hinder us from remembering Our Lord's excessive charity towards us, and thanking Him for it, from praying for His grace, from resolving to amend our lives? Must we, because we are unworthy, continue so still, by shunning the means of correcting and curing us? Must we increase our unworthiness, by transgressing our duty? (Isaac Barrow, *Brief Exposition*, Works, V, p. 608; *Angl.*, p. 505)

Menno Simons argued of excommunication not that it was the church's act of barring a member from the table, but rather the member's own self-determined absence from communication, or choice to remain separated:

No one is excommunicated or expelled by us from the communion of the brethren but those who have already separated and expelled themselves from Christ's communion either by false doctrine or by improper conduct. For we do not want to expel any, but rather to receive; not to amputate, but rather to heal; not to discard, but rather to win back; not to grieve, but rather to comfort; not to condemn, but rather to save. (Menno Simons, *A Kind Admonition on Church Discipline*, 1541, *CWMS*, p. 413)

In order to insure the proper administration of communion duly grounded in apostolic teaching, Ignatius stressed that the supper be celebrated only by one duly called and elected who stands faithfully in the apostolic tradition:

The sole Eucharist you should consider valid is one that is celebrated by the bishop himself, or by some person authorized by him. Where the bishop is to be seen, there let all his people be; just as wherever Jesus Christ is present, we have the world-wide Church. Nor is it permissible to conduct baptisms or love-feasts without the bishop. (Ignatius of Antioch, *Letter to Polycarp*, sec. 8, ECW, p. 121)

The connection with the bishop signified to Ignatius the connection with the authorized apostolic teaching of Christ's ministry. In the absence of a minister, can a lay person, even a child, serve the Eucharist in an emergency, under the guidance of an absent presbyter? Eusebius reports a letter from Dionysius of Alexandria concerning an unusual event of a child's providing emergency communion:

"I will give you this one example which occurred among us. There was with us a certain Serapion, an aged believer who had lived for a long time blamelessly, but had fallen during the times of persecution. He asked frequently to be restored, but no one gave heed to him, because he had sacrificed idolatrously. But he became sick, and for three successive days continued speechless and senseless. Having recovered somewhat on the fourth day he sent for his daughter's son, and said, 'How long do you detain me, my child? I beg you, make haste, and absolve me speedily. Call one of the presbyters to me.' And when he had said this, he became again speechless. And the boy ran to the presbyter. But it was night and the presbyter was sick, unable to come. But as I had commanded that persons at the point of death, if they requested it, and especially if they had asked for it previously, should receive remission, that they might depart with a good hope, he gave the boy a small portion of the Eucharist, telling him to soak it and let the drops fall into the old man's mouth. The boy returned with it, and as he drew near, before he entered, Serapion again arousing, said, 'You have come, my child, and the presbyter could not come; but do quickly what he directed and let me depart.' Then the boy soaked it and dropped it into his mouth. And when he had swallowed a little, immediately he gave up the ghost. Is it not evident that he was preserved?" (Eusebius, *Church History*, Bk. VI, Ch. XLIV, sec. 2-6, NPNF 2, I, p. 290)

IX ❧ THE BREAKING OF BREAD

If the act which epitomizes soul care is Supper with the resurrected Lord, it behooves the pastor to look carefully at the language of the eucharistic event to see how the ancient pastoral writers interpreted its meaning. The eucharistic prayers and rubrics yield the deepest insight. One of the earliest of such prayers is found in the *Didache*:

At the Eucharist, offer the eucharistic prayer in this way. Begin with the chalice: "We give thanks to thee, our Father, for the holy Vine of thy servant David, which thou hast made known to us through thy servant Jesus." *"Glory be to thee, world without end."* Then over the particles of bread: "We give thanks to thee, our Father, for the life and knowledge thou hast made known to us through thy servant Jesus." *"Glory be to thee, world without end."* "As this broken bread, once dispersed over the hills, was brought together and became one loaf, so may thy Church be brought together from the ends of the earth into thy kingdom." "*Thine is the glory and the power, through Jesus Christ, for ever and ever.*" No one is to eat or drink of your Eucharist but those who have been baptized in the Name of the Lord; for the Lord's own saying applies here, "Give not that which is holy unto dogs" (Matt. 7:6).

When all have partaken sufficiently give thanks in these words: "Thanks be to thee, holy Father, for thy sacred Name which thou hast caused to dwell in our hearts, and for the knowledge and faith and everlasting life which thou hast revealed to us through thy servant Jesus." "*Glory be to thee for ever and ever.*" "Thou, O Almighty Lord, hast created all things for thine own Name's sake; to all men thou hast given meat and drink to enjoy, that they may give thanks to thee, but to us thou hast graciously given spiritual meat and drink, together with life eternal, through thy Servant. Especially, and above all, do we give thanks to thee for the mightiness of thy power." "*Glory be to thee for ever and ever.*" "Be mindful of thy church, O Lord; deliver it from all evil, perfect it in thy love, sanctify it, and gather it from the four winds into the kingdom which thou hast prepared for it." "*Thine is the power and the glory for ever and ever.*" "Let His Grace draw near, and let this present world pass away." "*Hosanna to the God of David.*" "Whosoever is holy, let him approach. Whoso is not, let him repent." "*O Lord, come quickly. Amen.*" (Charismatists, however, should be free to give thanks as they please.) (*Didache*, sec. 9-10, ECW, pp. 231)

The Eucharist is a free act. It cannot be coerced:

We are to force no one to believe, or to receive the Sacrament, nor to fix any law, time, or place for it, but so to preach that they will be urged of their own accord, without our law, and will, as it were, compel us pastors to administer the Sacrament. (Luther, *Small Catechism*, Introduction, WA 30, I 264f; WLS 1, p. 118)*

On the frequency of holy communion, Anglican Isaac Barrow wrote:

The primitive Christians did very frequently use it, partaking in it, as it seems, every time they met for God's service. It is said of them by St. Luke that "they continued steadfastly in the Apostles' doctrine and communion, and in breaking of bread, and in prayers," (Acts 2:42) and "When you meet together, it is not (as according to the intent and duty of meeting it should be) to eat the Lord's Supper" (1 Cor. 11:20) said St. Paul. And Justin Martyr in his Second Apology, describing the religious service of God in their assemblies, mentions it as a constant part of it. And Epiphanius reports it a custom in the Church, derived from Apostolical institution, to celebrate the Eucharist three times each week, that is, so often as they met to pray and praise God." (Isaac Barrow, *A Brief Exposition of the Lord's Prayer and Decalogue*, Works, V, pp. 606-608; *Angl.*, p. 504)*

Luther wrote a Maundy Thursday discourse in 1521 which included this prayer for preparation for holy communion:

Lord, it is true that I am not worthy for you to come under my roof, but I need and desire your help and grace to make me godly. I now come to you, trusting only in the wonderful words I just heard, with which you invite me to your table and promise me, the unworthy one, forgiveness of all my sins through your body and blood if I eat and drink them in this sacrament. Amen. Dear Lord, I do not doubt the truth of your words. Trusting them, I eat and I drink with you. Do unto me according to your words. Amen. (Luther, *Sermon on the Worthy Reception of the Sacrament*, 1521, LW 42, p. 174)

Can beer or some other substitute be canonically offered instead of wine?

If any bishop or presbyter, otherwise than our Lord has ordained concerning the sacrifice, offer other things at the altar of God, as honey, milk, or strong beer instead of wine. . . . let him be deprived. (*Constitutions of the Holy Apostles*, Ch. XLVII, sec. 3, ANF VII, p. 500)

How are the bread and wine consecrated?

Do you wish to know how it is consecrated by heavenly words? Hear what those words are—the priest says: "Make for us this oblation ratified, reasonable, acceptable, because it is the figure of the body and blood of our Lord Jesus Christ." (Ambrose, *On the Mysteries*, Ch. IV, sec. 21, NPNF 2 X, 319; LCF, p. 184)

The crucial moment of the service, when the bread and wine are consecrated, was carefully set forth by John Chrysostom:

Christ is now also present. He who adorned that table [of the Last Supper] is he who now also adorns this. It is not man who makes the gift of the oblation to become the body and blood of Christ, but Christ himself, who was crucified. The priest stands, fulfilling the original pattern, and speaks those words; but the power and grace come from God. "This is my body" (Matt. 26:26; Mk. 14:22; Lk. 22:19), he says. This statement transforms the oblations. (Chrysostom, *De prod. Jud. 1.6*, IV.a; LCF p. 173)

The *epliklesis*, or invocation, is the prayer following and completing the consecration of the bread and wine, which calls upon God to pour out the Holy Spirit upon the bread and wine that their recipients may be filled with grace. Especially important in Eastern liturgies, its dramatic significance was set forth by John Chrysostom:

When the priest stands before the Table, holding up his hands to heaven, and invokes the Holy Spirit to come and touch the elements, there is a great silence, a great stillness. When the Spirit gives his grace, when he descends, when he touches the elements, when you see the sacrifice of the lamb completed; do you then indulge in uproar, riot, quarrelling or abuse? (John Chrysostom, *De coemet.*, IV.a; LCF, p. 173)

Hippolytus offered this account of the words spoken to accompany the fraction of the bread:

And when he breaks the Bread in distributing to each a fragment (*klasma*) he shall say: The Bread of Heaven in Christ Jesus. And he who receives shall answer: Amen. (Hippolytus, *The Apostolic Tradition*, XXIII.5-6, p. 41)

Thomas Aquinas set forth three reasons why the laity need the ministry of the eucharist, and why it is viewed as a pastoral remedy:

Sacraments are necessary unto man's salvation for three reasons. The first is taken from the condition of human nature which is such that it has to be led by things corporeal and sensible to things spiritual and intelligible. Now it belongs to Divine providence to provide for each one according as its condition requires. Divine wisdom, therefore, fittingly provides man with means of salvation, in the shape of corporeal and sensible signs that are called sacraments.

The second reason is taken from the state of man who in sinning subjected himself by his affections to corporeal things. Now the healing remedy should be given to a man so as to reach the part affected by disease. Consequently it was fitting that God should provide man with a spiritual medicine by means of certain corporeal signs; for if man were offered spiritual things without a veil, his mind being taken up with the material world would be unable to apply itself to them.

The third reason it taken from the fact that man is prone to direct his activity chiefly towards material things ... It follows, therefore, that through the institution of the sacraments man, consistently with his nature, is instructed through sensible things. (Thomas Aquinas, *Summa Theologica*, III, Q. 61, Art. 1, Vol. II, p. 2352)

Widely debated since the sixteenth century is the question of whether or to what extent a sacrifice is being offered in the mass. Here is a fourth century statement by Eusebius that combines the themes of mystery, memorial, and divine sacrifice:

We have received a memorial of this offering which we celebrate on a table by means of symbols of His Body and saving Blood. . . . Here it is plainly the mystic Chrism and the holy Sacrifices of Christ's Table that are meant, by which we are taught to offer to Almighty God through our great High Priest all through our life the celebration of our sacrifices, bloodless, reasonable, and well-pleasing to Him. . . . These were Isaiah's "wonders," the promise of the anointing with ointment of a good smell, and with myrrh made not to Israel but to all nations. . . . So, then, we sacrifice and offer incense: On the one hand when we celebrate the Memorial of His great Sacrifice according to the Mysteries He delivered to us, and bring to God the Eucharist for our salvation with holy hymns and prayers; while on the other we consecrate ourselves to Him alone and to the Word His High Priest, devoted to Him in body and soul. (Eusebius, *The Proof of the Gospel*, Bk. I, Ch. 10, sec. 4-5, pp. 60-62)

The Westminster Confession concisely stated the classical Reformed view of sacrament:

Sacraments are holy signs and seals of the covenant of grace, immediately instituted by God, to represent Christ and his benefits, and to confirm our interest in him: as also to put a visible difference between those that belong to the Church and the rest of the world; and solemnly to engage them to the service of God in Christ, according to his Word.

There is in every sacrament a spiritual relation or sacramental union, between the sign and the thing signified; whence it comes to pass that the names and the effects of the one are attributed to the other.

The grace which is exhibited in or by the sacraments, rightly used, is not conferred by any power in them; neither does the efficacy of a sacrament depend upon the piety or intention of the one who administers it, but upon the work of the Spirit, and the word of institution, which contains, together with a precept authorizing its use, a promise of benefit to worthy receivers.

There be only two sacraments ordained by Christ our Lord in the gospel, that is to say, Baptism and the Supper of the Lord; neither of which may be dispensed by any but by a minister of the Word lawfully ordained. (Westminister Confession, Ch. XXVII, sec. i-v, *CC*, pp. 223-224)*

The selections of Part Five have focussed upon confession and communion counsel. God's pardon is promised to those who sincerely confess sin. The offering of absolution is a crucial moment of pastoral activity. Holy communion is the fitting context for acts of contrition, confession, satisfaction, pardon, and restitution. The quintessential Christian pastoral act is one of feeding: eating and drinking, receiving spiritual nourishment for our souls in the Eucharist.

6 Pastor as Educator of the Soul

"APTNESS TO TEACH" (*didaktikos*, 2 Tim. 2:24) is requisite to the call to soul care. The pastor is not only preacher, liturgist, and empathic listener, but also to a significant degree teacher of the soul.

Soul care is education. The soul-friend is life-crisis mentor. The caregiving agent is also an agent of teaching of the truth. If the care of souls is a pedagogy of the inner life, then the pastor must develop the art of teaching.

I ❦ MINISTRY TO INQUIRERS

Each new generation will inquire with its own particular questions into the truth of Christianity. There is no standard format or predictable mode of inquiry. In each new culture and historical situation, the apostolic teaching seeks to be presented in ways that that emergent consciousness can understand and assimilate. Effective mission depends upon high competencies in teaching. Although laity in a given parish have many gifts for teaching that need to be channeled and utilized, the central burden of ordering, planning, and authenticating the teaching ministry in the parish falls primarily upon the pastor.

Yet the "pastor-knows-everything" syndrome may fail to understand the crucial function of doubt in faith. Consciousness of doubt is a preconditioning phase in which the truth can be constructively taught. The classical pastoral writers have welcomed unfettered, honest inquiry into the truth of Christianity. The following sayings, attributed to Peter in the pre-Nicene Clementine literature, demonstrate an early teaching style:

[They asked Peter]: "What will others think if they see you, like Socrates, pretending ignorance? . . . For if someone sees even you hesitating and doubting, then truly he will think that no one has knowledge of the truth." To this Peter answered: "Let us not concern ourselves about this. If indeed it is fitting that he enter the

166

gate of life, God will afford a fitting opportunity. Then the beginning shall be from God and not from man"....

[They asked Peter]: "Is it permitted to one to ask a question, if he wishes it? Or is silence enforced, after the manner of the Pythagoreans?" Then said Peter: "We do not compel those who come to us either to keep silence continually, or to ask questions; but we leave them free to do as they will, knowing that those who are anxious about their salvation, if they feel wounded in any part of the soul, that pain does not permit them to remain silent." (Clementina, *Recognitions of Clement*, Bk. X, Ch. IV, ANF VIII, p. 193)*

Although the Socratic method of "pretended ignorance" was not the standard method of early Christian teaching, it was available as a part of its teaching armamentarium. This imaginative recollection (presumably by Clement of Peter, but written much later) portrays the apostle as astutely fielding questions of inquirers, not anxious about the pretence of knowing everything, and willing to allow God time to plant and nurture the seeds of understanding in God's own time. There is an unusual degree of nondefensive freedom (to ask or not ask, to speak or keep silent) in this recollection.

Should special guidance be given to the best, so as to neglect the less advanced pupils?

There is no credit in spending all your affection on the cream of your pupils. Try rather to bring the more troublesome ones to order, by using gentleness. Nobody can heal every wound with the same unguent; where there are acute spasms of pain, we have to apply soothing poultices. So in all circumstances "be wary as serpents," though always "innocent as doves" (Matt. 10:16). (Ignatius of Antioch, *Letter to Polycarp*, sec. 2, ECW, p. 127, NEB)*

Clement of Alexandria, on the other hand, urged more pastoral attention to those who excel:

The Shepherd, then, cares for each of his sheep; and his closest inspection is given to those who are excellent in their natures and are capable of being most useful. (Clement of Alexandria, *The Stromata, or Miscellanies*, Bk. VI, Ch. XVII, ANF II, p. 577)

Some will come to Christian instruction with dubious motives or ambiguous intentions. Cyril showed high tolerance for various motivations to attend classes of inquiry into the Christian faith:

It is quite what might happen, that a man should be wanting to advance his suit with a Christian woman, and to that end has come here. And there is the like possibility the other way round. Or often it may be a slave that wanted to please his master, or a person that comes for the sake of his friend. I accept this as bait for the hook, and I welcome you as one who shall be saved, by a good hope, in spite of having come with an unsound intention. It may well be that you did not know where you were coming or what sort of a net it is that is taking you. And now you are inside the ecclesiastical fishnets. Let yourself be taken, do not make off, for Jesus is angling for you, not to make you die, but by his having died, to make you live. (Cyril of Jerusalem, *The Catechetical Letters*, Procatechesis, sec. 5, LCC, IV, p. 68)

Jewish pedagogy was greatly admired by some Christian pastoral writers:

During the Ten or Twelve years of their Education, their Youth are so much practised to the Scriptures, to weigh every word in them, and get them all by heart, that it is an Admiration to see how ready both Men and Women among them are at it; their Rabbis have it to that perfection that they have the concordance of their whole Bible in their memories. (Burnet, *Of the Pastoral Care*, Ch. VIII, p. 157)

The catechism seeks to bring the whole range of Christian teaching into a concise statement for elementary instruction in the faith:

The Catechism is an epitome and brief transcript of the entire Holy Scripture. (Luther, WA 30 I, p. 128; WLS 1, p. 124)

The usual practice was for the pastor to prove catechetical instruction of young people and inquirers at least once per year:

Great care must be taken in the Instruction of the Youth: The bare saying the Catechism by Rote is a small Matter; it is necessary to make them understand the weight of every Word in it: And for this end, every Priest, that minds his Duty, will find that no Part of it is so useful to his People, as once every year to go through the whole Church Catechism, Word by Word, and make his People understand the Importance of every Tittle in it. . . . By this means his people will come to have all this by heart; they will know what to say upon it at home to their children; and they will understand all his sermons the better when they have once had a clear notion of all those terms that run through them. (Burnet, *Of the Pastoral Care*, Ch. VIII, p.161; cf. *CS*, pp. 88-89)

Baxter argued that Christian education best proceeds through families under pastoral guidance:

It will be very necessary that we give one of the catechisms to every family in the parish, whether rich or poor, that so they may be without excuse: for if you leave it to themselves to buy them, perhaps the half of them will not get them. . . . As to the delivery of them, the best way is for the minister first to give notice in the congregation, that they shall be brought to their houses, and then to go himself from house to house and deliver them, and take the opportunity of persuading them to the work; and, as he goes round, to take a list of all the persons who have come of years of discretion in the several families, that he may know whom he has to take care of and instruct, and whom he has to expect when it cometh to their turn. . . . take the people in order, family by family, beginning a month or six weeks after the delivery of the catechisms, that they may have time to learn them. (Baxter, *RP*, pp. 235-236)

Cyril of Jerusalem, in speaking to inquirers into Christian truth (catechumens soon to be baptized), distinguished speaking and whispering in order to illustrate the difference between noisy den of elementary education toward the mystery of God's presence, and the solemn conclusion of that process—veritable baptismal entry into the living immediacy of that presence:

You were called catechumen, which means one into whom something is dinned from without. You heard of some hope, but you did not know what. You heard mysteries without understanding anything. You heard scriptures without plumbing their depth. It is not dinned in, any more, but whispered. (Cyril of Jerusalem, *The Catechetical Lectures*, Procatechesis, sec. 6, LCC, IV, p. 68)

Plain speaking is required more than fine theological distinctions in teaching young people of the faith:

All our teaching must be as plain and simple as possible. This best suits a teacher's ends. He that would be understood must speak to the capacity of his hearers. Truth loves the light, and is most beautiful when most naked. It is the sign of an envious enemy to hide the truth, but a work of a hypocrite to do this under pretence of revealing it. . . . There is no better way to make a good cause prevail than to make it as plain, and generally and thoroughly known as we can. . . . It is, at best, a sign that one has not well digested the matter himself, if one is not able to deliver it plainly to others. (Baxter, *RP*, pp. 115-116)*

Even deep points of truth can be patiently elicited from anyone, even a "silly tradesman" (as in Plato's *Meno*), if one learns to put the right question, as did Socrates:

Many say the catechism by rote, as parrots, without ever piercing into the sense of it. . . . The catechiser . . . will draw out of ignorant and silly souls even the dark, and deep points of religion. Socrates did thus in philosophy, who held that the seeds of all truths lay in every body; and accordingly, by questions well ordered, he found philosophy in silly tradesmen. (George Herbert, *CP*, Chap. XXI, CWS, pp. 83–84)

The Socratic method, drawing the truth out by questioning the learner, takes this form in Baxter:

When you perceive that they do not understand the meaning of your question, you must draw out their answer by an equivalent, or expository question; . . . I have often asked some very ignorant people, "How do you think that your sins, which are so many and so great, can be pardoned?" And they tell me, "By repenting, and amending their lives.". . . If you find them at a loss, and unable to answer your questions, do not drive them too hard, or too long, with question after question, lest they conceive you intend only to puzzle them, and disgrace them; but when you perceive that they cannot answer, step in yourself, and take the burden off them, and answer the question yourselves; and do it thoroughly and plainly, and give a full explanation of the whole truth to them. . . . (Baxter, *RP*, pp. 242-243)

II ❧ The Pastor as Pedagogue

The nature of pedagogy is the central concern of Clement of Alexandria's major treatise, *Christ the Educator (paidagogos)*. Its theme: how Christ teaches and guides the soul. The soul-guide mediates Christ's own guidance on the pathway toward behavioral excellence (virtue).

In a thoughtful description of what psychologists today call "neonate responsiveness" (the capacity of children to be immediately in touch with their own feelings), Clement clarified the sense in which the best learners are like children, and why "becoming a child" (an "uncontaminated lover of the horn of the unicorn") is a desirable quality of consciousness:

We define education as a sound training from childhood in the path of virtue. Be that as it may, the Lord once very clearly revealed what He means by the name "little child": A dispute having arisen among the Apostles as to which of them was greater, Jesus made a little child stand among them, saying: "Let a man humble himself till he is like this child, and he will be the greatest in the kingdom of Heaven" (Matt. 18:4). Therefore, He does not mean by "little child" one who has not yet reached the use of reason because of his immaturity, as some have thought. When He says: "Unless you turn round and become like children, you will never enter the kingdom of Heaven" (Matt. 18:3), we must not foolishly mistake His meaning. We are not little ones in the sense that we roll on the floor or crawl.... Children are those who look upon God alone as their father, who are simple, little ones, uncontaminated, who are lovers of the horn of the unicorn.... The name "little one" is not used in the sense of lacking intelligence. Childishness means that, but "little one" really means "one newly become gentle." (Clement of Alexandria, *Christ the Educator*, Bk. I, FC 23, pp. 17-19, NEB)*

Athanasius was among the first to recognize that God's way of teaching is by empathic participation in our limited situation—through incarnation:

He deals with them as a good teacher with his pupils, coming down to their level and using simple means. St. Paul says as much: "Because in the wisdom of God the world in its wisdom knew not God, God thought fit through the simplicity of the News proclaimed to save those who believe" (1 Cor. 1:21).... The Saviour of us all, the Word of God, in His great love took to Himself a body and moved as Man among men, meeting their senses, so to speak, half way. He became Himself an object for the senses. (Athanasius, *On the Incarnation*, sec. 15, p. 25)

The intriguing analogy between incarnation and empathic teaching was firmly grasped by the pastoral writers:

When Christ wished to attract and instruct men, He had to become a man. If we are to attract and instruct children, we must become children with them. (Luther, WA 19, p. 78; WLS 1, p. 447)

Ignatius did not despise the premise that the teacher is a fellow student who needs constantly to be taught by his students:

I am not giving you commands as if I were someone. For even though I am in bonds for the Name, I am not yet perfect in Jesus Christ; for now I am beginning to be a disciple, and I speak to you as my fellow students. For I needed to be anointed by you with faith, instruction, endurance, patience. But since love does not let me be silent about you, I have undertaken to exhort you [cf. Philem. 9], so that together you may run your race in accordance with God's purpose. For Jesus Christ, our inseparable life, is the expressed purpose of the Father, just as the bishops who have been appointed throughout the world exist by the purpose of Jesus Christ. (Ignatius of Antioch, *Letter to the Ephesians*, sec. 3:1-2, AF, p. 78)

Jesus taught the disciples through gradual stages of development, according to Origen. Education is a developmental process. It does not happen all at once:

[Christ] wished first to give catechetical instruction as it were to those of the Apostles who were to hear the name of Christ, then to permit this, so to speak, to be digested in the minds of the hearers, that, after there had been a period of silence in the proclamation of something of this kind about Him, at a more seasonable time there might be built up upon the former rudiments "Christ Jesus crucified and raised from the dead," which at the beginning not even the Apostles knew.... For our Saviour wished, when He enjoined the disciples to tell no man that He was the Christ, to reserve the more perfect teaching about Him to a more fitting time, when to those who had seen Him crucified, the disciples who had seen Him crucified and risen could testify the things relating to His resurrection. For if the Apostles, who were always with Him and had seen all the wonderful things which He did, and who bore testimony to His words that they were words of eternal life, were offended on the night on which He was betrayed,—what do you suppose would have been the feelings of those who had formerly learned that He was the Christ? To spare them, I think, He gave this command. (Origen, *Commentary on Matthew*, sec. 17, ANF X, pp. 460-461)

At one point in *Paedogogos*, Clement of Alexandria described the teaching method of his own teachers. The account is shaped by two metaphors: bees gathering pollen from widely diverse sources, and good seeds being carefully planted.

Now this work of mine in writing is not artfully constructed for display; but my memoranda are stored up against old age, as a remedy against forgetfulness, truly an image and outline of those vigorous and animated discourses which I was privileged to hear, and of blessed and truly remarkable men.

Of these the one, in Greece, an Ionic; the other in Magna Graecia: the first of these from Coele-Syria, the second from Egypt, and others in the East. The one was born in the land of Assyria, and the other a Hebrew in Palestine.

When I came upon the last (he was the first in power), having tracked him out concealed in Egypt, I found rest. He, the true, the Sicilian bee, gathering the spoil of the flowers of the prophetic and apostolic meadow, engendered in the souls of his hearers a deathless element of knowledge.

Well, they preserving the tradition of the blessed doctrine derived directly from the holy apostles, Peter, James, John, and Paul, the sons receiving it from the father (but few were like the fathers), came by God's will to us also to deposit those ancestral and apostolic seeds. (Clement of Alexandria, *The Stromata, or Miscellanies*, Bk. I, Ch. I, ANF II, p. 301)

No names are mentioned, although Tatian, Theodotus and Pantaenus were probably among them. The principal feature of the teaching was the transmission of tradition through effective seed-planting (from which comes the word "seminary") of genuine, undistorted apostolic teaching.

III ❧ COHERENCE IN EDUCATING THE SOUL

The better pastor is the one more ready to respond to emergent situations that require particular insights into the larger body of Christian teaching. Hence it is commended that the pastor study the whole range of Christian teaching as an internally consistent witness. Good teaching proceeds in a definite order, through sequential development, with internal congruity. Early pastoral writers sought a meaningful order for instruction in the faith that would correspond with scriptural requirements and manifest the intuitive coherence found in the apostolic witness.

Stone must follow stone in the appointed order, and corners be turned in each successive course. Unevennesses must be levelled off, so that the building may rise without fault. So we are proffering to you, as it were, building-stones of knowledge. You have to be told about the living God, you have to be told about the judgement, you have to be told about Christ, you have to be told about the resurrection. There are many things to be said, and in their proper order. As they are being said, they appear casual, but afterwards they present themselves as all connected together. (Cyril of Jerusalem, *The Catechetical Lectures*, Procatechesis, sec. 11, LCC, IV, p. 72)

Cyril understood that even though the pastor might seem to be contextually applying scriptural teaching to various situations, such insight can only emerge out of a deep inward grasp of a congruent whole. The practice of ministry needs both a sense of the integrity of the whole and the specificity of its application. Martin Luther thought that the surest and simplest way to organize the whole range of Christian teaching was to adhere closely to the primary texts of the Lord's Prayer, the Apostles' Creed and the Ten Commandments. All of these texts were memorized by every believer in Luther's time:

The ordinary Christian, who cannot read the Scriptures, is required to learn and know the Ten Commandments, the Creed, and the Lord's Prayer; and this has not come to pass without God's special ordering. For these three contain fully and completely everything that is in the Scriptures, everything that ever should be preached, and everything that a Christian needs to know, all put so briefly and so plainly that no one can make complaint or excuse, saying that what he needs for his salvation is too long or too hard to remember.

Three things a man needs to know in order to be saved. First, he must know what he ought to do and what he ought not to do. Second, when he finds that by his own strength he can neither do the things he ought, nor leave undone the things he ought not to do, he must know where to seek and find and get the strength he needs. Third, he must know how to seek and find and get this strength.

When a man is ill, he needs to know first what his illness is,—what he can do and what he cannot do. Then he needs to know where to find the remedy that will restore his health and help him to do and leave undone the things he ought. Third, he must ask for this remedy, and seek it, and get it or have it brought to him. In like manner, the Commandments teach a man to know his illness, so that he feels and sees what he can do and what he cannot do, what he can and what he cannot leave undone, and thus knows himself to be a sinner and a wicked man. After that the Creed shows him and teaches him where he may find the remedy,—the grace which helps him to become a good man and to keep the Commandments; it shows him God, and the mercy which He has revealed and offered in Christ. In the third place, the Lord's Prayer teaches him how to ask for this grace, get it, and take it to himself, to wit, by habitual, humble, comforting prayer; then grace is given and by the fulfilment of God's commandments he is saved. (Luther, *Brief Explanation*, WML II, pp. 354-355)

The first three commandments of the decalogue correlate with the petitions of the Lord's Prayer in a way that constitutes a reliable introduction to Christian teaching. Luther summarized:

See, therefore, what a pretty, golden ring these three Commandments and their works naturally form, and how from the First Commandment and faith the Second flows on to the Third, and the Third in turn drives through the Second up into the First. For the first work is to believe, to have a good heart and confidence toward God. From this flows the second good work, to praise God's Name, to confess His grace, to give all honor to Him alone. Then follows the third, to worship by praying, hearing God's Word, thinking of and considering God's benefits, and in addition chastising oneself, and keeping the body under. . . . Thus faith goes out into the works and through the works comes to itself again. . . . This order of good works we pray in the Lord's Prayer. The first is this, that we say: "Our Father, Who art in heaven"; these are the words of the first work of faith, which, according to the First Commandment, does not doubt that it has a gracious Father in heaven. The second: "Hallowed be Thy Name," in which faith asks that God's Name, praise and honor be glorified, and calls upon it in every need, as the Second Commandment says. The third: "Thy kingdom come," in which we pray for the true Sabbath and rest, peaceful cessation of our works, that God's work alone be done in us, and so God rule in us as in His own kingdom, as He says, Luke 17:21, "Behold, God's kingdom is nowhere else except within you." The fourth petition is "Thy will be done"; in which we pray that we may keep and have the Seven Commandments of the Second Table, in which faith is exercised toward our neighbor; just as in the first three it is exercised in works toward God alone. (Luther, *Treatise on Good Works*, WML I, pp. 248-250)

The extent to which catechectical teaching should pursue the meaning of the triune teaching was discussed by Cyril in his pre-baptismal lectures:

Every grace is given by the Father, through the Son, who also acts together with the Holy Spirit. There are not some graces that come from the Father, and different graces from the Son, and others again from the Holy Spirit. There is but one salvation, one giving of power, one faith, and yet there is one God the Father, our Lord, his only-begotten Son, and one Holy Spirit, the Paraclete. Let us be content with this knowlege and not busy ourselves with the questions about the divine nature or hypostasis. I would have spoken of that had it been contained in Scripture. Let us not venture where Scripture does not lead, for it suffices for our salvation to know that there is Father, and Son, and Holy Spirit. (Cyril of Jerusalem, *Catechetical Lectures*, Lecture XVI, sec. 24, LCC, IV, p. 173)

Luther warned against constantly revising and changing the curricular resources for catechetical study:

The minister should above all things avoid the use of different texts and forms of the Ten Commandments, the Lord's Prayer, the Creed, the Sacraments, etc. Let him adopt one form and adhere to it, using it one year as the other; for young and ignorant people must be taught one certain text and form, and will easily become confused if we teach thus today and otherwise next year, as if we thought of making improvements. In this way all effort and labor will be lost. This our honored fathers well understood, who all used the Lord's Prayer, the Creed, the Ten Commandments in one and the same manner. Therefore we also should so teach these forms to the young and inexperienced as not to change a syllable, nor set them forth and recite them one year differently from the other. (Luther, *Small Catechism*, 1529, Introduction, WA 30, I p. 263f.; WLS 1, p. 117-118)

IV ❧ TRUE TEACHING

The first responsibility of the educator of the soul is to have reasonable knowledge of the subject matter—the health of the soul. One cannot guide others in a path never taken. One cannot teach what one does not know:

Who can defend that which he has not learned, or make clear to others that which he himself does not know? (Lactantius, *On the Workmanship of God*, Ch. XX, ANF VII, p. 299)

Not only must the teacher know what he teaches, but also follow his own teaching. Merely intending to do so is not enough. Lactantius distinguished the effective from the defective teacher largely by behavioral fruits:

If any one should diligently inquire into their [false teachers'] character, he will find that they are passionate, covetous, lustful, arrogant, wanton, and, concealing their vices under a show of wisdom, doing those things at home which they had censured in the schools.

Perhaps I speak falsely for the sake of bringing an accusation. Does not Tullius both acknowledge and complain of the same thing? "How few," he says, "of philosophers are found of such a character, so constituted in soul and life, as reason demands! how few who are obedient to themselves, and submit to their own decrees! We may see some of such levity and ostentation, that it would be better for them not to have learned at all; others eagerly desirous of money, others of glory; many the slaves of lusts, so that their speech wonderfully disagrees with their life." Cornelius Nepos also writes to the same Cicero: "So far am I from thinking that philosophy is the teacher of life and the completer of happiness, that I consider that none have greater need of teachers of living than many who are engaged in the discussion of this subject. For I see that a great part of those who give most elaborate precepts in their school respecting modesty and self-restraint, live at the same time in the unrestrained desires of all lusts." Seneca also, in his Exhortations, says: "Many of the philosophers are of this description, eloquent to their own condemnation: for if you should hear them arguing against avarice, against lust and ambition, you would think that they were making a public disclosure of their own character, so entirely do the censures which they utter in public flow back upon themselves. . . . It makes no difference with what intention you act, when the action itself is vicious; because acts are seen, the intention is not seen.". . . Tullius rightly gives the preference, above teachers of philosophy, to those men employed in civil affairs, who govern the state, who found new cities or maintain with equity those already founded, who preserve the safety and liberty of the citizens either by good laws or wholesome counsels, or by weighty judgements. For it is right to make men good rather than to give precepts about duty to those shut up in corners, which precepts are not observed even by those who speak them. . . . They who merely teach without acting, of themselves detract from the weight of their own precepts; for who would obey, when they who give the precepts themselves teach disobedience? . . . Since they are the advisers of actions, and do not themselves act at all, they are to be regarded as mere talkers. (Lactantius, *The Divine Institutes*, Bk. III, Ch. XV, ANF VII, pp. 84-85)

Athanasius set forth Jesus as exemplar of one who taught so as to embody his teaching:

He not only taught, but also accomplished what he taught, so that everyone might hear when he spoke, and seeing as in an image, receive from him the model for acting, hearing him say, "Learn from me, for I am gentle and lowly in heart" (Matt. 11:29). A more perfect instruction in virtue one could not find than that which the Lord typified in himself. For whether the issue is forbearance of evil, or love of mankind, or goodness, or courage, or compassion, or pursuit of justice, one will discover all present in him, so that nothing is lacking for virtue to one who considers closely this human life of his. Cognizant of this, Paul said, "Be imitators of me, as I am of Christ" (1 Cor. 11:1). (Athanasius, A Letter to Marcellinus, ACW 10, p. 112)

Should a lecherous teacher be entrusted to teach children?

Aristippus, the master of the Cyrenaics, had a criminal intimacy with Lais, the celebrated courtesan; and that grave teacher of philosophy defended this fault by saying, that there was a great difference between him and the other lovers of Lais because he himself possessed Lais, whereas others were possessed by Lais. O illustrious wisdom, to be imitated by good men! Would you, in truth, entrust your children to this man for education, that they might learn to possess a harlot? . . . Nor was it enough to live in this manner, but he began also to teach lusts; and he transferred his habits from the brothel to the school, contending that bodily pleasure was the chief good. (Lactantius, *The Divine Institutes*, Ch. XV, ANF VII, p. 84)

Are there restrictions on the laity in teaching of Christian doctrine?

It does not benefit a layman to dispute or teach publicly, thus claiming for himself authority to teach, but he should yield to the order appointed by the Lord, and to open his ears to those who have received the grace to teach, and be taught by them divine things; for in one Church God has made "different members," according to the word of the Apostle: and Gregory the Theologian, wisely interpreting this passage, commends the order in vogue with them saying: "This order brethren we revere, this we guard. Let this one be the ear; that one the tongue, the hand or any other member. Let this one teach, but let that one learn." And a little further on: "Learning in docility and abounding in cheerfulness, and ministering with alacrity, we shall not all be the tongue which is the more active member, not all of us Apostles, not all prophets, nor shall we all interpret" (cf. 1 Cor. 12:29-30). And again: "Why dost thou make thyself a shepherd when thou art a sheep? Why become the head when thou art a foot? Why dost thou try to be a commander when thou art enrolled in the number of the soldiers?" And elsewhere: "Wisdom orders, Be not swift in words; nor compare thyself with the rich, being poor; nor seek to be wiser than the wise." (Synod of Quinisext, A.D. 692, Canon LXIV, The Seven Ecumenical Councils, NPNF 2, XIV, p. 394; quotations from Gregory of Nazianzus, *Theological Orations*, First Oration, Against Eunomians, NPNF 2, VII, p. 286)

V ❧ FALSE TEACHING

Wherever Christian instruction proceeds, it must deal with alternative views of history, God, humanity, reality, and ethics. These views may come from within the Christian community or from the culture it confronts. A *heterodox* opinion is other than that received in ecumenical teaching, while *hairesis* simply means an opinion self-chosen in opposition to the received teaching. The task of differentiating authentic from inauthentic teaching does not end with any given generation. True teaching must distinguish itself in each new cultural situation from its spurious or dubious alternatives.

Pastoral writers thought that an unintended providential purpose was at work in false teaching: to challenge, test out, and improve true teaching.

The character of the times in which we live is such as to call forth from us even this admonition, that we ought not to be astonished at the heresies which abound, neither ought their existence to surprise us. For it was foretold that they should come to pass. Nor need we be surprised that they subvert the faith of some, for their final purpose is, by affording a trial to faith, to give it also the opportunity of being approved. . . .

The Lord teaches us that many "ravening wolves shall come in sheep's clothing" (Matt. 7:15). Now, what are these sheep's clothings other than the external surface of the Christian profession? Who are the ravening wolves but those deceitful senses and spirits which are lurking within to waste the flock of Christst? . . . Heresies, at the present time, will no less rend the church by their perversion of doctrine, than will Antichrist persecute her at that day by the cruelty of his attacks, except that persecution makes martyrs while heresy makes only apostates. And therefore "dissensions are necessary if only to show which of your members are sound" (1 Cor. 11:19), both those who remained steadfast under persecution, and those who did not wander out of their way into heresy. . . . It was owing to the prospect of the greater evil that Paul readily affirmed the meaning of the lighter ones; and so far indeed was he from believing, in the face of evils of such a kind, that heresies were good, that his object was to forewarn us that we ought not to be surprised at temptations of even a worse stamp, since (he said) they tended to "show which of your members are sound" (1 Cor. 1:19). (Tertullian, *Prescription Against Heretics*, Ch. I, IV-V, ANF III, pp. 243, 245, NEB)*

This does not make *hairesis* good as such, but only divinely permissible within the frame of reference of God's purpose of freedom and redemption. Both heresy and persecution test the mettle of the believing church. These false teachings, however, win only temporary victories over true teaching. Where do heresies derive their strength? Believers who have to face repeatedly the buffetings of false teachers may become like a boxer with lowered morale:

False teachings would have less power if everyone would cease to be amazed at their alleged potency. . . . In a combat of boxers and gladiators, generally speaking, it is not simply because a man is physically strong that he gains the victory, or loses it because he is not strong, but often because he vanquished a smaller man. And sometimes it happens that this very conqueror, when afterwards matched against a really powerful man, actually retires crest-fallen from the contest. In precisely the same way, heretical teachings derive such strength as they have from the infirmities of individuals. They have no strength whatever when they encounter a really powerful faith. (Tertullian, *Prescription Against Heresies*, Ch. II, ANF III, pp. 243, 244)*

Hippolytus provided an account of how the motives, internal consistencies, and scriptural grounds of false teachings might be critically examined, as in the case of Noetus:

Some others are secretly introducing another doctrine, who have become disciples of one Noetus, who was a native of Smyrna, and lived not very long ago. This person was greatly puffed up and inflated with pride, being inspired by the conceit of a strange spirit. He alleged that Christ was the Father Himself, and that the Father Himself was born, and suffered, and died. You see what pride of heart and what a strange inflated spirit had insinuated themselves into him. From his other actions, then, the proof is already given us that he did not speak with a pure spirit; for he who blasphemes against the Holy Spirit is cast out from the holy inheritance. He alleged that he was himself Moses, and that Aaron was his brother. When the blessed presbyters heard this, they summoned him before the Church, and examined him. But he denied at first that he held such opinions. Afterwards, however, taking shelter among some, and having gathered round him some others who had embraced the same error, he wished thereafter to uphold his dogma openly as correct. And the blessed presbyters called him again before them, and examined him. But he stood out against them, saying, "What evil, then, am I doing in glorifying Christ?" And the presbyters replied to him, "We too know in truth one God; we know Christ; we know that the Son suffered even as He suffered, and died even as He died, and rose again on the third day, and is at the right hand of the Father, and cometh to judge the living and the dead. And these things which we have learned we allege." Then, after examining him, they expelled him from the Church. And he was carried to such a pitch of pride, that he established a school. (Hippolytus, *Against the Heresy of One Noetus*, sec. 1, ANF V, p. 223)*

It was not an incidental error (claiming oneself to be Moses, confusing the Father and the Son, blaspheming the Holy Spirit). The case of Noetus showed very early in the pastoral tradition that there was an orderly procedure for the examination of idiosyncratic, unecumenical, unorthodox, unworthy pastors who teach heresy but call it Christian faith. Later Jeremy Taylor would warn that Christian education does not invite in all opinions equally so as to pretend or appear to be merely a debating society:

Receive not the people to doubtful disputations: and let no names of sects or differing religions be kept up amongst you, to the disturbance of the public peace and private charity: and teach not the people to estimate their piety by their distance from any opinion. (Jeremy Taylor, *RAC*, Bk. III, sec. 29; *CS*, p. 11)

Some highly controversial (yet widely received) Christian teachings, like predestination and divine foreknowledge, need to be taught cautiously in such a way as not to lead to the abuse of other teachings:

We should not make predestination an habitual subject of conversation. If it is sometimes mentioned we must speak in such a way that no person will fall into error, as happens on occasion when one will say, "It has already been determined whether I will be saved or lost, and in spite of all the good or evil that I do, this will not be changed." As a result, they become apathetic and neglect the works that are conducive to their salvation and to the spiritual growth of their souls.

In like manner, we must be careful lest by speaking too much and with too great emphasis on faith, without any distinction or explanation, we give occasion to the people to become indolent and lazy in the performance of good works, whether it be before or after their faith is founded in charity.

Also in our discourse we ought not to emphasize the doctrine that would destroy free will. We may therefore speak of faith and grace to the extent that God enables us to do so, for the greater praise of His Divine Majesty. But, in these dangerous times of ours, it must not be done in such a way that good works or free will suffer any detriment or be considered worthless. (Ignatius Loyola, *Spiritual Exercises*, p. 141)

It is not only the clergy who have responsibility to recognize, judge, and reject false teaching, but the laity as well:

To recognize and judge doctrine behooves each and every Christian, so much so that he is accursed who infringes upon this right by as little as a hairsbreadth. For Christ Himself has established this right by various and unassailable statements, such as Matt. 7:15: "Beware of false prophets, which come to you in sheep's clothing." He is certainly speaking this word to the people in opposition to those who teach, and He commands them to avoid false teachings. But how can they avoid them if they do not recognize them? And how can they recognize them if they do not have the right to judge them? (Luther, WA 10 II, p. 217; WLS 1, p. 418)

False teaching should be approached by persuasion, not by persecution. However skewed the false teaching, it should not be resisted by coercion:

We should vanquish heretics with books, not with burning; for so the ancient fathers did. If it were a science to vanquish the heretics with fire, then the hangmen would be the most learned doctors on earth. (Luther, *An Open Letter to the Christian Nobility*, WML II, p. 142)

Selections of Part Six have focussed upon the pastor as educator of the soul, the aptness to teach required of ministry, the pedagogy of the inner life. The soul-guide mediates Christ's own guidance on the pathway toward behavioral excellence. God teaches by empathic participation in the limited situation of the learner. True teaching must distinguish itself in each new cultural situation from its spurious alternatives, under the guidance of apostolic teaching.

7 Care of the Community

PASTORS DO NOT DIRECT their soul care exclusively to individuals within the Church. Their care is also extended to the congregation as a body, and beyond the congregation to the secular sphere, the world. The pastor's care within the domestic order and economic order are treated in another volume of this series on *Crisis Ministries*. In this Part we will deal with four ever-widening circles of community to which the pastor is responsible: church institutions, inter-institutional relationships, the political order, and the world.

First, curacy requires the nurture of institutional processes within the Church that they may better serve the education and growth of souls effected by them. Modern seminary courses of study call these tasks by various names: church and ministry, church management, and "church administration." We prefer to call it, "administry," or that which leads to and prepares for ministry. Secondly, curacy involves dealing with other pastors, and with alternative church structures that interface in various inter-institutional relationships. In earlier periods this part of the pastoral task was sometimes called "pastoral etiquette," which referred to the maintenance of cordial relationships with others in Christian ministry. Third, curacy involves dealing with economic and political structures that confront and affect the lives of Christian communicants, and the society at large. The church has thought long and hard about the extent of the pastor's involvement in political activities. This task involves the political ethics of the pastor. Fourth, curacy is called to care more largely for the *saeculum*, the world, the structures of secularity given to the church by God at a particular time, for service, intercession, responsible love, and the search for justice. There are varied interpretations of the relationship of the church to the world.

I ❧ ADMINISTRY: PASTORAL CARE THROUGH INSTITUTIONS

"Administry" is an old English word derived from the Latin *administrare*, to manage as a steward. Administry is literally "toward ministry," or do-

184

ing that which one must do to enable ministry. Ministry cannot proceed without administry, without working patiently with institutions and group processes seeking to elicit responsiveness to the church's mission of care.

From the earliest centuries, the pastor has been called to be steward not only of the mysteries of God but also of the temporal life of the congregation. The pastor will expend much time and energy in planning which seeks to avert future problems, scarcities, or needless limitations upon Christian mission:

But you, O steward, who receive all offerings that come from the churches, conceal nothing from the bishop. In the same spirit, the bishop must set aside nothing for himself personally. But the management of resources of the Lord shall be under the steward and the seals under the bishop. . . . And the treasuries of the house of the Lord you are charged with keeping filled, because scarcity may befall the city or its outlying district. (*Athanasian Canons*, sec. 89, p. 55)*

A letter from Theonas of Alexandria to Lucianus shows how important the pastoral writers thought it was to keep accurate accounts and properly designate fiscal accountability:

Keep every thing in an exact reckoning. He should be ready at any time to give an accurate account of all things. He should note down everything in writing, if it is at all possible, before giving money to another. He should never trust such things to his memory, which, being drawn off day by day to other matters, readily fails us, so that, without writing, we sometimes honestly certify things which have never existed; neither should this kind of writing be of a commonplace order, but such as easily and clearly unfolds all things, and leaves the mind of the inquirer without any scruple or doubt on the subject. This will easily be effected if a distinct and separate account is kept in writing of all receipts, and of the time when, and the person by whom, and the place at which they were made. (Theonas of Alexandria, *Epistle to Lucianus*, sec. IV, ANF VI, p. 159)

Clement of Rome thought that the willingness voluntarily to give up leadership roles, and to put oneself at the disposal of others, was the key to integrity in pastoral leadership:

Is there any man of noble mind among you? A man who is compassionate? A man overflowing with love? Then let such a one say, "If it is I who am the cause of any disorder, friction, or division among you, I will remove myself. I will go away, any-

where you wish, and I will do anything the congregation says."
(Clement of Rome, *To the Corinthians*, sec. 54, ECW, p. 51)

Baxter suggested a deliberate principle of time distribution for pastoral priorities:

A preacher must be oft upon the same things, because the matters of necessity are few. We must not either feign necessaries, or fall much upon unnecessaries, to satisfy them that look for novelties. . . . As Gregory Nazianzen and Seneca often say, "Necessaries are common and obvious; it is superfluities that we waste our time for, and labour for, and complain that we attain them not." Ministers, therefore, must be observant of the care of their flocks, that they may know what is most necessary for them, both for matter and for manner; and usually the matter is to be first regarded, as being of more importance than the manner. (Baxter, *RP*, p. 114)

Jeremy Taylor, a moderate Anglican defender of toleration, argued that the pastor must provide leadership, and not simply follow a perceived consensus:

Let not the humours and inclinations of the people be the measures of your doctrines, but let your doctrines be the measure of their persuasions. Let them know from you what they ought to do; but if you learn from them what you ought to teach, you will give but a very ill account at the day of judgment of the souls committed to you. He that receives from the people what he shall teach them is like a nurse that asks of her child what physic she shall give him. (Jeremy Taylor, *RAC*, Bk. III, sec. 43; *CS*, p. 15)

Luther, concerned about the quality of governance of church institutions, advised that such institutions should not be continued that cannot be well managed:

Of spiritual power we have much; but of spiritual government nothing or little. Meanwhile may he help who can, that endowments, monastic houses, parishes and schools be well established and managed. . . . It is much better that there be no monastic house or endowment than that there be evil government in them, whereby God is the more provoked to anger. (Luther, *Treatise on Good Works*, Sec. VIII, WML II, p. 259)

Lay persons may justly withhold money from corrupted clergy.

Now our prelates are perverted on the side of the devil, not so sustaining the poor by hospitality, but rather secular lords and tyrants, who do not need such alms, but are commonly gorged with inhuman and gluttonous feasts, and yet are satiated sumptuously without a qualm from the goods of the poor. . . . From these considerations the faithful conclude that when a curate is notoriously negligent in his pastoral office, they as subjects should, yea, ought, to withdraw offerings and tithes from him and whatever might offer occasion for the fostering of such wickedness. . . . In all such cases it is permitted to the parishioners wisely to withdraw their alms, lest they seem to defend and foster the obstinacy of such a so-called pastor. (John Wyclif, *On the Pastoral Office*, sec. 4, 8, 17, LCC XIV, pp. 35, 38, 45-46)*

Pastors often seem to be found promoting community events, encouraging persons to get together, eat together, celebrate occasions, enjoy processions and feasts, and experience themselves as a community. George Herbert is one of the few pastoral writers who thought deliberately about the theological-liturgical rationale for this sort of activity:

The Country Parson is a Lover of old Customs, if they be good and harmless; and the rather, because Country people are much addicted to them; so that to favour them therein is to win their hearts, and to oppose them therein is to deject them. If there be any ill in the custom, which may be severed from the good, he pares the apple, and gives them the clean to feed on. Particularly, he loves Procession, and maintains it; because there are contained therein four manifest advantages. First, a blessing of God for the fruits of the field; secondly, justice in the Preservation of bounds; thirdly, Charity in loving, walking and neighborly accompanying one another, with reconciling of differences at that time, if there be any; fourthly, Mercy relieving the poor by a liberal distribution and largess, which at that time is, or ought to be used. . . . and sometimes where he knows there hath been or is a little difference, he takes one of the parties, and goes with him to the other; and all dine or sup together. There is much preaching in this friendliness. (George Herbert, *CP*, Ch. XXXV, CWS, p. 109)

In order to maintain contact with the parish through regular visitation, the pastor may have to make rigorous choices about the distribution of his time. Richard Baxter offered this practical suggestion:

Before we undertook this work [of pastoral visitation] our hands were full, and now we are engaged to set apart two days every

week, from morning to night, for private catechizing and instruction; so that any man may see that we must leave undone all that
other work that we were wont to do at that time: and we are ne-
cessitated to run upon the public work of preaching with small
preparation, and so must deliver the message of God so rawly and
confusedly, and unanswerably to its dignity and the need of men's
souls, that it is a great trouble to our minds to consider it, and a
greater trouble to us when we are doing it. And yet it must be so;
there is no remedy: unless we will omit this personal instruction. . . . [If we] set apart two whole days a week for this work, it
will be as much as we shall be able to do, to go over the parish
once in a year (being about 800 families). Otherwise we would be
forced to cut it short, or do it less effectually. We have above fifteen families a week to deal with. And, alas! how small a matter is
it to speak to a man only once in a year. (Baxter, *RP*, pp. 183–
184)*

The number of people in the church is hardly an accurate indicator
of its spiritual strength. Salvian the Presbyter (c. 400–c. 480) worried
about the overemphasis upon numbers:

When the people in the faith are multiplied, their faith is weak-
ened. When the children are growing, their mother sickens. You,
the Church, have become weaker as your fertility has progressed.
You fall back as you go forward, and, as it were, you are weaker
by reason of your strength. Indeed, you have spread throughout
the whole world members who bear the name of Christians, but
who do not possess the force of religion. Thus, you have begun
to be rich in number and poor in faith. The richer you are in
multitudes, the more needy you are in devotion. The bigger your
body, the more limited your soul. You are, so to speak, both
greater in yourself and lesser in yourself. You increase and de-
crease at the same time by a new and almost unheard of progres-
sion and recession. (Salvian the Presbyter, *The Four Books of
Timothy to the Church*, Bk. 1, sec. 1, FC 3, p. 270)

Luther also urged the pastor not to allow numbers to become a special preoccupation of ministry, but rather to focus primarily upon being
faithful to the Word:

The point of importance is not whether many or few people
believe or do not believe, are damned or saved. On the contrary,
the point of importance is what God has commanded or forbidden, what is His Word or what is not His Word. To this one

should look, and about this one should think; and one should ignore the entire world. (Luther, *Sermon on Matthew* 7, 1532, WA 30 II, p. 192; WLS III, p. 1208)

The pastor has a duty to oversee the physical caring for the church building. The biblical grounding of this task was set forth by George Herbert as follows:

The Country Parson has a special care of his Church, that all things there be decent, and befitting his Name by which it is called. Therefore, first, he takes order, that all things be in good repair; as walls plastered, windows glazed, floors paved, seats whole, firm and uniform, especially that the Pulpit, and Desk, and Communion table, and Font be as they ought, for those great duties that are performed in them. . . . And all this he does not as out of necessity, or as putting a holiness in the things themselves, but because he desires to keep the middle way between superstition and slovenliness, and to follow the Apostle's two great and admirable Rules in things of this nature; the first of which is, *Let all things be done decently and in order*, and the second, *Let all things be done to edification* (1 Cor. 14:[26,40]). For these two rules comprise and include the double object of our duty, God and our neighbor; the first being for the honor of God, the second for the benefit of our neighbor. (George Herbert, *CP*, Ch. XIII, CWS, pp. 74f.)*

The Synod of Quinisext prohibited the use of church property for the making of money:

It is not right that those who are responsible for reverence to churches should place within the sacred bounds an eating place, nor offer food there, nor make other sales. For God our Saviour teaching us when he was tabernacling in the flesh commanded not to make his Father's house a house of merchandise. (Synod of Quinisext, A.D. 692, Canon LXXVI, The Seven Ecumenical Councils, NPNF 2, XIV, pp. 398-399)

II ❧ THE PASTOR'S RELATION TO OTHER PASTORS

The pastor is charged with a flock and a parish, which traditionally was defined as a distinct geographical area. Most of the pastoral tradition has assumed that there would only be one pastor in charge of a parish. The term parish derives from *para oikos*, beside the house, i.e., nearby the pastor's residence, or within a day's walk of the church. From the outset there has been an assumption of territoriality of ministry. Potential conflicts between clergy may emerge when this sense of territory has been upset, intruded, or challenged. The notion of a parish antedated the explosion of denominations after the Protestant Reformation, which itself intensified and complicated the problem of territoriality of ministry. The pastoral writers have had a long-standing concern about how to avert, adjudicate, and deal with conflicts between ministers.

Let no preacher envy any other who has a greater audience, or more fame in preaching, than himself; let him not detract from him or lessen his reputation directly or indirectly; for he that cannot be even with his brother but by pulling him down, is but a dwarf still; and no man is the better for making his brother worse. (Jeremy Taylor, *RAC*, Bk. III, sec. 60; *CS*, p. 19)*

The Second Council of Constantinople urged that pastors gather together often to discuss their mutual pastoral tasks and needs:

For although the grace of the Holy Spirit abounded in each one of the Apostles so that no one of them needed the counsel of another in the execution of his work, yet they were not willing to define on the question then raised touching the circumcision of the Gentiles, until being gathered together they had confirmed their own several sayings by the testimony of the divine Scriptures. (Second Council of Constantinople, A.D. 553, The Sentence of the Synod, The Seven Ecumenical Councils, NPNF 2, XIV, p. 306)

Yet it is no simple matter to cross over these territorial lines and still maintain good relationships:

Entertain no persons into your assemblies from other parishes unless upon great occasion, or in the destitution of a minister, or by contingency and seldom visits, or with leave; lest the labour of your brother be discouraged, and you yourself be thought to preach Christ out of envy, and not of good-will. (Jeremy Taylor, *RAC*, Bk. III, sec. 37; *CS*, p. 13)*

Earlier the Apostolic Constitutions had recognized the problem of territoriality in episcopal administration:

A bishop ought not to leave his own parish and leap to another. (*Constitutions of the Holy Apostles*, Ecclesiastical Canons, sec. 14, ANF VII, p. 501)

Nor should clergy wander from parish to parish without the advice and consent of the bishop:

If any presbyter or deacon, or any one of the catalogue of the clergy, leaves his own parish and goes to another, and, entirely removing himself, continues in that other parish without the consent of his own bishop, him we command no longer to go on in his ministry, especially in case his bishop calls upon him to return, and he does not obey, but continues in his disorder. However, let him communicate there as a layman. (*Constitutions of the Holy Apostles*, Ecclesiastical Canons, sec. 15, ANF VII, p. 501)

The First Council of Nicaea was similarly concerned about wandering, unattached ministries:

Neither bishop, presbyter, nor deacon shall pass from city to city. And if any one, after this decree of the holy and great Synod, shall attempt any such thing, or continue in any such course, his proceedings shall be utterly void, and he shall be restored to the Church for which he was ordained bishop or presbyter. . . . Such presbyters or deacons as desert their own Church are not to be admitted into another, but are to be sent back to their own diocese. (First Council of Nicea, A.D. 325, Canon XV; Ancient Epitome of Canon XVI, The Seven Ecumenical Councils, NPNF 2, XIV, pp. 32, 35)

Yet it was thought to be proper for the church of a well-resourced region to send missionary personnel and free-will gifts to a region that lacks resources:

News has come to me that, in response to your prayers and your loving sympathy in Christ Jesus, peace now reigns in the church at Antioch in Syria. It would therefore be very fitting for you, as a church of God, to appoint one of your deacons to go there as God's ambassador, and when they are all assembled together to offer them your felicitations and give glory to the Name. The man whom you think suitable for such a mission will have the blessing of Jesus Christ. (Ignatius of Antioch, *To the Phillipians*, sec. 10, ECW, p. 114)

Clergy from other parishes are to be received with dignity and mutuality:

If a presbyter comes from another parish, let him be received to communion by the presbyters; if a deacon, by the deacons; if a bishop, let him sit with the bishop, and be allowed the same honour with himself; and thou, O bishop, shalt desire him to speak to the people words of instruction: for the exhortation and admo-

nition of strangers is very acceptable, and exceeding profitable. . . . Thou shalt also permit him to offer the Eucharist.
(*Constitutions of the Holy Apostles*, Bk. II, Sec. VII, lviii, ANF VII,
p. 422)

Strong measures were proposed by the Council of Ancyra against one
bishop invading another's territory:

If any who have been constituted bishops, but have not been received by the parish to which they were designated, shall invade
other parishes and wrong the constituted (bishops) there, stirring
up seditions against them, let such persons be suspended from
office and communion. (Council of Ancyra, A.D. 314, Canon
XVIII, The Seven Ecumenical Councils, NPNF 2, XIV, p. 71)

The Council of Chalcedon (451 A.D.) provided measures to prevent
one group of clergy from conspiring against other clergy:

The crime of conspiracy or banding together is utterly prohibited even by the secular law, and much more ought it to be forbidden in the Church of God. Therefore, if any, whether
clergymen or monks, should be detected in conspiring or banding together, or hatching plots against their bishops or fellow-
clergy, they shall by all means be deposed from their own rank.
(Council of Chalcedon, A.D. 451, Canon XVIII, The Seven Ecumenical Councils, NPNF 2, XIV, p. 281)

It is not beyond the reach of pastoral care to seek also to heal the
divisions of the church. Here is a seventeenth century form of the ecumenical vision:

That is necessary to us as we are fellow-labourers in the same
work; and that is this, we must be very studious of union and
communion among ourselves, and of the unity and peace of the
churches that we oversee. We must be sensible how needful this is
to the prosperity of the whole, the strengthening of our common
cause, the good of the particular members of our flock, and the
further enlargement of the kingdom of Christ. And, therefore,
ministers must smart when the Church is wounded, and be so far
from being the leaders in divisions, that they should take it as a
principal part of their work to prevent and heal them. Day and
night should they bend their studies to find out means to heal
such breaches. They must not only hearken to motions for unity,
but propound them and prosecute them; not only entertain an
offered peace, but even follow it when it flies from them. They

must, therefore, keep close to the ancient centre of catholic unity. (Baxter, *RP*, p. 123)

III 𝓎 THE POLITICAL ETHICS OF THE PASTOR

An entire book could be justifiably written of the classical pastoral tradition on this theme alone. For ministry exists always within some political order, and the relation of ministry and statecraft has fascinated the pastoral writers. We will limit our observations primarily to those that seek to define the boundary between pastoral care and care of the *polis* (the city, the political order).

Luther argued that the church's responsibility to temporal and political authority is not absolute, and that there are limits of legitimate civil power:

But if it should happen, as it often does, that the temporal power and authorities, as they are called, should urge a subject to do contrary to the Commandments of God, or hinder him from doing them, there obedience ends, and that duty is annulled. Here a man must say as St. Peter says to the rulers of the Jews: "We ought to obey God rather than men" (Acts 5:29). . . . Thus, if a prince desired to go to war, and his cause was manifestly unrighteous, we should not follow nor help him at all; since God has commanded that we shall not kill our neighbor, nor do him injustice. (Luther, *Treatise on Good Works*, sec. XXI, WML III, p. 271)

The search for justice is doubly difficult, first to find, then to preserve:

It is a problem to find where justice lies, and it is hard not to pervert it when found. . . . Many of those who have suffered wrong hate those who cannot help them just as much as those who did the wrong. (John Chrysostom, *On the Priesthood*, Ch. III, sec. 18, p. 101)

Luther defined the legitimacy and limits of pastoral authority in the political sphere in this way:

Although governmental authority is an ordinance of God, God has nonetheless reserved for Himself the right to rebuke its faults. And so government, too, is to be censured that the possessions of the lower classes may not be drained by usury and because of bad supervision. But it is not proper for a preacher to want to prescribe regulations to government concerning the price of bread and meat and the manner of imposing taxes. (Luther, *Table Talk*, W-T 5, #5258; WLS 3, p. 1114)

The extent to which church bodies and leaders may rightly and prudently enter into the political sphere has been much debated. The Westminster Confession stated a majority Reformed opinion in urging caution:

Synods and councils are to handle or conclude nothing but that which is ecclesiastical: and are not to intermeddle with civil affairs which concern the commonwealth, unless by way of humble petition in cases extraordinary; or by way of advice for satisfaction of conscience, if they be thereunto required by the civil magistrate. (Westminister Confession, Ch. XXXI, sec. v, *CC*, p. 228)

Shall the pastor seek political office and influence?

To be able clearly to distinguish between these two kingdoms is a great art, for few people make the proper distinction. This is what commonly happens: the temporal lords want to rule the church, and, conversely, the theologians (*die Geistlichen*) want to play the lord in the town hall. Under the papacy mixing the two was considered ruling well, and it is still so considered. But in reality this is ruling very badly. When bishops were still pious, they observed the distinction well, took care of the churches, and let the emperor do his ruling. But their descendants subsequently mixed the two, grabbed for the sword, and turned into worldly lords. The same thing is happening today: noblemen and young lords want to rule consciences and issue commands in the church. And someday, when the theologians get back on their feet, they will again take the sword from the temporal authorities, as happened under the papacy. (Luther, *Christmas Day Sermon on Luke 2*, WA 34 II, p. 502; WLS 1, pp. 294-295)

Elsewhere, Luther stated forthrightly:

A minister must not go in for politics. Christ was the sole Lord, and yet He said to Pilate: You are My lord (cf. John 19:10f). (Luther, *Table Talk*, W-T 1, #181; WLS 2, p. 937)

Athanasius thought that one of the most heinous aspects of the Arian heresy is that it sought to coerce belief through political force:

Our fathers called an Ecumenical Council, when three hundred of them, more or less, met together and condemned the Arian heresy, and all declared that it was alien and strange to the faith of the Church. Upon this its supporters, perceiving that they were dishonoured, and had now no good ground of argument to insist upon, devised a different method, and attempted to vindicate it by means of external power. . . . . If anyone so much as speaks against them, he is dragged before the Governor or the General. . . . .

The other heresies also, when the very Truth has refuted them on the clearest evidence, are wont to be silent, being simply confounded by their conviction. But this modern and accursed heresy, when it is overthrown by argument, when it is cast down and covered with shame by the very Truth, forthwith endeavours to coerce by violence and stripes and imprisonment those whom it has been unable to persuade by argument. (Athanasius, *History of the Arians*, sec. 66,67, NPNF 2, IV, pp. 294-295)

Ministry and statecraft are generally thought to be distinguishable caring functions, alike in their office of governance, but different in their sphere of operation:

I admonish you who are someday to become the instructors of consciences and of Christian churches to see to it that you continue to observe the difference [between church and state]. For nothing good comes of a mixing of these two. And this mixing takes place as soon as the prince says: Listen, you preacher, I want you to teach in this and that way on my behalf; do not criticize and rebuke in the way you are doing. Conversely, it is also wrong for a preacher to propose: Listen, you government officials or judges, you are to pass judgment according to my will. (Luther, *Exposition of John 2*, 1538, WA 46, pp. 184f.; WLS 2, p. 937)

How does pastoral care of the church differ from the prince's care of the *polis*?

The spiritual power is to reign only over the soul, seeing to it that it comes to Baptism and the Sacrament of the Altar, to the Gospel and true faith, over which matters emperors and kings have no jurisdiction. . . . Power over temporal affairs has not been committed to us (clergymen). The spiritual ban, which Christ preached and used, belongs to us. Beyond this ban we must not go, nor should we arrogate to ourselves the ban which belongs only to the government and the executioner. (Luther, *Sermon on Matthew 18*, WA 47, p. 284; WLS 1, p. 294)

Allan of Lille provided this penetrating instruction on how governmental authorities are to be counseled by pastors:

O prince, if you wish to judge the earth rightly, judge rightly the earth of your own body. For there is a three-fold earth: the earth which we tread, the earth which we live in, and the earth which we seek. The earth we tread is the material earth, which is to be trampled on; the earth which we live in is the earth of our own body, which must be tended; the earth which we seek is everlasting life, which must be cultivated. . . . What will your spirit say to you then, O prince of the earth, when it, a pauper, will judge you on the Day of Judgement, if you have ruled your sphere ill, and unjustly judged the poor? (Alan of Lille, *The Art of Preaching*, Ch. xlii, CFS 23, pp. 154-155)

There is no reason for the spiritual guide to quake with fear in the presence of governmental power. Among many accounts of kings visiting pastors, this one of St. Severin is outstanding:

Batavis is the name of a town situated between the two rivers, Inn and Danube. There blessed Severin had built a monastery for a few monks in his usual manner because he was often asked by the citizens to come to that place, especially in view of the frequent invasions of the Alamanni, whose king, Gibuldus, greatly honored and loved him. At one time the king, wishing ardently to see Severin, even went there to see him. The saint, fearing that the king's coming might be a burden to the city, went outside to meet him. He addressed the king so firmly that the latter began to tremble vehemently in his presence; after they had parted, the king declared to his army that never before, either in battle or in any peril, had he been shaken by such trembling. When he gave the servant of God his choice to demand of him what he wanted, the wise teacher asked him that, in his own interest, he should restrain his people from the devastation of Roman territory, and that he should graciously release those who were being held prisoners by his men. (Eugippius, *The Life of Saint Severin*, 5, Memorandum, 19.1-3, FC 55, p. 77)

IV ❧ CARE OF THE SAECULUM

The world is the object of God's care (John 3:16). In this light, the pastor cares not only for the church, but also for the world, the *saeculum*, the whole secular sphere. Augustine made a distinction between the heavenly city characterized by the selfless love of God, and the earthly city characterized by the godless love of self. These two cities interact in this world. Wheat and tares are mixed together in the visible church. The pastor has primary responsibility for the nurture and guidance of the flock and the eliciting of virtue and the health of the soul. But pastoral responsibility also reaches out to the world, to whatever extent possible.

Augustine thought that the city of God was a universal human community embracing all languages and cultures:

This heavenly city, then, while it sojourns on earth, calls citizens out of all nations, and gathers together a society of pilgrims of all languages, not scrupling about diversities in the manners, laws, and institutions whereby earthly peace is secured and maintained, but recognising that, however various these are, they all tend to one and the same end of earthly peace. It therefore is so far from rescinding and abolishing these diversities, that it even preserves and adapts them, so long only as no hindrance to the worship of the one supreme and true God is thus introduced. (Augustine, *The City of God*, Bk. XIX, sec. 17, p. 696)

John Chrysostom argued that the parish ministry that engages in the rough and tumble life of the world is not inferior to that ministry that withdraws from the world to a life of prayer. The double metaphor is that of a ship at sea and at anchor:

For just in the same way as the man who is always at anchor in harbor, is not the man who requires his ship to be fitted out, and who needs a pilot and a crew, but he who is always out at sea; so is it with the man of the world and the monk. The one is entered as it were into a waveless harbor, and lives an untroubled life, and far removed from every storm; whilst the other is ever on the ocean, and lives out at sea in the very midst of the ocean, battling with billows without number. (John Chrysostom, *Homilies on Ephesians*, XX, NPNF 1, XIII, p. 155)

The Epistle of Diognetus viewed the Christian life as existing in a paradoxical relation to the world.

The difference between Christian and the rest of mankind is not a matter of nationality, or language, or customs. Christians do not live apart in separate cities of their own, speak any special dialect, nor practise any eccentric way of life. The doctrine they profess is not the invention of busy human minds and brains, nor are they, like some, adherents of this or that school of human thought. They pass their lives in whatever township—Greek or foreign—each man's lot has determined; and conform to ordinary local usage in their clothing, diet, and other habits. Nevertheless, the organization of their community does exhibit some features that are remarkable, and even surprising. For instance, though they are residents at home in their own countries, their behaviour there is more like that of transients; they take their full part as citizens, but they also submit to anything and everything as if they were aliens. For them, any foreign country is a motherland, and any motherland is a foreign country. . . . They obey the prescribed laws, but in their own private lives they transcend the laws. . . . They repay calumny with blessings, and abuse with courtesy. For the good they do, they suffer stripes as evildoers; and under the strokes they rejoice like men given new life. (*The Epistle to Diognetus*, sec. 5, ECW, pp. 176-177)

The Christian community's relation to the world is something like the relation of soul and body:

To put it briefly, the relation of Christians to the world is that of a soul to the body. As the soul is diffused through every part of the body, so are Christians through all the cities of the world. The soul, too, inhabits the body, while at the same time forming no part of it; and Christians inhabit the world, but they are not part of the world. The soul, invisible herself, is immured within a visible body; so Christians can be recognized in the world, but their Christianity itself remains hidden from the eye. The flesh hates the soul, and wars against her without any provocation, because she is an obstacle to its own self-indulgence; and the world similarly hates the Christians without provocation, because they are opposed to its pleasures. All the same, the soul loves the flesh and all its members, despite their hatred for her; and Christians, too, love those who hate them. The soul, shut up inside the body, nevertheless holds the body together; and though they are confined within the world as in a dungeon, it is Christians who hold the world together. The soul, which is immortal, must dwell in a mortal tabernacle; and Christians, as they sojourn for a while in the midst of corruptibility here, look for incorruptibility in the heavens. Finally, just as to be stinted of food and drink makes the soul's improvement, so when Christians are every day subjected to ill-treatment, they increase the more in numbers. Such is the high post of duty not to shrink from it. (*The Epistle to Diognetus*, sec. 6, ECW, pp. 177-178)

Selections in Part Seven have focussed upon the ever-widening circles of community in and to which the pastor is responsible: church institutions, inter-institutional relationships, the civic and political order, and the world. Curacy requires the upbuilding of institutional processes both within the church and society on behalf of the health of souls. The pastor must learn to deal with other pastors, and with para-church structures to elicit improved contexts for soul care. Curacy, although distinguishable from civic and political office, requires dealing with economic and political structures that effect the lives of communicants. The pastor guides not only individual souls but the redemptive community as a body in the hope that the Christian community may enter into a responsible, intercessory, prophetic, and healing relationship to the world.

8 On Enabling Support and Limiting Abuse

THE WORK OF MINISTRY requires the confidence and support of laity. If this support system is not consistent with everything else that ministry says about itself, its integrity is suspect. Consequently the pastoral writers have paid careful attention to better and worse means of funding and resourcing pastoral care, rejecting fees for service, and urging voluntary contributions from the laity on the basis of biblical imperatives. They have also thought carefully about how abuses of ministry are properly to be corrected, with due process, amid conflicting interests.

I ❧ REJECTION OF FEES FOR PASTORAL SERVICE

Unlike pastors in the classical tradition, some modern "pastoral counseling" has looked toward an excessively professionalized medical realm as a model for financial support. Professional pastoral counselors have been happy to provide the counseling services clients want, receive fees for those services, and call the whole operation "pastoral care." Few objections have been raised by theologians to this dubious procedure. Yet such practice demonstrates a lack of awareness of the support systems for pastoral care as conceived and sustained for almost two millenia.

There is no traditional objection to receiving *fees for services other than pastoral care*. The problem arises when one borrows the term "pastoral" from ministry and calls such services *pastoral* care or *pastoral* psychotherapy, tending toward a misunderstanding of the adjective "pastoral." It tends to separate the individual from the caring community, to disjoin the pastor from the apostolic witness, and to provide services primarily for those who can pay for them, thus reinforcing class differences rather than seeking to reconcile them. It is appropriate, therefore, in connection with the discussion of abuses of the pastoral office, to state the time-tested reasons why the classical pastoral writers have so persistently rejected the fee-for-service conception of support for ministry.

In professions other than ministry, the pastoral writers have voiced no objection to the reception of reasonable fees. Thomas Aquinas in fact provided a solid argument in defense of the justice of physicians and attorneys receiving fees:

Augustine says that an advocate may lawfully sell his pleading, and a lawyer his advice. . . . A man may justly receive payment for granting what he is not bound to grant. Now it is evident that an advocate is not always bound to consent to plead, or to give advice in other people's causes. Wherefore, if he sells his pleading or advice, he does not act against justice. The same applies to the physician who attends on a sick person to heal him, and to all like persons; provided, however, they take a moderate fee, with due consideration for persons, for the matter in hand, for the labor entailed, and for the custom of the country. (Thomas Aquinas, *Summa Theologica*, Pt. II-II, Q. 71, Art. 4, II, p. 1499)

Criteria here applied to the assessment of a just fee are fairness, moderation, contextual needs of the client, amount of work, and custom. The classical pastoral writers' objection is not to the idea of fees, but to the application of the fee system to pastoral acts that are presumably based on the idea of service. Freely bestowed gifts for the support of the church's ministry are not to be thought of as analogous to just payments for services rendered:

These gifts are not prices, purchases, or sales. We must have our daily sustenance, food and drink; but absolution is not paid for with these. For who would be able to pay it? What are 100 or 1,000 guldens in comparison with the incalculable gift of the forgiveness of sins?
Therefore when we receive sustenance from the church, it is not a price equivalent to this gift, which is worth so much that the wealth of the whole world cannot pay for it. But because this stupendous and incalculable gift cannot be administered except by men who need food and clothing, it is necessary to nourish and support them. This, however, is not payment for the gift; it is payment for the service and the work. (Luther, "Lectures on Genesis Chapters 21 to 25," LW 4, p. 204; cf. WA 43, 282)

Giving freely to support ministry is not an attempt to pay for the services pastors offer, for a price cannot be put on the mediation of God's forgiveness. Support for ministry is not primarily to be viewed as an act of economic justice, but an act of thanksgiving, love, and the praise of God. Gifts are given in gratitude for God's goodness which is manifested through duly called, well-prepared and well-performed pastoral service. But when these are put on a monetary scale of regularized expectation, such as a per hour figure, the whole basis of the relationship is essentially distorted.

Over a millenium before Luther, Tertullian had clarified the reasoning behind a free, voluntary offering, rejecting the contractual fee-for-service conception:

There is no buying and selling of any sort in the things of God. Though we have our treasure-chest, it is not made up of money paid in entrance fees, as if religion were a matter of contract. Everyone once a month brings some modest coin—or whenever he wishes, and only if he does wish, and if he can; for nobody is compelled; it is a voluntary offering. You might call them the trust funds of piety. For they are not spent upon banquets nor drinking-parties nor thankless eating-houses; but to feed the poor and to bury them, to supply the wants of boys and girls destitute of means and parents, and for slaves grown old and ship-wrecked mariners; and if there happen to be any in the mines, or banished to the islands, or shut up in the prisons for no reason except their fidelity to the cause of God's church. These are among those who shall receive support from the confessing church. (Tertullian, *Apology*, 39. 1-6, Loeb, pp. 175-177; cf. ANF I, p. 46)*

Early canon law especially provided that fees were not to be associated in any way with the giving and receiving of holy communion:

That no one, whether bishop, presbyter, or deacon, when giving the immaculate Communion, shall exact from him who communicates fees of any kind. For grace is not to be sold, nor do we give the sanctification of the Holy Spirit for money; but to those who are worthy of the gift it is to be communicated in all simplicity. (Synod of Quinisext, A.D. 692, Canon XXIII, The Seven Ecumenical Councils, NPNF 2, XIV, p. 376)

Menno Simons argued that pastoral services are unpriceable, and therefore not to be viewed primarily as residing within the realm of fees. Nonetheless, voluntary support for ministry to the poor is welcomed and urged:

As they had received the knowledge of the kingdom of God, the truth, love, and Spirit of God, without price, so they were again prepared to dispense it diligently and teach it without price, to their needy brethren. And as for the temporal necessities of life, the begotten church was sufficiently driven by love, through the Spirit and Word of God, to give unto such faithful servants of Christ and watchers of their souls all the necessities of life, to assist them and provide for them all such things which they could not obtain by themselves. O brethren, flee from avarice! (Menno Simons, Brief and Clear Confession, 1544, *CWMS*, p. 443)

Fully attentive "watchers of souls" (pastors) cannot be part-time tradesmen. The Word which was freely given cannot be bought and sold. Those who are unconditionally stewards of sacred mysteries cannot also be entrepreneurs. A pastoral service contingent upon a direct fee may tend to distort or trivialize the pastoral relationship. Nonetheless, the church's ministry needs the support of all who have benefited by it, who understand it and wish to share it. As early as the fourth century, in the Clementine literature, this sort of rationale was provided to lay persons for pastoral support:

[The pastor] having given himself up wholly to labour for you, and needing sustenance, and not being able to attend to his own affairs, how can he procure necessary support? Is it not reasonable that you are to take forethought for his living, not waiting for his asking you, for this is the part of a beggar? But he will rather die of hunger than submit to do this.... Let no one say: Is, then, the word sold which was freely given? Far be it.... If he who has not takes support in order to live—as the Lord also took at supper and among His friends, having nothing, though He alone is the owner of all things—he sins not. Therefore suitably honour elders, catechists, useful deacons, widows who have lived well, orphans as children of the Church. But wherever there is need of any provision for an emergency, contribute all together. (Clementina, *Homilies*, Hom. III, Ch. LXX, ANF VI, p. 251)*

Since Jesus was willing to sit down at the table of many sorts of people and receive food, it was reasoned, so are Christian pastors called upon to accept support for worthy ministry.

Some sort of surveillance may be required in order to prevent fee-for-service support of ministry. If we examine pastoral practice in the Church of England in 1635, we find Archbishop Laud asking annually in each episcopal visitation to a congregation whether any pastor had abused the pastoral office by taking any extraordinary (i.e., outside of the due ordering of ministry) fees for services:

Do you know, or have you heard, that any ecclesiastical judge, officer, or minister, has received or taken any extraordinary fees, or other rewards or promises, by any ways or means, directly or indirectly, from any person or persons whatsoever? (William Laud, Visitation Articles, 1635, sec. 4; *Angl.*, p. 714)*

There have doubtless been in most periods of the church's history incidental exceptions to the rule against reception of fees for pastoral services. This would apply to occasional events such as weddings, etc., upon which the minister's livelihood does not fundamentally depend, but which have been thought in some cultures to be occasions in which token acts of gratitude are considered appropriate, especially if the proceeds are directly to poor relief. But it is quite a different matter when monetary entanglements, billings, payments, or compensations begin fundamentally to preoccupy the pastor or become central or conditional to the offering of pastoral services. Bishop Jeremy Taylor sought to distinguish between more and less fitting forms of pastoral engagement in business affairs:

Let not the name of the Church be made a pretence for personal covetousness. . . . Never exact the offerings, or customary wages, and such as are allowed by law, in the ministration of the sacraments; nor condition for them, nor secure them beforehand: but first do your office, and minister the sacraments purely, readily, and for Christ's sake and when that is done, receive what is your due. . . . Let every minister be careful to live a life as abstracted from the affairs of the world as his necessity will permit him; but in no way immersed and principally employed in the affairs of the world. (Jeremy Taylor, *RAC*, Bk. IV, sec. 6-12; *CS*, pp. 6-8) *

The Anabaptist left wing of Protestantism was especially determined to resist the practice of receiving fees for pastoral service:

One is a hireling who has hired himself out as a servant at certain wages and a stipend. This stands contrary to the example of Christ and of all the true messengers who have been sent by Him. (Menno Simons, Reply to Gellius Faber, 1554, *CWMS*, p. 648)*

Even voluntary gifts to the church's mission to the poor are subject to abuse by those who might deceitfully raise money or peddle influence. Among the charges that Appolonius made against Montanus (c. 211) were self-aggrandizement, deception, and a kind of advertising mentality that abused voluntary offerings. Note the full list of charges:

But who is this new teacher? His works and teaching tells who he is. This is the one who taught the dissolution of marriage; who inculcated fasting; who called two small towns of Phrygia "Jerusalem" (they were Peruga and Tymius), because he wanted to bring people there from all about the country!; who set up exactors of money; who craftily contrived the taking of gifts under the name of voluntary offerings; who even granted stipends to those who would publish his doctrine abroad. (Apollonius, *Concerning Montanism*, sec. 1, ANF VIII, p. 775)*

Thus as early as the third century we find the church having to deal with those who abused ministry in order to make a profit. This appears to be an extraordinarily bold scam based on misrepresentation of facts, not wholly unlike some modern television ministry practices that focus on collecting money, engendering intense enthusiasms, and sometimes taking offerings under false pretenses. On the contrary, learning contempt for riches was thought by Ambrose to be a crucial precondition for becoming a good counselor:

Is it not better that the clergy know how not to be excited at the thought of money, have a contempt for riches, and look down as if from a higher vantage point upon the human passions? . . . It is more fitting that the clergy be superior in soul rather than treasures, and in willing service to friends. . . . But if it is desirable to have one's soul free from this failing, how much more desirable is it to gain the love of the people by liberality which is neither too freely shown to those who are unsuitable, nor too sparingly bestowed upon the needy. . . . The highest kind of liberality is to redeem captives, to save them from the hands of their enemies, to snatch men from death, and most of all, women from shame, to restore children to their parents, parents to their children, and to give back a citizen to his country. (Ambrose, *Duties of the Clergy*, Bk. II, Ch. XIV-XV, sec. 66-70, NPNF 2, X, pp. 53-54)*

II ❧ PASTORAL DISENGAGEMENT FROM WORLDLY PREOCCUPATIONS

It is a common assumption of pastoral writers that upon entry into curacy, the care-giver will systematically disengage from business activities in order to give undivided attention to soul care. The Athanasian Canons stated the point succinctly:

No priest shall sell in the market. (*Athanasian Canons*, sec. 38, p. 33)

The rationale for this restriction hinged largely upon the notion of set-apartness, of priestly separation, purity and the life of holiness:

O thou levitical priest, to what purpose do you sell or buy? For to you is given the first fruits of all. . . . The priests are chosen that they may be more holy than the people and that unto them the offerings may be given, that they may be holy, praying for the people, entreating for their sins, even as Moses said of them that they are those whom "the Lord God hath chosen" (Deut. 18:1-5). And when the priest shall sin like the people, who then will intercede for them? (*Athanasian Canons*, sec. 3, p. 8)*

Although Paul served as a tentmaker for temporal support during portions of his ministry, in subsequent centuries more definite restrictions were placed upon the secular employment of *presbuteroi* who were expected to offer full and undivided energies to the life of prayer and proclamation:

Shake off all the cares of life, being neither a bondsman, nor an advocate, nor involved in any other secular business. For Christ does not wish to appoint you either a judge or an arbitrator in business, or negotiator of the secular affairs of the present life, lest, being confined to the present cares of men, you should not have leisure by the word of truth to separate the good. . . . from the bad. (Clementina, *Epistle of Clement to James*, Ch. V-VI, ANF VIII, p. 219)*

In the Apostolic Constitutions the practice by clergy of usurious lending was rigorously constricted:

Let a bishop, or presbyter, or deacon who requires usury of those he lends to either leave off to do so, or let him be deprived. (*Constitutions of the Holy Apostles*, Ecclesiastical Canons, Canon 44, ANF VII, p. 502)

With the specific exception of business activities necessary to care for the poor, widows and minors, and of assigned ecclesiastical business, clergy were not permitted by the Council of Chalcedon to engage in entrepreneurial management of businesses:

It has come to (the knowledge of) the holy Synod that certain of those who are enrolled among the clergy have, through lust of gain, become hirers of other men's possessions, and make contracts pertaining to secular affairs, lightly esteeming the service of God, and slip into the houses of secular persons, whose property they undertake through covetousness to manage. Wherefore the great and holy Synod decrees that henceforth no bishop, clergyman, nor monk shall hire possessions, or engage in business, or occupy himself in worldly engagements, unless he shall be called by the law to the guardianship of minors, from which there is no escape; or unless the bishop of the city shall commit to him the care of ecclesiastical business, or of unprovided orphans or widows and of persons who stand especially in need of the Church's help, through the fear of God. (Chalcedon, A.D. 451, Canon III, The Seven Ecumenical Councils, NPNF 2, XIV, p. 269)

Ministry is to be freed from temporal affairs in order to study and serve:

Sirach says, 38:24-26: "The wisdom of a scribe (namely for the kingdom of heaven) requires opportunity for leisure; and it is necessary for him to be free of other matters, who wants either to obtain that wisdom for himself or impart it to others. For how can he deal with wisdom, who must hold the plow and drive oxen, etc.?" The office of a minister of the church therefore is that he diligently study the holy Scriptures and give himself to reading them (1 Ti 4:13), moreover, that he labor in the Word and doctrine (1 Ti 5:17), that he feed the flock of Christ and the church of God (1 Ptr 5:2; Acts 20:28); that is, he is to serve the church with the preaching of the Word and administration of the Sacraments and the use of the keys. As Origen aptly writes on Lev. 8: "These two are works of a priest: First, that he learn of God by reading the Holy Scriptures and frequent meditation, and that he teach the people, but that he teach the things that he himself has learned from God. There is also another work, which Moses does: he does not go to war, but prays for the people." (Chemnitz, *MWS*, Part 2, sec. 33, p. 38)

Wherever the pastor becomes preoccupied with financial affairs, Luther thought, the caring tasks easily become displaced. It is better that the pastor entrust temporal support to the laity and live without complaint on whatever resources are available:

A true minister of Christ should not be concerned about money and creature comforts (*deliciis*), which are a cause of avarice, but about the care which he exercises in his actual calling. And money is not worth arguing about, because it makes proud and does this only for a little while; it does not go with us when we die. (Luther, W-T 2, #2796; WLS 2, pp. 940-941)

More dangerous, according to Menno Simons, was the temptation of clergy to neglect the poor in pursuing their own economic interest:

O preachers, dear preachers, where is the power of the Gospel you preach? Where is the thing signified in the Supper you administer? Where are the fruits of the spirit you have received? And where is the righteousness of your faith which you dress up so beautifully before the poor, ignorant people? Is it not all hypocrisy that you preach, maintain, and assert? Shame on you for the easygoing gospel and barren bread-breaking, you who have in so many years been unable to effect enough with your gospel and sacraments so as to remove your needy and distressed members from the streets, even though the Scripture plainly teaches and says, "But if a man has enough to live on, and yet when he sees his brother in need shuts up his heart against him, how can it be said that the divine love dwells in him?" (1 John 3:17). Also Moses said: "There will never be any poor among you if only you obey the Lord your God" (Deut. 15:4). (Menno Simons, Reply to False Accusations, 1554, *CWMS*, p. 559)

III ❧ Support of Ministries

It is clear from the above selections that the pastoral writers rejected direct fee support from individuals for pastoral services contingent upon payment. Some might therefore prematurely conclude that the pastoral writers rejected all regularized arrangements for the support of ministries, but this is not the case. Proper means of temporal support of soul care has been a much-debated question from New Testament times to the present. It is now useful to set forth the reasons why the mainstream pastoral tradition has appealed not to individual fees for services, but to a biblically and theologically grounded system of support for ministry in which gratitude, stewardship, and mutually shared responsibility are interrelated themes. They appealed to earlier Hebraic traditions of tithing and first-fruits in their reasoning about support of Christian ministries. Thomas Aquinas drew together much of this reasoning in his treatise on tithes:

"It is a duty to pay tithes, and whoever refuses to pay them takes what belongs to another" [Augustine, Append. Serm. cclxxiv]. I answer that: In the Old Law tithes were paid for the sustenance of the ministers of God; hence it is written (Malachi 3:10): "Bring the tithes into the treasury, all of them; let there be food in my house." Hence the precept about the paying of tithes was partly moral and instilled in the natural reason; and partly judicial, deriving its force from its divine institution. Natural reason dictates that the people should administer the necessities of life to those who minister the divine worship for the welfare of the whole people even as it is the people's duty to provide a livelihood for their rulers and soldiers and so forth. Hence the Apostle proves this from human custom, saying (1 Cor. 9:7): "Did you ever hear of a man serving in the army at his own expense? or planting a vineyard without earning the fruit of it?". . . For ten is, in a way, the perfect number (being the first numerical limit since the figures do not go beyond ten but begin over again from one), and therefore he that gave a tenth, which is the sign of perfection, reserving the nine other parts for himself, acknowledged by a sign that imperfection was his part, and that the perfection which was to come through Christ was to be hoped for from God. . . . The right to receive tithes is a spiritual thing, for it arises from the debt in virtue of which the ministers of the altar have a right to the expenses of their ministry, and temporal things are due to those who sow spiritual things. This debt concerns none but the clergy who have care of souls, and so they alone are competent to have this right. (Thomas Aquinas, *Summa Theologica*, Pt. II-II, Q. 87, Art. 1-3, II, pp. 1562-1565, NEB)*

Several pivotal principles undergird Thomas' interpretation: temporal support is pertinent to and needed for those who offer spiritual gifts; the fruits of tithing are intrinsically connected with the idea of caring for souls; both mystical significance and moral reasoning have become attached to the idea of a tenth. For giving the first tenth and keeping the remainder meant that one was giving the perfect to God and withholding the imperfect for oneself. One of the earliest Christian writings, the Didache, appealed to the tradition of offering first-fruits as tithe. It assumed that one gives the first and best quality of the ten parts, not the last or least:

Take the first products of your winepress, your threshing-floor, your oxen and your sheep, and give them as firstfruits to the charismatists, for nowadays it is they who are your "High Priests." If there is no charismatist among you, give them to the poor. And when you bake a batch of loaves, take the first of them and give it away, as the commandment directs. Similarly when you broach a jar of wine or oil, take the first portion to give to the charismatists. So, too, with your money, and your clothing, and all your possessions; take a tithe of them in whatever way you think best, and make a gift of it, as the commandment bids you. (*Didache*, sec. 13, ECW, p. 234)

The same texts were appealed to in the Apostolic Constitutions:

You shall give a tenth of your produce to the orphan and to the widow, and to the poor, and to the stranger. The first-fruits of your hot bread, your barrels of wine, oil, honey, nuts, grapes, and the first-fruits of other things you shall give to the *presbuteroi*. But those of silver, and of garments, and of all sort of possessions, give to the orphan and to the widow. (*Constitutions of the Holy Apostles*, Bk. VII, Sec. II, Ch. XXIX, ANF VII, p. 471)*

Distributions to the poor were to be made through the office of ministry. Origen argued that it is proper that Christian *presbuteroi*—analogous to priests in the Levitical tradition—should live from the freely-given voluntary support of laity, in order to devote undivided energies to the care of souls:

The levites and priests, on the other hand, have no possessions but tithes and first fruits. . . . The same is the case with those who approach Christian studies. Most of us devote most of our time to the things of this life, and dedicate to God only a few special acts, thus resembling those members of the [non-Levitical] tribes. . . . But those who devote themselves to the divine word and have no other employment but the service of God may not unnaturally . . . be called our levites and priests. . . . Now our whole activity is devoted to God, and our whole life, since we are bent on progress in divine things. (Origen, *Commentary on John*, sec. 3-4, ANF X, p. 298)

The Apostolic Constitutions coalesced the ox-muzzling, levitical, and first-fruits analogies:

It is written, "You shall not muzzle an ox while it is treading out the corn" (Deut. 25:4). . . . The ox that labours in the threshing-floor without a muzzle does indeed eat but does not eat up everything. Similarly, you who labour in the threshing-floor, that is, in the Church of God, feed from the resources of the Church. This was also the case of the Levites, who served in the tabernacle of the testimony, which was in every way a type of the Church. Furthermore its very name implied that the earlier tabernacle was providentially given as a testimony to the Church. Levites who attended the tabernacle received those things that were offered to God by all the people—gifts, offerings, first-fruits, tithes, sacrifices, and oblations. . . . Those who exercise care for the Church ought to be maintained by the Church as similar to priests, Levites, presidents, and ministers of God. It is written in the book of Numbers concerning the priests: "I give you all the choicest of the oil, the choicest of the new wine and the corn, the firstfruits which are given to the Lord. The first-ripe fruits of all produce in the land which are brought to the Lord shall be yours" (Numbers 18:12,13). (*Constitutions of the Holy Apostles*, Bk. II, Sec. IV, Ch. XXV, ANF VII, p. 409, NEB)*

Diaconal, presbuteral and episcopal support begins with gifts gratefully and freely given by the laity. The supported ministries are then thought to be responsible to God to administer resources faithfully, mercifully and fairly:

Give to the priest that which is due, the first-fruits of your harvest, of your wine-press, and sacrificial offerings, as if he were mediating between God and those who stand in need of purgation and forgiveness. It is your duty to give and his to administer, since he is the steward and disposer of churchly matters. You are not in a position to call your bishop to account, or watch his administration, how he does what, when, to whom, or where, or whether he does it well or poorly or indifferently. For the bishop already has Another who will call him sufficiently to an account, the Lord God, who put this administration into his hands, and thought him worthy of an office of such great importance. (*Constitutions of the Holy Apostles*, Bk. II, sec. IV, Ch. XXXV, ANF VII, p. 413)*

Funds assigned to Christian ministry are not to be diverted for private use:

Let the bishop have the care of ecclesiastical revenues, and administer them as in the presence of God. But it is not lawful for him to appropriate any part of them to himself, or to give the things of God to his own kindred. (*Constitutions of the Holy Apostles*, Bk. VIII, Sec. V, Ch. XLVII, ANF VII, p. 502)

The Athanasian canons warned against left-over, second-rate, or tawdry offerings for the support of soul care. The bread is to be "fresh and whole," for it is God's own mission and ministry that one is supporting:

All the first-fruits of corn, wine and beasts of burden shall be given to the priests of the church, and from it there shall be taken a choice offering into the sanctuary; and what remains the servants of the Lord shall eat. An offering that remains over from yesterday shall not be offered, nor any offering that has already been divided into pieces previously in any church. Rather use bread that is warm, fresh and whole. (*Athanasian Canons*, sec. 63-64, p. 42)*

The pastor to whom is given the task of serving the poor shall be willing to share in their poverty:

If you shall still say that you cannot live so meanly as poor people do, I further ask whether your parishioners can better endure damnation than you can endure want and poverty. . . . Should you not rather beg your bread than put to risk or disadvantage so great a matter as salvation? . . . This poverty is not so intolerable and dangerous a thing as it is pretended to be. If you have but food and rainment, must you not be content? . . . "A man's life consisteth not in the abundance of the things that he possesseth" (Luke 12:15). If your clothing be warm, and your food be wholesome, you may be as well supported by it to do God's service as if you had the fullest satisfaction to your flesh. (Baxter, *RP*, pp. 92-94)*

Appeals were made to encourage laity in the sharing of God's ministry to the world, but with a solemn awareness that both wealth and lack of it stand equally reduced before the majesty of God:

What good is what we possess if we do not make God a sharer in what we possess? If there is someone poor like Elias' widow, or sick like the lame man who received alms, he shall be honored as one who is making an offering of himself to God. And even if what he offers is small, yet shall it be a remembrance of himself. For not only is he remembered who gives gold to the sanctuary, but he that gives an earthen cup or bread or a little wine or a water-vessel, or who fills up a tankard with water as a gift. God remembers him as much as another who gives out of his riches. (*Athanasian Canons*, sec. 84, p. 51)*

Clergy as well as laity are called upon to offer tithes:

It it fitting not only for the laity to give tithes, but the clergy also, from the bishop to the door-keeper. (*Athanasian Canons*, sec. 83, p. 50)*

IV 🕏 Answering Critics

Since the pastor is in a highly visible public office which cannot altogether avoid criticism, it is necessary to learn to face conflicts, hear out critics, assess them appropriately, and answer proportionally. It is better that the pastor not compulsively ignore criticism, but promptly respond, before the imagination of greater error grows in the minds of the doubtful:

The right course is neither to show disproportionate fear and anxiety over ill-directed abuse (for the president will have to put up with unfounded criticism), nor simply to ignore it. We should try to extinguish criticisms at once, even if they are false and are levelled at us by quite ordinary people. . . . We should leave nothing untried that might destroy an evil report. (John Chrysostom, *On the Priesthood*, Ch. V, sec. 3, p. 129)

Pastors do better to utilize limited energies defending the Word than focussing upon their own personal integrity:

If anyone undeservedly persecutes, slanders, and curses my person, I should and will say *Deo gratias* (thank God) for this, because God will richly bless me for suffering such injustice. But if anyone assails the Baptism, Sacrament, and ministry committed to me by God and thus does not attack me but God, it does not become me to be silent, merciful, and friendly; then I must maintain the office committed to me and "use argument, reproof, and appeal," as St. Paul says, "with all the patience that the work of teaching requires" (2 Tim. 4:2), in season and out of season, for those who do not teach and believe correctly or do not amend their lives, no matter who they may be or how they may like it. (Luther, WA 22, pp. 62ff.; WLS 3, pp. 1113-1114)*

John Chrysostom, in his analysis of challenges distinctive to ministry, correctly realized that defects tend to be exceptionally long remembered:

Men are so made that they overlook their neighbour's successes, however many or great; yet if a defect comes to light, however commonplace and however long since it last occured, it is quickly noticed, fastened on at once, and never forgotten. So a trifling and unimportant fault has often curtailed the glory of many fine achievements. (John Chrysostom, *On the Priesthood*, Ch. V, sec. 5, p. 131)

Chrysostom noted a special temptation in pastoral service to love and desire applause overmuch. This may make clergy especially sensitive to even the hint of censure, or more subtly, the lack of being constantly praised:

We should not be much elated by their praise nor much dejected by their censure, when we get these things from them out of season. This is not easy, my friend, and I think it may be impossible. I do not know whether anyone has ever succeeded in not enjoying praise. If he enjoys it, he naturally wants to receive it. And if he wants to receive it, he cannot help being pained and distraught at losing it. People who enjoy being wealthy take it hard when they fall into poverty, and those who are used to luxury cannot bear to live frugally. So, too, men who are in love with applause have their spirits starved not only when they are blamed off-hand, but even when they fail to be constantly praised. (John Chrysostom, *On the Priesthood*, Ch. V, sec. 4, p. 130)

One who tells the truth may as well expect resistance:

The truth is something men do not like; they become angry with him who tells them the truth. (Luther, W-T 6, #6784; WLS 3, p. 1169)

Luther regarded his greatest temptation the wish to remain at peace and uncondemned by everyone:

I know that if my cause is just, it must be condemned on earth, and approved only by Christ in heaven; for all the Scriptures show that the cause of Christians and of Christendom must be judged by God alone. Such a cause has never yet been approved by men on earth, but the opposition has always been too great and strong. It is my greatest care and fear that my cause may remain uncondemned, by which I should know for certain that it was not yet pleasing to God. (Luther, "An Open Letter to the Christian Nobility," WML II, p. 164)

Some decry mostly those who excel them. Thus it may happen ironically that the higher quality of one's work may be attested by the lower quality of one's detractors. In defending a theological master like Origen from his less-gifted critics, the Constantinopolitan Church historian, Socrates (c. 380-450) wrote:

Worthless characters, and such as are destitute of ability to attain eminence themselves, often seek to get into notice by decrying those who excel them. And first Methodius, bishop of a city in Lycia named Olympus, labored under this malady; next Eustathius, who for a short time presided over the church at Antioch; after him Apollinaris; and lastly Theophilus. This quaternion of revilers has traduced Origen. . . . But I affirm that from the censure of these men, greater commendation accrues to Origen. (Socrates Scholasticus, *Ecclesiastical History*, Ch. XIII, VI. 13, NPNF 2, II, p. 147)

Jerome was sadly aware of the temptation of some persons in ministry to gain public favor by discrediting others. In writing Augustine

(402 A.D.) on an issue that might have divided them, he pleaded for a spirit of mutual correction, and reflected upon the spirit of divisiveness:

Far be it from me to presume to attack anything which your Grace has written. For it is enough for me to prove my own views without controverting what others hold. But it is well known to one of your wisdom, that every one is satisfied with his own opinion, and that it is puerile self-sufficiency to seek, as young men have of old been wont to do, to gain glory to one's own name by assailing men who have become renowned. I am not so foolish as to think myself insulted by the fact that you give an explanation different from mine; since you, on the other hand, are not wronged by my views being contrary to those which you maintain. But that is the kind of reproof by which friends may truly benefit each other, when each, not seeing his own bag of faults, observes, as Persius has it, the wallet borne by the other. Let me say further, love one who loves you, and do not because you are young challenge a veteran in the field of Scripture. I have had my time, and have run my course to the utmost of my strength. It is but fair that I should rest, while you in your turn run and accomplish great distances; at the same time (with your leave, and without intending any disrespect), lest it should seem that to quote from the poets is a thing which you alone can do, let me remind you of the encounter between Dares and Entellus, and the proverb, "The tired ox treads with a firmer step." With sorrow I have dictated these words. Would that I could receive your embrace, and that by converse we might aid each other in learning! (Jerome, To Augustine, in Augustine, *Letters*, LXVIII, NPNF 1, I, p. 324-325)

Hugh Latimer, burned with Ridley at the Oxford stake in 1555, had to defend himself against false and absurd charges that viciously blamed him for consequences which he did not cause. In this case, he had been falsely accused of preaching rebellion. He adroitly examined the *non sequitur* of his accusers:

It is we preachers that trouble England. We preached against covetousness last year in Lent, and the next summer followed rebellion. Ergo, preaching against covetousness was the cause of the rebellion! A fine argument!

Here now I remember an anecdote of Master More's (Lord-Chancellor Sir Thomas More) set forth in a book he wrote against Bilney. I will tell you the pleasant tale. Master More was once sent in commission into Kent, to find out if he could what might be the cause of movement of the Goodwin Sands, and the shelf that stopped up Sandwich haven. Along came Master More, and called out from around the country such as were thought to be men of experience, who could most likely reason with him concerning the stopping of the movement of Sandwich haven. Among others there came before him an old man with a white head who was thought to be little less than a hundred years old. When Master More saw this aged man, he thought it expedient to hear him speak his mind in this matter; for, being so old a man, it was likely that he knew most of any man in that company. So Master More called this old aged man unto him, and said, "Father, tell me, if you can, what is the cause of this great rising of the sands and shelves here about this haven, which stop it up so that no ships can arrive here? You are the oldest man that I can find in all this company, so that if any man can tell any cause of it, you it is likely can say most in it, or at least more than any other man here assembled." "Yea, forsooth, good master," said this old man, "for I am well-nigh a hundred years old, and no man here in this company is anything near to my age." "Well, then," said Master More, "how say you in this matter? What think you are the causes of these shelves and flats that stop up Sandwich haven?" "Forsooth, sir," said he, "I am an old man; I think that Tenterden steeple is the cause of Goodwin Sands. For I am an old man, sir," said he, "and I may remember the building of Tenterden steeple, and I remember when there was no steeple at all there. And before that Tenterden steeple was built, there was no speaking of any flats or sands that stopped the haven, and therefore I think that Tenterden steeple is the cause of the destroying and decay of Sandwich haven." Thus said this old man, and even so to my purpose is preaching of God's Word the cause of rebellion, as Tenterden steeple was the cause that Sandwich haven is decayed!" (Hugh Latimer, Defense, OCC I, pp. 57-58)*

V ❧ Dealing with False Accusations

When ministry is under unjust attack by those who would seek to discredit it, it is fitting to respond proportionally in a way that is consistent with everything else that the care of souls stands for. This may require astute efforts to preserve the community from devisiveness. From Jesus' ministry to the present, the care of souls has had to deal with serious challenges from determined detractors. Nothing is more salutary, under such circumstances, than to reflect fundamentally upon the nature of the church as a redemptive community:

Jesus was called a winebibber, a blasphemer, and one possessed of the devil. Paul was called mutinous and an apostate Jew, etc. Behold, thus in their time the mission of the faithful servants of the Lord, nay, of the Lord and Messiah Himself, was despised, although bolstered by many miracles. How much more then shall we be despised, who are such weak and insignificant instruments, and come to a seven fold more wicked and evil world than theirs was. Inasmuch then as we are so reviled by our opponents, the learned ones, that we are not called of a church of God, but of false prophets, or a false church, therefore I would briefly admonish the reader to weigh well with the Scriptures who, how, and what the church of God is. It is not a collection of proud, avaricious, usurers, pompous, drunkards, and impenitent as the church of the world is, of whom the learned ones are called, but a gathering or congregation of saints, as the Holy Scriptures and the Nicene Creed clearly teach and present, namely, those who through true faith are regenerated by God unto Christ Jesus and are of a divine nature, who would gladly regulate their lives according to the Spirit, Word, and example of the Lord, who are actuated by His Spirit, and are willing and ready patiently to bear the cross of their Lord Jesus Christ. (Menno Simons, Reply to Gellius Faber, 1554, *CWMS*, pp. 666-667)*

False accusations against the pastor are best answered through a life lived in congruence with one's teachings. Those who make such accusations should be brought to realize that they may cause great harm, as happened in the suffering of Menno Simons, who for many years was hunted down as an outlaw on the basis of false accusations by ordained ministers:

Some alas, from a perverted heart, say that I eat more roasted than they do seethed; and that I drink more wine than they do beer. My Lord and Master, Jesus Christ, was also called a winebibber and a glutton by the perverse. I trust that through the grace of the Lord I am innocent in this matter, and stand acquitted before God. He who purchased me with the blood of His love, and called me, who am unworthy, to His service, knows me, and He knows that I seek not wealth, nor possessions, nor luxury, nor ease, but only the praise of the Lord, my salvation, and the salvation of many souls. Because of this, I with my poor, weak wife and children have for eighteen years endured excessive anxiety, oppression, affliction, misery, and persecution. At the peril of my life I have been compelled everywhere to drag out an existence in fear. Yes, when the preachers repose on easy beds and soft pillows, we generally have to hide ourselves in out-of-the-way corners. When they at weddings and baptismal banquets revel with pipe, trumpet, and lute; we have to be on our guard when a dog barks for fear the arresting officer has arrived. When they are greeted as doctors, lords, and teachers by everyone, we have to hear that we are Anabaptists, bootleg preachers, deceivers, and heretics, and be saluted in the devil's name. In short, while they are gloriously rewarded for their services with large incomes and good times, our recompense and portion must be fire, sword, and death. (Menno Simons, Reply to Gellius Faber, 1554, *CWMS*, pp. 673-674)

Calvin often had to deal with accusations that were fabricated out of whole cloth. Here are some of his reflections on why these stories seem so delicious to his detractors:

Because I affirm and maintain that the world is managed and governed by the secret providence of God, a multitude of presumptuous men rise up against me, and allege that I represent God as the author of sin. This is so foolish a calumny, that it would of itself quickly come to nothing, did it not meet with persons who have tickled ears, and who take pleasure in feeding upon such discourse. But there are many whose minds are so filled with envy and spleen, or ingratitude, or malignity, that there is no falsehood, however preposterous, yea, even monstrous, which they do not receive, if it is spoken to them. . . . Others circulated ridiculous reports concerning my treasures; others, of the extravagant authority and enormous influence which they say I possess; others speak of my delicacies and magnificence. . . . And if there are some whom I cannot persuade whilst I am alive that I am not rich, my death at length will prove it. I confess, indeed, that I am not poor; for I desire nothing more than what I have. All these are invented stories, and there is no colour whatever for any one of them, but many nevertheless are very easily persuaded of their truth, and applaud them; and the reason is, because the greatest part judge that the only means of cloaking their enormities is to throw all things into disorder. (John Calvin, Preface to Psalms, SW, pp. 30-32)

Innocent pastors have a right to be defended, and to have their rights protected by ecclesiastical due process and civil guarantees. As bishop, Augustine often came to the defense of pastors falsely accused, as in the case of Boniface:

Let me therefore say in a few words to your Charity, that the presbyter Boniface has not been discovered by me to be guilty of any crime, and that I have never believed, and do not yet believe, any charge brought against him. How, then, could I order his name to be deleted from the roll of presbyters? . . . As a bishop, I ought not rashly to suspect him; and as being only a man, I cannot decide infallibly concerning things which are hidden from me. (Augustine, *Letters*, LXXVII, NPNF 1, I, p. 345)

Nonetheless, Augustine argued that a magnanimous resignation could be exceedingly honorable in cases where it might serve to protect the unity and peace of the church:

It is a far more magnanimous thing to have resigned the onerous responsibilities of the bishop's dignity in order to save the Church from danger, than to have accepted these in order to have a share in her government. He truly proves that he was worthy of holding that office, had the interests of peace permitted him to do so, who does not insist upon retaining it when he cannot do so without endangering the peace of the Church. . . . In laying down that ministry of stewardship of the mysteries of God, he was not deserting his duty under the pressure of some worldly desire, but acting under the impulse of a pious love of peace, lest, on account of the honour conferred upon him there should arise among the members of Christ an unseemly and dangerous, perhaps even fatal, dissension. (Augustine, *Letters*, LXIX, sec. 1, NPNF 1, I, p. 325)

Among principle values under such conditions of conflict are the tranquility and cohesion of the caring community. John Chrysostom went further in arguing that it is not always a disgrace to be expelled from an order of ministry. Rather under some circumstances it could be an extraordinary badge of honor:

"Blessed are ye" says our Lord, "when men shall reproach you and persecute you, and say all manner of evil against you falsely for my sake. Rejoice and be exceeding glad; for great is your reward in heaven" (Matt. 5:11-12). This is surely true even when anyone is expelled by men of his own order, either through envy or to please others or through enmity or any other wrong motive. But when he gets this treatment from his enemies, I do not think any argument is needed to prove how great a benefit they confer on him by their wickedness. (John Chrysostom, *On the Priesthood*, Ch. III, sec. 11, p. 81)

Great pastors have handled conflicted periods in imaginative ways. An amazing story is told by Palladius concerning Athanasius, who patiently waited for seven years for an opposing tyrannical Arian regime to fold, willing to risk scandal in order to persist in his mission:

In Alexandria I knew a virgin whom I met when she was about seventy years old. All the clergy confirmed that when she was a young maiden of about twenty she was exceedingly pretty and really to be avoided because of her beauty, lest one be suspected of having been with her. Now it happened that the Arians were in conspiracy against Saint Athanasius, the Bishop of Alexandria, working through Eusebius while Constantius was Emperor. They were bringing false charges and accusing Athanasius of unlawful deeds, and he fled to avoid the risk of being judged by a corrupt court. He trusted his person to no one, not to relative, friend, cleric, or anyone else. But when the prefects came suddenly into the bishop's palace looking for him, he fled in the middle of the night, taking only his tunic and cloak, and went to the maiden. She was astonished and frightened by this.

He told her: "Since the Arians are searching for me and have informed on me unjustly, I made up my mind to flee so that I might not get a bad reputation and be the cause of a crime by those who want to punish me. Just this night now God made it clear to me that I will be saved by no one but you."

With great joy then she cast all doubts to the wind and became an instrument of the Lord. She hid the most holy man for six years, until the death of Constantius. She washed his feet and cared for all his bodily needs and his personal affairs, obtaining the loan of books for his use. During these six years no one in Alexandria knew where Saint Athanasius was spending his time.

When news of the death of Constantius reached him, he got dressed and appeared in the church at night. All were amazed and looked on him as one risen from the dead. (Palladius, *The Lausiac History*, Ch. 63, sec. 1-4, ACW 34, pp. 144-145)

Palladius is the source of another case study of an unjust accusation by and toward clergy. The lector of this story was innocently accused. His ministry under these entangled conditions focussed upon a redemptive attempt to help those who had been harmed, and to appeal in prayer to divine mercy and justice:

A maiden, daughter of a priest in Caesarea of Palestine, fell, and she had been coached by her despoiler to accuse a certain lector in the city. And as she was now pregnant and her father was asking questions, she put the blame on the lector. The bishop called the priests together and had the lector called in also. The whole matter was investigated and the lector, upon being questioned, did not confess—for how could he admit something which had never happened?

The bishop was vexed and spoke to him severely: "You will not confess, you wretched and miserable man, glutted with impurity?"

The lector replied: "I told you that it was not of my doing. I am innocent of any design upon her. But if you insist on hearing something, even if it is not true, then I did it."

When the lector said this, the bishop deposed him. Then he came to the bishop and said: "Well, since I have made a mistake, command her to be given to me in marriage, for I am no longer a cleric, nor is she a maiden."

Then he gave her over to the lector, supposing that the young man would stay by her and could not help but continue his relations with her. But the young man took her from the bishop and her father and entrusted her to a monastery of women. He enjoined the deaconess of the sisterhood there to care for her until it was time for the child to be born.

It was not long before it was the time for her to give birth. The decisive hour had come. Sighs, pangs, labors, visions of the underworld—and still the child was not born!

Then passed the first, the second, the third day, a week—the woman, in hell with her pain, did not eat, drink, or sleep, but kept calling out, saying: "Miserable me, I am in danger for having accused this lector falsely."

They hurried off and told this to her father. He was afraid of being condemned as an informer and kept his peace for two more days. The young lady did not die, but she also did not deliver her child. As they could no longer bear her outcries, they ran and told the bishop: "This woman has confessed, crying out for days now that she falsely accused the lector."

Then the bishop sent deacons to the lector with a message for him: "Pray that the woman who accused you falsely may deliver her child."

He gave them no answer, he did not even open the door, but he had been praying to God from the day he went inside.

Again the father went to the bishop and prayers were recited in church—and still she did not give birth. Then the bishop got up and went to the lector, knocked on the door, went in, and said to him: "Eustathius, arise, and open the door you have closed."

At once the lector knelt down with the bishop and the woman was delivered of the child. His prayer and persistence had prevailed both to show the chicanery and to teach a lesson to the one who had made the false accusation. From this we may learn to devote ourselves to prayer and to know its power. (Palladius, *The Lausiac History*, No. 70, sec. 1-5, ACW 34, pp. 151-152)

With his usual generosity and wisdom, George Herbert commented on the varied ways that pastors may respond to those who hold them in contempt:

The Country Parson knows well, that,—both for the general ig-nominy which is cast upon the profession, and much more for those rules which out of his choicest judgment he hath resolved to observe, and which are described in this book,—he must be despised. . . . Nevertheless, according to the apostle's rule, he endeavors that none shall despise him; especially in his own parish he suffers it not, to his utmost power, for that, where contempt is, there is no room for instruction. . . . He that will be respected, must respect; . . . when any despises him, he takes it either in an humble way, saying nothing at all; or else in a slighting way, showing that reproaches touch him no more than a stone thrown against heaven, where he is and lives; or in a sad way, grieved at his own and others' sins. (George Herbert, CP, Ch. XXVIII, CWS, p. 95)

VI ❦ Inquiry into Pastoral Abuses

When abuses of the pastoral office have been charged, circumspect inquiry is required. Careful procedures have been worked out over the course of much historical experience to seek to protect the conflicting rights of various parties. Efforts at reconciliation must come first, which if unsuccessful, must be followed by rigorous efforts at equity.

Polycarp, Bishop of Smyrna (c. 69-c. 155), a direct link between the apostlic age and the second century writers, set a moderating pattern.

He thought it inappropriate to be harsh on clergy who have fallen. He plead for serious efforts at reconciliation rather than a hasty, judgmental attitude:

I feel the deepest sorrow for that man [Valens] and his wife; may the Lord grant them real repentance. You too, for your part, must not be over severe with them, for people of that kind are not to be looked on as enemies; you have to restore them, like parts of your own person that are ailing and going wrong, so that the whole body can be maintained in health. Do this, and you will be promoting your own spiritual welfare at the same time. (Polycarp, *To the Philippians*, ECW, pp. 148-149)

The motive of accusers requires careful analysis. Justin Martyr (c. 100-c. 165), stated an early form of the protection of the rights of the accused:

If anyone brings an accusation and proves that the men referred to have done anything contrary to the laws, you will assign penalties in accordance with the character of the offenses. But you must certainly take the greatest care, that if anyone accuses any of these people merely for the sake of calumny, you will punish him with severe penalties for his offense. (Justin Martyr, *First Apology*, sec. 68, LCC I, pp. 288-289)

Accusations were to be supported by more than one or two witnesses, to protect against personal invective:

There shall no accusation be received against any man that is reckoned of the priesthood, from the bishop unto the doorkeeper, except it be with three witnesses. (*Athanasian Canons*, sec. 53, p. 37)

In Augustine's struggle with the Donatists, he chided them for their lack of interest in dialogue, and for their neglect of due process and abuse of fair procedures:

Some of your predecessors, in whose impious schism you obstinately remain, delivered up to persecutors the sacred manuscripts, and the vessels of the Church (as may be seen in municipal records), . . . [and] condemned others without a hearing. . . . Let your bishops answer these questions to your laity at least, if they will not debate with us; and do you, as you value your salvation, consider what kind of doctrine that must be about which they refuse to enter into discussion with us. If the wolves have prudence enough to keep out of the way of the shepherds, why have the flock so lost their prudence, that they go into the dens of the wolves? (Augustine, *Letters*, LXXVI, sec. 3-4, NPNF 1, I, p. 344)

In seeking to sustain a high ethic of ministry, Calvin's *Draft Ecclestical Ordinances* set forth a list of possible charges against clergy, and an order for guaranteeing due process:

To obviate all scandals of living, it will be proper that there be a form of correction to which all submit themselves. It will also be the means by which the ministry may retain respect, and the Word of God be neither dishonoured nor scorned because of the ill reputation of the ministers. For as one is to correct those who merit it, so it will be proper to reprove calumnies and false reports which are made unjustly against innocent people.

But first it should be noted that there are crimes which are quite intolerable in a minister, and there are faults which may on the other hand be endured while direct fraternal admonitions are offered.

Of the first sort are:

heresy, schism, rebellion against ecclesiastical order, blasphemy open and meriting civil punishment, simony and all corruption in presentations, intrigue to occupy another's place, leaving one's Church without lawful leave or just calling, duplicity, perjury, lewdness, larceny, drunkenness, assault meriting punishment by law, usury, games forbidden by the law and scandalous, dances and similar dissoluteness, crimes carrying with them loss of civil rights, crime giving rise to another separation from the Church.

Of the second sort are:

strange methods of treating Scripture which turn to scandal, curiosity in investigating idle questions, advancing some doctrine or kind of practice not received in the Church, negligence in studying and reading the Scriptures, negligence in rebuking vice amounting to flattery, negligence in doing everything required by his office, scurrility, lying, slander, dissolute words, injurious words, foolhardiness and evil devices, avarice and too great parsimony, undisciplined anger, quarrels and contentions, laxity either of manner or of gesture and like conduct improper to a minister. (John Calvin, *Draft Ecclesiastical Ordinances*, 1541, SW, p. 232)

Augustine thought that it would not be good order if a minister in disrepute in one diocese should be readily welcomed and well-received by another:

If you come to us while debarred from communion with the venerable bishop Aurelius, you cannot be admitted to communion with us; but we would act towards you with that same charity which we are assured shall guide his conduct. Your coming to us, however, should not on this account be embarrassing to us, because the duty of submission to this, out of regard to the discipline of the Church, ought to be felt by yourself, especially if you have the approval of your own conscience, which is known to yourself and to God. (Augustine, *Letters*, LXIV, NPNF 1, I, p. 321)

The early church synods sought to guarantee the right of appeal and to protect pastors against the wrath of irrascible bishops. The presumption of innocence was assumed:

If some bishop is perchance quick to anger (which ought not to be the case) and, moved hastily and violently against one of his presbyters or deacons, decides to cast him out of the Church, provision must be made that an innocent man be not condemned or deprived of communion. Therefore let him that is cast out be authorized to appeal to the neighbouring bishops and let his case be heard and examined into more diligently. For a hearing ought not to be denied one who asks it. (Council of Sardica, A.D. 343 or 344, Canon XIV, The Seven Ecumenical Councils, NPNF 2, XIV, p. 428)

The principle of assuming innocence was clearly operative in this concluding epistle by Augustine. He argued that clergy under charges should not be prematurely barred from Christian community:

Even in secular affairs, when a perplexing case is referred to a higher authority, the inferior judges do not presume to make any change while the reference is pending. Moreover, it was decreed in a Council of bishops that no clergyman who has not yet been proved guilty be suspended from communion, unless he fail to present himself for the examination of the charges against him. (Augustine, *Letters*, LXXVIII, sec. 4, NPNF, I, p. 346)

The selections of Part Eight have sought to show reasons why ministry is better supported by free gifts than by contracted fees for services, and why ministry has traditionally been regarded as a full-time calling requiring disengagement from worldly occupations and temporal affairs. In the event of accusations of conduct unbecoming to a minister, the classic pastoral tradition has provided guidelines for fair hearing, due process, and the presumption of innocence.

Conclusion

EIGHT CONCLUSIONS FOLLOW from these selections on soul care in the classical pastoral literature:

(1) Pastors owe a duty not only to care for the flock, but to care for themselves, since caring for the flock cannot occur unless one first cares for oneself, in the sense of feeding and nurturing one's own soul. Pastors are enjoined by scripture to "keep watch over yourselves" (Acts 20:28), as a prior condition to watching over the flock.

(2) Pastoral care occurs not only in individuated conversation but also through preaching, a public task intrinsic to the care of souls.

(3) Soul care occurs within a caring commuity whose primary corporate act is the praise of God's care. The worshipping community is the necessary spiritual matrix for individual care of souls. Guidance of the community at prayer is an indispensable aspect of pastoral guidance.

(4) Soul care is mediated powerfully through sacramental actions, the first of which is a ministry of beginnings—baptism—a decisive starting point in the care of a particular person within the community of faith.

(5) The quintessential Christian pastoral act is one of feeding: eating and drinking, receiving spiritual nourishment for our souls. No pastoral act is more central to the care of souls than the Supper where the resurrected Christ is present at table with the community. Confession is intrinsically connected with holy communion. The pastor attends the communicant through penitential confession with its trenchant challenge to the human spirit, through pardon to restitution.

(6) The pastor is a teacher of the soul, educating the soul toward behavioral excellence. The soul-friend is a life-crisis mentor, and reliable teacher of the good life. If care of souls is a pedagogy of the inner life, then the pastor must develop the art of teaching.

(7) The care of souls occurs not only individualistically, but extends to institutional nurture and accountability, and beyond the parameters of the congregation to the nurture of community in the parish, the civil sphere, the *polis*, and ultimately to the world.

(8) Soul care requires the support of the laity through voluntary gifts grounded in biblical imperatives, rather than on a fee-for-service basis, which tends to separate the individual from the caring community, to

disjoin the pastor from the apostolic witness, and to provide services primarily for those who can pay for them. When pastoral abuses occur, they require rigorous inquiry which presumes innocence and seeks procedures for fair hearing and due process.

Abbreviations

ACW Ancient Christian Writers. Edited by J. Quasten, J. C. Plumpe, and W. Burghardt. 44 Vols. New York: Paulist Press, 1946–1985.

AF *The Apostolic Fathers.* Edited by J. N. Sparks. New York: Thomas Nelson, 1978.

AF-Ltft The Apostolic Fathers. Edited by J. B. Lightfoot, revised by J. R. Harmer, London, New York: Macmillan, 1907.

ANF Ante-Nicene Fathers. Edited by A. Roberts and J. Donaldson. 10 vols. 1866–1896. Reprint ed., Grand Rapids: Eerdmans, 1979.

Angl. *Anglicanism: The Thought and Practice of the Church of England, Illustrated from the Religious Literature of the Seventeenth Century.* Edited by P. E. More and F. L. Cross. London: S.P.C.K., 1935.

BCP *Book of Common Prayer* (1662 unless otherwise noted). Royal Breviar's edition. London: S.P.C.K., n.d.

BPR *Book of Pastoral Rule.* Gregory the Great, NPNF 2nd X, pp. 1–94.

CC *Creeds of the Churches.* Edited by John Leith. Richmond: John Knox Press, 1979.

CFS Cistercian Fathers Series. 44 vols. Kalamazoo, MI: Cistercian Publications, 1968ff.

COCL Classics of the Contemplative Life. Edited by J. M. Hussey. 8 vols. London: Faber and Faber, 1960ff.

CS *The Curate of Souls.* Edited by John R. H. Moorman, London: S.P.C.K., 1958.

CSS Cistercian Studies Series. 68 vols. Kalamazoo, MI: Cistercian Publications, 1968ff.

CWMS *Complete Writings of Menno Simons* (c. 1496–1561). Edited by John C. Wenger, Scottdale, PA: Herald Press, 1956.

CWS Classics of Western Spirituality. 37 vols. to date. Edited by Richard J. Payne et al. New York: Paulist Press, 1978ff.

ECF *Early Christian Fathers.* Edited by H. Bettenson. London: Oxford University Press.

ECW Early Christian Writers: The Apostolic Fathers. Translated by Maxwell Staniforth. London: Penguin Books, 1968.

FC Fathers of the Church. Edited by R. J. Deferrari. 73 vols. Washington, DC: Catholic University Press, 1947ff.

FER The Fathers for English Readers. 15 vols. London: S.P.C.K., 1878–1890.

Inst. Institutes of the Christian Religion, by John Calvin. LCC, vols. 21–22. Philadelphia: Westminster Press, 1960.

KVJ King James Version, 1611 (also called the Authorized Version).

LACT Library of Anglo-Catholic Theology. 99 vols. Oxford University Press, 1841–63.

LCC Library of Christian Classics. 26 vols. Edited by J. Baillie, J. T. McNiell, and H. P. Van Dusen. Philadelphia: Westminster Press, 1953–61.

LCF *Later Christian Fathers*. Edited by H. Bettenson. London: Oxford University Press, 1970.

LF A Library of Fathers of the Holy Catholic Church. Edited by E. B. Pusey, J. Kebel, J. H. Newman, and C. Marriott. 50 vols. Oxford: J. H. Parker, 1838–88.

Loeb Loeb Classical Library. Edited by Page, Capps, Rouse. Cambridge, MA: Harvard University Press, 1912ff.

LPT Library of Protestant Thought. Edited by John Dillenberger. 13 vols. New York: Oxford University Press. 1964–72.

LW Luther's Works. Edited by J. Pelikan and H. T. Lehmann. 54 vols. St. Louis: Concordia, 1953ff.

MPG J. B. Migne, ed., Patrologia Graeca. 162 vols. Paris: Migne, 1857–76.

MPL J. B. Migne, ed., Patrologia Latina. 221 vols. Paris: Migne, 1841–1865. General Index, Paris, 1912.

MPLS J. B. Migne, ed., Patrologia Latina: Supplementum. 4 vols. Edited by A. Hamman, Turnhout, Belgium: Editions Brepols.

MWS *Ministry of Word and Sacrament: An Enchiridion,* by Martin Chemnitz (1595). St. Louis: Concordia, 1981.

NE *A New Eusebius: Documents Illustrative of the History of the Church to A.D. 337.* Edited by J. Stevenson (based on B. J. Kidd). London: S.P.C.K., 1957.

NEB New English Bible.

NIV New International Version.

NPNF A Select Library of the Nicene and Post-Nicene Fathers of the Christian Church. 1st Series, 14 vols; 2nd series, 14 vols. Edited by H. Wace and P. Schaff. New York: Christian, 1887–1900.

OCC Our Christian Classics, ed. James Hamilton. London: Nisbet, 1858.

PW Practical Works, Richard Baxter. 23 vols. London: James Duncan, 1830.

RAC   *Rules and Advices to the Clergy of the Dicoese of Noum and Connor,* by Jeremy Taylor (1661), Works, ed. R. Heber, 1839, vol. xiv.

RD   *Reformed Dogmatics.* Edited by J. W. Beardslee. Grand Rapids: Baker, 1965.

RSV   Revised Standard Version.

SC   *Spiritual Conferences* (1628), St. Francis de Sales. Westminster MD: Newman, 1943.

SCG   Summa contra Gentiles, On the Truth of the Catholic Faith, Thomas Aquinas. 4 vols. New York: Doubleday, 1955–57.

SED   Standard English Divines. 19 multi-volume series. Oxford: Parker, 1855ff.

SSW   *Selected Sacred Writings,* Hugh of St. Victor. London: Faber and Faber, 1962.

ST   Summa Theologica, Thomas Aquinas. Edited by English Dominican Fathers. 3 vols. New York: Benziger, 1947–48.

SW   *John Calvin, Selections from His Writings.* Edited by John Dillenberger. Missoula, MT: Scholars' Press, 1975.

TCL   Translations of Christian Literature. Edited by Sparrow Simpson and Lowther Clarke. London: S.P.C.K., 1917ff.

TPW   Taylor's Practical Works, by Jeremy Taylor. 2 vols. London: H. G. Bohn, 1854.

WA   "Weimarer Ausgabe," D. Martin Luthers Werke. Kritische Gesamtausgabe, Weimar, 1883ff.

W-Br.   Weimarer Ausgabe, D. Martin Luther, Briefwechsel, Kritische Gesamtausgabe, Weimar, 1930ff., Letters.

WLS   What Luther Says. Edited by E. Plass. 3 vols. St. Louis: Concordia, 1959.

WML   Works of Martin Luther. Philadelphia Edition. 6 vols. Philadelphia: Muhlenberg Press, 1943.

WA-T   Weimarer Ausgabe. D. Martin Luther, Tischreden, Kritische Gesamtausgabe, Table Talk, 1912ff.

WSD   *Writings on Spiritual Direction,* ed. J. M. Neufelder, and Mary C. Coelho. New York: Seabury Press, 1982.

Acknowledgments

THE AUTHOR IS GRATEFUL to the following for the use of the selections listed below in the four volumes of this series.

Benziger Bros., Inc.: Thomas Aquinas, *Summa Theologica.*

Catholic University of America: R. J. Deferrari, ed., Fathers of the Church Series.

Cistercian Publications, Inc., Kalamazoo, MI: Cistercian Studies Series, Cistercian Fathers Series.

Concordia Press: J. Pelikan, ed., Martin Luther, *Luther's Works;* E. Plass, ed., *What Luther Says.*

Faber and Faber, Inc.: Classics of the Contemplative Life Series.

Herald Press: Menno Simons, *Complete Writings of Menno Simons.*

Holy Transfiguration Monastery Press: John Climacus, *Ladder of Divine Ascent.*

Muhlenberg Press: Works of Martin Luther.

Oxford University Press: John Dillenberger, ed., Library of Protestant Thought; and E. B. Pusey et al., eds., A Library of Fathers of the Holy Catholic Church; Library of Anglo-Catholic Thought.

Paulist Press: Richard J. Payne, ed., Classics of Western Spirituality; and J. Quasten et al., eds. Ancient Christian Writers Series.

Scholars Press and the American Academy of Religion: John Dillenberger, ed., *John Calvin: Selections from His Writings.*

S.P.C.K.: S. Simpson and L. Clarke, eds., Translations of Christian Literature, The Fathers for English Readers; and P. W. Moore and F. L. Cross, eds., *Anglicanism.*

Thomas Nelson: Jack Sparks, ed., *The Apostolic Fathers: New Translations of Early Christian Writings.*

University of Michigan Press: John Donne, *Devotions Upon Emergent Occasions.*

Viking-Penguin Inc.: *Early Christian Writings: The Apostolic Fathers,* trans. Maxwell Staniforth.

Westminster Press: J. Baille, J. T. McNeill, and H. P. Van Dusen, eds., The Library of Christian Classics.